The Norton Book of
Light Verse

THE NORTON BOOK OF LIGHT VERSE

Edited by RUSSELL BAKER

With the assistance of

KATHLEEN LELAND BAKER

W·W·NORTON & COMPANY·NEW YORK·LONDON

Published simultaneously in Canada by Penguin Books Canada Ltd., 2801 John Street,
Markham, Ontario L3R 1B4.
Printed in the United States of America.

The text of this book is composed in Avanta (Electra), with display type set in Bernhard
Modern. Composition and manufacturing by The Haddon Craftsmen, Inc.
Book design by Antonina Krass.

First Edition

Library of Congress Cataloging-in-Publication Data
The Norton book of light verse.
1. Humorous poetry, English. 2. English poetry.
3. Humorous poetry, American. 4. American poetry.
I. Baker, Russell, 1925–
PR1195.H8N67 1986   821'.08'08   86–18172

ISBN 0-393-02366-4

W. W. Norton & Company, Inc., 500 Fifth Avenue, New York, N.Y. 10110
W. W. Norton & Company Ltd., 37 Great Russell Street, London WC1B 3NU

1 2 3 4 5 6 7 8 9 0

ACKNOWLEDGMENTS

Franklin Pierce Adams: "The Reconciliation: A Modern Version," "The Rich Man," and "To a Thesaurus" from *Tobogganning on Parnassus*. Reprinted by permission of Doubleday & Co., Inc.

Conrad Aiken: "Limberick" from *A Seizure of Limbericks* by Conrad Aiken. Copyright © 1963, 1964 by Conrad Aiken. Reprinted by permission of Brandt and Brandt as literary agents for the author.

Jon Anderson: "Ye Bruthers Dogg." Reprinted from *In Sepia*, by Jon Anderson by permission of the University of Pittsburgh Press. © 1974 by Jon Anderson.

Maya Angelou: "Pickin Em Up and Layin Em Down." Copyright © 1975 by Maya Angelou. Reprinted from *Oh Pray My Wings are Gonna Fit Me Well*, by Maya Angelou, by permission of Random House, Inc.

Richard Armour: "Money" from *Yours for the Asking* by Richard Armour. Reprinted by permission of the author.

W.H. Auden: "The Aesthetic Point of View." Copyright © 1960 by W.H. Auden. Reprinted from *Homage to Clio* by W. H. Auden, by permission of Random House, Inc. "The Unknown Citizen" and "Doggerel by Senior Citizen." Copyright 1940 and renewed 1968 by W.H. Auden. Copyright © 1969 by W.H. Auden. Reprinted from *W.H. Auden: Collected Poems*, edited by Edward Mendelson, by permission of Random House, Inc. (and Faber and Faber Ltd. for "The Unknown Citizen").

Kathleen Leland Baker: "Moon Guest" and "The Baby Hilary, Sir Edmund" reprinted by permission of the author.

Max Beerbohm: "Thomas Hardy and A.E. Housman" and "Brave Rover" from *Men and Memories, Recollections of William Rothenstein 1900–1922*, edited by William Rothenstein. Reprinted by permission of G.P. Putnam's, Inc.

Hilaire Belloc: "Epitaph on the Politician," "Fatigue," "Henry King Who Chewed Bits of String, and Was Early Cut Off in Dreadful Agonies," "Franklin Hyde Who Caroused in the Dirt and was Corrected by His Uncle," "Lord Finchley," "Lord Lucky," "On His Books," "On Jam," "The Yak," and "The Lion" from *Complete Verse*. Reprinted by permission of Gerald Duckworth & Co. Ltd.

Stephen Vincent Benét: "For City Spring" by Stephen Vincent Benét from *Selected Works of Stephen Vincent Benet*, Holt, Rinehart and Winston. Copyright 1935 by Stephen Vincent Benét. Copyright renewed © 1963 by Thomas C. Benét, Stephanie B. Makim, and Rachel Benét Lewis. "Hernando De Soto" by Rosemary and Stephen Vincent Benét from *A Book of Americans* by Rosemary and Stephen Vincent Benét. Copyright 1933 by Rosemary and Stephen Vincent Benét. Both selections reprinted by permission of Brandt and Brandt as literary agents for the authors.

Gerard Benson: "The Probatioun Officeres Tale" reprinted from *The New Statesman*.

John Betjeman: "In Westminster Abbey" from *Collected Poems*. Reprinted by permission of John Murray (Publishers) Ltd.

Helen Bevington: "Mrs. Trollope in America" from *Dr. Johnson's Waterfall*. Copyright 1945, 1946 by Helen Bevington. Copyright © renewed 1974 by Helen Bevington. Reprinted by permission of Houghton, Mifflin Company.

Ambrose Bierce: "Don't Steal . . ." from *The Devil's Dictionary*. Reprinted by permission of Doubleday & Co., Inc.

Morris Bishop: Limerick stanza from "Sonnet and Limerick," "Public Aid for Niagara Falls," and "Ozymandias Revisited." Reprinted by permission of The Putnam Publishing

Group from *Spilt Milk* by Morris Bishop. Copyright © 1942 by Morris Bishop, renewed 1969 by Morris Bishop. Fragment from "The Maladjusted: A Tragedy," "Sales Talk for Annie," "The Anatomy of Humor," and "The Naughty Preposition" from *The Best of Bishop* (Cornell University Press) and *A Bowl of Bishop* (Dial Press). © 1941, 1947, 1949, 1950 Alison Kingsbury Bishop; copyright duly renewed. Originally published in *The New Yorker*. "Diogenes" reprinted from *The Saturday Evening Post*. Copyright 1931 The Curtis Publishing Company. Reprinted by permission.

Margaret Blaker: "Pippa Passes, But I Can't Get Around This Truck" from *Light Year '85*. Reprinted by permission of the author.

Roy Blount: "Song Against Broccoli" from *One Fell Soup, or, I'm Just a Bug on the Windshield of Life* by Roy Blount, Jr. Copyright © 1982 by Roy Blount, Jr. Reprinted by permission of Little, Brown and Company in association with The Atlantic Monthly Press.

Burma Shave signs from *The Verse by the Side of the Road* by Frank Rowsome, Jr. Copyright © 1966 by Frank Rowsome, Jr. Reprinted by permission of the Stephen Greene Press, a wholly owned subsidiary of Viking Penguin, Inc.

Fred Chappell: "My Mother Shoots the Breeze" from *Wind Mountain* by Fred Chappell. Copyright © 1979 by Fred Chappell. "Guess Who" from *The World Between the Eyes* by Fred Chappell. Copyright © 1963, 1964, 1966, 1969, 1970 and 1971. Reprinted by permission of Louisiana State University Press.

G.K. Chesterton: "A Ballad of Suicide," from "Variations on an Air Composed on Having to Appear in a Pageant as Old King Cole" from *The Collected Poems of G.K. Chesterton*. Copyright 1932 by Dodd, Mead & Company, Inc. Copyright renewed 1959 by Oliver Chesterton. Reprinted by permission of Dodd, Mead & Company, Inc. and A.P. Watt Ltd. on behalf of Miss D.E. Collins.

John Ciardi: "Censorship" is reprinted from *For Instance, Poems by John Ciardi*, by permission of W.W. Norton & Company, Inc. Copyright © 1979 by John Ciardi. "Back Through the Looking Glass to This Side" copyright John Ciardi 1978, "Suburban" copyright John Ciardi 1984. Reprinted from *Selected Poems*. Used by permission of the University of Arkansas Press.

Joseph Clancy: translation of Dafydd Ap Gwillym "Medieval Welsh Lyrics" from *The Rattle Bag* published by Faber & Faber Ltd. Reprinted by permission of the author.

William Cole: "Oh. Noa Noa!" Copyright 1971 William Cole. Reprinted by permission of the author.

Jack Conway: "Clothes Make the Man" from *The Nantucket Review* (#26). Reprinted by permission of The Nantucket Review.

Noel Coward: "A Bar on the Piccola Marina," "Mad Dogs and Englishmen," "He Never did that to ME," "I've Been to a Marvelous Party," "Irish Song," "The Little Ones' A.B.C.," and "What's Going to Happen to the Tots?" from *The Lyrics of Noel Coward*, published by The Overlook Press, Woodstock, NY 12498 (1973). "Any Part of Piggy" by Noel Coward reprinted by permission of Graham Payn for the Estate of Noel Coward.

Richard Cumbie: "New Jersey Turnpike" originally published in *Boxspring*. Reprinted by permission of the author.

E.E. Cummings: "spring omnipotent goddess thou dost" Reprinted from *Tulips & Chimneys* by E.E. Cummings, edited by George James Firmage, with the permission of Liveright Publishing Corporation. Copyright 1923, 1925 and renewed 1951, 1953 by E.E. Cummings. Copyright © 1973, 1976 by the Trustees for the E.E. Cummings Trust. Copyright © 1973, 1976 by George James Firmage. "next to of course god america i" and "nobody loses all the time" Reprinted from *Is 5* by E.E. Cummings, edited by George

James Firmage, with the permission of Liveright Publishing Corporation. Copyright ©
1985 by E.E. Cummings Trust. Copyright 1926 by Horace Liveright. Copyright © 1954
by E.E. Cummings. Copyright © 1985 by George James Firmage. "may i feel said he"
Reprinted from *No Thanks* by E.E. Cummings, edited by George James Firmage, with
the permission of Liveright Publishing Corporation. Copyright 1935 by E.E. Cummings.
Copyright © 1968 by Marian Morehouse Cummings. Copyright © 1973, 1978 by the
Trustees for the E.E. Cummings Trust. Copyright © 1973, 1978 by George James
Firmage. "a politician is an arse upon" Copyright 1944 by E.E. Cummings. Reprinted
from his volume *Complete Poems 1913–1962* by permission of Harcourt Brace Jovano-
vich, Inc.

T.A. Daly: "Mia Carlotta" from *Carmina,* copyright 1908, 1937 by T.A. Daly. Reprinted
by permission of Harcourt Brace Jovanovich, Inc.

Peter Davison: "Motley" from *Praying Wrong.* Copyright © 1984 by Peter Davison.
Reprinted with the permission of Atheneum Publishers.

Clarence Day: "Might and Right" from *After All* by Clarence Day. Copyright 1936 and
renewed 1964 by Katherine Briggs Day. Reprinted by permission of Alfred A. Knopf, Inc.
"The Egg" and "Wife and Home" from *Thoughts Without Words* by Clarence Day.
Copyright 1928 by Clarence Day and renewed 1956 by Mrs. Clarence Day. Reprinted
by permission of Alfred A. Knopf, Inc.

Peter De Vries: "Bacchanal" copyright 1950 by Peter DeVries. First appeared in *The New
Yorker.* "Sacred and Profane Love, Or, There's Nothing New Under the Moon Either"
copyright 1951 by Peter DeVries. First appeared in *Harpers.* "Christmas Family Reun-
ion" copyright 1949 by Peter DeVries. First appeared in *The New Yorker.* All of the above
from *The Tents of Wickedness* by Peter DeVries. Reprinted by permission of Little,
Brown and Company, Inc. "To His Importunate Mistress" copyright © 1986 by Peter
DeVries. Appeared in *The New Yorker,* 1986. Reprinted by permission of Watkins,
Loomis, Inc.

Emily Dickinson: "I'm Nobody! Who Are You?" Reprinted by permission of the publish-
ers and the Trustees of Amherst College from *The Poems of Emily Dickinson,* edited by
Thomas H. Johnson. Cambridge, Mass.: The Belknap Press of Harvard University Press.
Copyright 1951, © 1955, 1979, 1983 by The President and Fellows of Harvard College.

Thomas Disch: "La, La, La!" from *ABCDEFGHIJKLMNOPQRSTUVWXYZ* by
Thomas M. Disch, reprinted by permission of Anvil Press Poetry Ltd.

T.S. Eliot: "Lines for Cuscuscaraway and Mizra Murad Ali Beg" and "Lines to Ralph
Hodgson Esqre" from *Collected Poems 1909–1962* by T.S. Eliot, copyright 1936 by
Harcourt Brace Jovanovich, Inc.; Copyright © 1963, 1964 by T.S. Eliot. Reprinted by
permission of Harcourt Brace Jovanovich, Inc. and Faber and Faber Ltd. "The Naming
of Cats" and "Macavity: The Mystery Cat" from *Old Possum's Book of Practical Cats*
by T.S. Eliot, copyright 1939 by T.S. Eliot; renewed 1967 by Esme Valerie Eliot. Re-
printed by permission of Harcourt Brace Jovanovich, Inc. and Faber and Faber Ltd.

Gavin Ewart: "Ending" from *The Collected Ewart 1933–1980.* Reprinted by permission
of Century Hutchinson Limited.

James Facos: "Fable" from *Light Year '85.* Reprinted by permission of the author.

Robert N. Feinstein: "Woolly Words" from *Oysters in Love* (Stronghold Press). First
published in *Light Year '85.* Reprinted by permission of the author.

F. Scott Fitzgerald: "Obit on Parnassus." Reprinted by permission of Harold Ober
Associates Incorporated. Copyright 1937, 1965 by The New Yorker Magazine Inc. First
published in *The New Yorker.*

Elizabeth Flynn: "After Grave Deliberation" from *The Literary Review.*

Barbara Fried: "The Good Old Days," reprinted by permission of the author.

Robert Frost: "The Objection to Being Stepped On" from *The Poetry of Robert Frost* edited by Edward Connery Lathem. Copyright © 1962 by Robert Frost. Copyright © 1969 by Holt Rinehart and Winston. Reprinted by permission of Henry Holt and Company.

John Fuller: "De Sade," reprinted by permission of the author.

Walker Gibson: "Advice to Travelers" from *Come As You Are* by Walker Gibson. This poem first appeared in *Saturday Review*, May 5, 1956. Reprinted by permission of the author.

Strickland Gilliland: "On the Antiquity of Microbes," published in *What Cheer*, edited by David McCord.

Allen Ginsberg: "I Am a Victim of Telephone" copyright © 1964 by Allen Ginsberg and "Sweet Levinsky" copyright 1949 by Allen Ginsberg from *Collected Poems 1947–1980* by Allen Ginsberg. Reprinted by permission of Harper & Row, Publishers, Inc.

Harry Graham: "Indifference," "L'Enfant Glace," and "Tender-heartedness" from *Ruthless Rhymes*. Reprinted by permission of Edward Arnold (Publisheshers) Ltd.

Virginia Graham: "Disillusionment." © Copyright Punch/Rothco. Reprinted by permission.

Robert Graves: translation from the Welsh of "Welcome to the Caves of Arta!" from *Welchman's Hose*, and "Traveler's Curse after Misdirection" from *Collected Poems 1961*, reprinted by permission of A.P. Watt Ltd. on behalf of the Executors of the Estate of Robert Graves.

Arthur Guiterman: "Anthologistics" copyright 1939 from *Lyric Laughter* by Arthur Guiterman. "Everything in its Place" copyright 1939 from *Brave Laughter* by Arthur Guiterman. "Local Note" and "On the Vanity of Earthly Greatness" copyright 1936 from *Gaily the Troubadour*. Reprinted by permission of Louise H. Sclove.

James Harrison: "Helen" from *Flying Dutchmen* (1983), reprinted with the permission of Sono Nis Press.

Anthony Hecht: "Samuel Sewall" from *A Summoning of Stones*. Copyright 1954 by Anthony E. Hecht. Copyright renewed © 1982. "The Dover Bitch" from *The Hard Hours*. Copyright © 1967 by Anthony E. Hecht. Both selections reprinted with the permission of Atheneum Publishers.

Anthony Hecht and John Hollander: "Heliogabalus," "Paradise Lost," "Danish Wit," and "The Russian Soul II" from *Jiggery Pokery*. Copyright © 1966 by Anthony Hecht and John Hollander. Reprinted with the permission of Atheneum Publishers.

Graham Lee Hemminger: "This Smoking World" reprinted from the *Penn State Froth*.

A.P. Herbert: "Saturday Night," "Triangular Legs," and "I Like Them Fluffy" from *Plain Jane*. Reprinted by permission of A.P. Watt Ltd.

Samuel Hoffenstein: "Nothing from a straight line swerves," "Your little hands," "With rue my heart is laden," "The early bird may catch the worm," "Babies haven't any hair," "Of all the birds that sing and fly," "Birdie McReynolds," "Miss Millay says something too," and "Come, live with me and be my love," reprinted from *A Treasury of Humorous Verse* including *Poems in Praise of Practically Nothing* by Samuel Hoffenstein, by permission of Liveright Publishing Corporation. Copyright 1928 by Samuel Hoffenstein. Copyright 1946 by Liveright Publishing Corporation.

Mark Hollis: "'Twixt Cup and Lip" and "Careless Talk" © Copyright Punch/Rothco. Reprinted by permission.

A.E. Housman: "Inhuman Henry or Cruelty to Fabulous Animals," "As into the garden Elizabeth ran," "The shades of night were falling fast," "Hallelujah!" and "When I was born in a world of sin (G. K. Chesterton on His Birth)" from *My Brother*, A.E. Housman. Copyright 1937, 1938 Laurence Housman; copyrights renewed © 1965, 1966 Lloyds Bank Limited. Reprinted with the permission of Charles Scribner's Sons, and The Society of Authors as the literary representative of the Estate of A.E. Housman, and Jonathan Cape Ltd., publishers of A.E. Housman's *Collected Poems*.

Langston Hughes: "Advice" from *Montage of a Dream Deferred*. Reprinted by permission of Harold Ober Associates Incorporated. Copyright 1951 by Langston Hughes. Copyright renewed 1979 by George Houston Bass. "Life is Fine," "Little Lyric," "Morning After," and "What" copyright 1942 and renewed 1970 by Arna Bontemps and George Houston Bass. Copyright 1948 by Alfred A. Knopf, Inc. Reprinted from *Selected Poems of Langston Hughes* by permission of the publisher.

M. Keel Jones: "Election Reflection" © copyright Punch/Rothco. Reprinted by permission.

X.J. Kennedy: "Brats" and "In a Prominent Bar in Secaucus One Day" from *Cross Ties* © 1985 by X.J. Kennedy. Reprinted by permission of the University of Georgia Press. "Emily Dickinson in Southern California" from *Emily Dickinson in Southern California* by X.J. Kennedy. Copyright © 1973 by X.J. Kennedy. Reprinted by permission of David R. Godine Publishers, Inc.

Hugh Kingsmill: "What, Still Alive" from *The Best of Hugh Kingsmill*, edited by Michael Holroyd. Reprinted by permission of Lady Dorothy Hopkinson.

Galway Kinnell: "In a Parlor Containing a Table" from *What a Kingdom It Was*. Copyright © 1960 by Galway Kinnell. Reprinted by permission of Houghton Mifflin Company.

Rudyard Kipling: "A Dead Statesman" from *Rudyard Kipling's Verse: Definitive Edition*. Reprinted by permission of The National Trust, Doubleday & Company, Inc., and A.P. Watt, Ltd.

Peter Klappert: "For the Poet Who Said Poets are Struck by Lightning Only Two or Three Times" from *Lugging Vegetables to Nantucket* (volume 66 of Yale Series of Younger Poets). Reprinted by permission of Yale University Press.

Ronald Knox: "Idealism" from *The Faber Book of Comic Verse*. Reprinted by permission of A.P. Watt Ltd. on behalf of the Earl of Oxford and Asquith.

Kenneth Koch: "Variations on a Theme by William Carlos Williams" copyright © Kenneth Koch 1962 from *Selected Poems 1950–1982* (Random House). Reprinted by permission of the author.

Felicia Lamport: "Poll Star" from *Political Plumlines* by Felicia Lamport. Copyright © 1984 by Felicia Lamport. Reprinted by permission of Doubleday & Company, Inc. "Eggomania" from *Light Meters* and "Mother, Mother Are You There?" from *Scrap Irony*. Reprinted by permission of the author.

Philip Larkin: "Annus Mirabilis" from *High Windows* by Philip Larkin. Copyright © 1974 by Philip Larkin. Reprinted by permission of Farrar, Straus & Giroux, Inc. and Faber and Faber Ltd.

D.H. Lawrence: "Intimates" from *The Complete Poems of D.H. Lawrence*, Collected and Edited by Vivian de Sola Pinto and F. Warren Roberts. Copyright © 1964, 1971 by Angelo Ravagli and C.M. Weekley, Executors of the Estate of Frieda Lawrence Ravagli. Reprinted by permission of Viking Penguin, Inc.

Naomi Lazard: "In Answer to Your Query" from *Ordinances*. Reprinted by permission of Owl Creek Press.

Tom Leher: "Alma" © 1965 Tom Leher. Used by permission of the author.

John Lennon: "The Fat Budgie" from *A Spaniard in the Works* by John Lennon. Reprinted by permission of Jonathan Cape Ltd. for the Estate of John Lennon.

C. Day Lewis: "Come, live with me and be my love" from *Two Songs* from *Collected Poems 1954.* Reprinted by permission of the Executors of the Estate of C. Day Lewis, Jonathan Cape Ltd., The Hogarth Press and A.D. Peters & Co. Ltd.

Vachel Lindsay: "Simon Legree: A Negro Sermon." Reprinted with permission of Macmillan Publishing Company from *Collected Poems* by Vachel Lindsay. Copyright 1917 by Macmillan Publishing Company, renewed 1945 by Elizabeth C. Lindsay.

James Lipton: "Misericordia." Copyright © 1986 by News America Publishing, Inc. Reprinted with permission of *New York* Magazine.

Louis MacNeice: "Bagpipe Music" from *Collected Poems of Louis MacNeice.* Reprinted by permission of Faber and Faber Ltd.

John Manifold: "Fife Tune" from *Collected Verse.* Reprinted by permission of the University of Queensland Press.

Don Marquis: "archy at the zoo," "certain maxims of archy," "mehitabel and her kittens," and "the song of mehitabel" from *archy and mehitabel* by don marquis. Copyright 1927 by Doubleday & Company, Inc. Reprinted by permission of the publisher. "When One Loves Tensley" by Don Marquis. Copyright 1921 by Sun Printing & Publishing Association. From the book *Love Sonnets of a Caveman.* Reprinted by permission of Doubleday & Company, Inc.

David McCord: "Ascot Waistcoat" from *And What's More* by David McCord. "Baccalaureate" and "Epitaph on a Waiter" from *Bay Window Ballads* by David McCord. Reprinted by permission of the author.

Phyllis McGinley: "Ballad of Lost Objects" from *Times Three* by Phyllis McGinley. Copyright 1953 by Phyllis McGinley, renewed © 1981 by Phyllis Hayden Blake. Originally published in *The New Yorker.* "Notes for a Southern Road Map" from *Times Three* by Phyllis McGinley. Copyright 1953 by Phyllis McGinley, renewed © 1968 by Julie Elizabeth Hayden and Phyllis Hayden Blake. Originally published in *The New Yorker.* "Ode to the End of Summer" from *Times Three* by Phyllis McGinley. Copyright 1938 by Phyllis McGinley, renewed © 1966 by Julie Elizabeth Hayden and Phyllis Hayden Blake. Originally published in *The New Yorker.* "Public Journal" from *Times Three* by Phyllis McGinley. Copyright 1946 by Phyllis McGinley, renewed © 1974 by Julie Elizabeth Hayden and Phyllis Hayden Blake. Originally published in *The New Yorker.* "Reflections at Dawn" and "A Garland of Precepts" from *Times Three* by Phyllis McGinley. Copyright 1954 by Phyllis McGinley, renewed © 1982 by Phyllis Hayden Blake. Originally published in *The New Yorker.* All of the above reprinted by permission of Viking Penguin, Inc.

Laurence McKinney: "Oboe" from *People of Note.* Copyright 1939, 1940 by Crowell-Collier Publishing Co., renewed 1967 by Laurence McKinney. Reprinted by permission of the publisher, E.P. Dutton, a division of New American Library.

Spike Milligan: "A Thousand Hair Savages" from *Silly Verse for Kids.* Reprinted by permission of Spike Milligan Productions Ltd., London.

Adrian Mitchell: "Giving Potatoes" from *The Apeman Commeth.* Reprinted by permission of Jonathan Cape Ltd.

Christopher Morley: "Dial Call" from *Gentlemen's Relish* by Christopher Morley. Reprinted by permission of The Spectator Ltd. "Pennsylvania Deutsch" and "Public Beach" reprinted from *Gentlemen's Relish,* by permission of W.W. Norton & Company, Inc.

Keith Preston: "Chicago Analogue" and "Lapsus Linguae" from *Pot Shots from Pegasus.* Copyright 1929 by Covici, Friede, Inc. Copyright renewed 1957 by Crown Publishers, Inc. Used by permission of Crown Publishers, Inc.

Sir Arthur Quiller-Couch: "Sage Counsel" published in *The Home Book of Light Verse* (reprinted by permission of G.P. Putnam's Sons).

John Crowe Ransom: "Survey of Literature." Copyright 1927 by Alfred A. Knopf, Inc. and renewed 1955 by John Crowe Ransom. Reprinted from *Selected Poems,* Third Edition, Revised and Enlarged by John Crowe Ransom, by permission of the publisher.

Henry Reed: "Chard Witlow" from *A Map of Verona.* Reprinted by permission of the author and Jonathan Cape Ltd.

Laura E. Richards: "Eletelephony" from *Tirra Lirra* by Laura E. Richards. Copyright 1932 by Laura E. Richards; renewed © 1960 by Hamilton Richards. Reprinted by permission of Little, Brown and Company.

James Whitcomb Riley: "Little Orphant Annie" from *The Complete Works of James Whitcomb Riley,* Biographical Edition (Indianapolis: Bobbs-Merrill, 1913).

Theodore Roethke: Excerpt from "Praise to the End" ("Mips and Ma and the Mooly Moo"), "Song for a Squeeze Box," "For an Amorous Lady," and "The Lady and the Bear" copyright 1939, 1950, 1951, 1953, by Theodore Roethke. "Pipling" and "The Mistake" copyright © 1954, 1957 by Beatrice Roethke, as administratrix of the Estate of Theodore Roethke. "My Papa's Waltz" copyright 1942 by Hearst Magazines, Inc. All poems from *The Collected Poems of Theodore Roethke,* reprinted by permission of Doubleday & Company, Inc.

Maurice Sagoff: "Robinson Crusoe," "Preface Shrinklit, Elements of Style" from *Shrinklits.* Reprinted by permission of Workman Publishing Company, Inc.

May Sarton: "Eine Kleine Snailmusik" and "The Snow Light" reprinted from *Selected Poems of May Sarton,* edited by Serena Sue Hilsinger and Lois Brynes, by permission of W. W. Norton & Company, Inc. Copyright © 1978 by May Sarton.

Stanley Sharpless: "Hamlet," "In Praise of Cocoa, Cupid's Nightcap," and "Low Church" reprinted from *The New Statesman.*

Shel Silverstein: "Slithergadee" from *Don't Bump the Glump!* Copyright © 1964 by Shel Silverstein. Reprinted by permission of Simon & Schuster, Inc.

Stevie Smith: "Autumn," "Correspondence Between Mr. Harrison in Newcastle and Mr. Sholto Peach Harrison in Hull," "Major Macroo," "The Jungle Husband," "Our Bog is Dood," "Lord Barrenstock" reprinted from *The Poems of Stevie Smith.* Copyright © 1972 by Stevie Smith. Reprinted by permission of New Directions Publishing Corporation, Inc.

George Starbuck: excerpt from "High Renaissance" in *Desperate Measures* by George Starbuck. Copyright © George Starbuck 1978. Reprinted by permission of David R. Godine, Publishers, Inc.

Timothy Steele: "Here Lies Sir Tact." Reprinted by permission of Louisiana State University Press from *Uncertainties and Rest* by Timothy Steele. Copyright © 1979.

James Stephens: "A Glass of Beer" reprinted with permission of Macmillan Publishing Company and The Society of Authors on behalf of the copyright owner, Mrs. Iris Wise, from *Collected Poems by James Stephens.* Copyright 1918 by Macmillan Publishing Company, renewed 1946 by James Stephens.

L.A.G. Strong: "The Brewer's Man" from *The Body's Imperfection.* Reprinted by permission of Methuen & Co.

Henry Taylor: "Riding Lesson," "Speech," and "The View from a Cab" from *Afternoon of Pocket Billiards* by Henry Taylor (1975). Reprinted by permission of the author and the University of Utah Press.

Anne Tibble: "Trials of a Tourist" from *The Faber Book of Comic Verse*

John Updike: "Insomnia the Gem of the Ocean" copyright © 1972 by John Updike. Reprinted from *Tossing and Turning* by John Updike, by permission of Alfred A. Knopf, Inc. "Some Frenchmen" copyright © 1963 by John Updike. Reprinted from *Midpoint and Other Poems* by John Updike, by permission of Alfred A. Knopf, Inc.

Peter Veale: "I put my hat upon my head," reprinted from *The New Statesman.*

Judith Viorst: "Mother Doesn't Want a Dog" from *If I Were in Charge of the World and Other Worries* by Judith Viorst. Copyright © 1981 Judith Viorst. Reprinted with the permission of Atheneum Publishers.

Carolyn Wells: "How to Tell the Wild Animals" from *Baubles* by Carolyn Wells. Reprinted by permission of Dodd, Mead & Company, Inc. Copyright 1917 by Dodd, Mead & Company, Inc. Copyright renewed 1945 by Bridget M. O'Connell. "The Universal Favorite" reprinted by permission of Maurice O'Connell.

E.B. White: "I Paint What I See," copyright 1933 by E.B. White. "The Critic," copyright 1925 by E.B. White. "The Red Cow is Dead," copyright 1946 by E.B. White. "Window Ledge in the Atom Age," copyright 1946 by E.B. White. "Commuter," copyright 1925 by E.B. White, from *Poems and Sketches of E.B. White.* All reprinted by permission of Harper & Row Publishers, Inc. All poems originally appeared in *The New Yorker.* "To a Lady Across the Way" reprinted by permission of the Estate of E.B. White.

Richard Wilbur: "A Summer Morning" copyright © 1960 by Richard Wilbur. "Two Voices in a Meadow" and "Pangloss's Song: A Comic-Opera Lyric" copyright © 1957 by Richard Wilbur. Reprinted from his volume *Advice to a Prophet and Other Poems* by permission of Harcourt Brace Jovanovich, Inc. "The Prisoner of Zenda," "The Star System," and "What's Good for the Soul Is Good for Sales" copyright © 1975 by Richard Wilbur. Reprinted from his volume *The Mind-Reader* by permission of Harcourt Brace Jovanovich, Inc. "To an American Poet Just Dead" copyright © 1978 by Richard Wilbur. Reprinted from his volume *Ceremony and Other Poems* by permission of Harcourt Brace Jovanovich, Inc.

Tennessee Williams: "Carrousel Tune" from *In the Winter of Cities.* Copyright © 1956 by Tennessee Williams. Reprinted by permission of New Directions Publishing Corporation.

Jonathan Williams: "Uncle IV Surveys his Domaine from his Rocker of a Sunday Afternoon as Aunt Dory Starts to Chop Kindling" from *An Ear in Bartram's Tree* (University of North Carolina Press)

Robert Williams Wood: "The Pecan. The Toucan," "The Pen-guin. The Sword-fish," and "The Elk. The Whelk" from *How to Tell the Birds from the Flowers and Other Woodcuts,* published by Dodd, Mead & Company, Inc.

Kit Wright: "A New World Symphony" from *The Bear Looked Over the Mountain,* published by Salamander.

W.B. Yeats: "The Fiddler of Dooney" from *Collected Poems of W.B. Yeats* (New York: Macmillan, 1956). Reprinted by permission of A.P. Watt Ltd. on behalf of Michael B. Yeats and Macmillan London Ltd.

Contents

Arts and Letters · 63

Contents 17

SOME FUN WITH THE MOTHER TONGUE · 103

ONLY HUMAN · 114

Contents

LIFE'S LOSERS · 138

PERSONALITIES · 155

FOOD AND DRINK · 166

OCCUPATIONS AND PREOCCUPATIONS · 187

Ports of Call · 219

Love · 241

FAMILY PLEASURES · 287

P.G. · 307

Nature's Blessings · 333

Words to Live By · 376

BILE · 392

DEPARTURES · 410

INTRODUCTION

The first light verse I ever heard was alarming, but fortunately I didn't know a word of English at the time, so was not distressed.

It was the one that begins, "Rock-a-bye baby, on the treetop" and ends with that nasty business of the breaking bough hurling baby, cradle and all, down to earth.

After learning enough English to grasp what was going on in that verse, I found it mysterious that mothers should be so fond of crooning it to helpless infants. A sweet little lullaby? Hardly. "Down will come baby, cradle and all" is a sour warning that life's finest moments, those moments when you are sitting on top of the world, or at least on top of the tree, are fraught with peril.

It is a poem with a message: don't let them lull you, kid, or you'll end up broken.

So life begins: with mother using verse to caution us, long before we can understand her words, that the world is no place for the unwary. It is a dark message concealed in pleasant music. Deceptive packaging of this sort is a frequent characteristic of light verse, which has a fondness for dark messages.

Of course it is the sound of the thing that charms the child. As toddlers we fall under the spell of having our toes pinched to the rhythmic beat of "This little piggy went to market," but feel none of the tragedy of the piggy who got no roast beef or the one who cried all the way home.

"The north wind doth blow, and we shall have snow" began the verse that introduced me to compassion. The thought of poor robin having to sit in the barn to keep himself warm and tuck his head under his wing, poor thing, brought me great sorrow when my mother first read it aloud. To this day, as soon as the first storm of winter starts to howl, my wife has to put up with me reciting, "The north wind doth blow, and we shall have snow, and what will poor robin do then?"

Poetry is so vital to us until school spoils it. By kindergarten most of us are so sophisticated about it that if we could spell "hexameter" and "caesura" we would make passable poetry critics. Is there anybody here who, at age five or thereabouts, didn't know with absolute certainty that the ending of "Old Mother Hubbard" needed to be rewritten because rhyming "bone" and "none" just didn't work?

Then we went to school and had to read "Idylls of the King." After that, Shakespeare, who was a great poet. The teacher said so. There is something to be said for Tennyson and a lot to be said for Shakespeare, but something terrible is done to children's innate love of poetry when Tennyson and Shakespeare are force-fed into them as part of an educational pudding containing equal parts of binomial theorem, the *Orations* of Cicero, Boyle's Law of Gases, and French irregular verbs.

In adolescence we are not only constantly embarrassed and sexually maddened, but also highly observant. We look around and note that the people the world calls great do not speak poetry, nor seem to have any poetry in them. They are, all too often, tediously droning windbags or solemn asses. Though we do not articulate very effectively at this age, if we did we would say something like, "Hey, this is a prose world, and the prosier your prose, the more they respect you."

Thus the poetry in the childish soul is slowly covered with dust, then stored away in the attic of the mind, there to lie forgotten until, driving some endless turnpike, the adult trying to fight off sleep finds himself reciting, "When I was sick and lay a-bed," and, "This is the house that Jack built," and, "If seven maids with seven mops swept it for half a year . . ."

The child's instinctive sense for poetic rhythms stays in our bones long after the ponderous, long-winded prose culture of modern life has deadened our ears, leaving us indifferent, puzzled, or hostile to poetry. This childish love of verse comes bursting now and then out of prose-calloused adults in the most improbable settings, sometimes with macabre results.

In 1961 when New York City Republicans offered the voters a ticket led by three men named Gilhooley, Fino, and Lefkowitz, some Republican whose childhood poetic instinct had survived a career in politics composed one of the most memorable campaign slogans I have ever heard:

Gilhooley and Fino
Will handle things nice,
And Lefkowitz
Smash to bits
Corruption and vice.

Of course it's terrible, but after twenty-five years it still refuses to get out of my skull. Perhaps it is the thought of Gilhooley and Fino handling things nice that enchants me. During eleven years as a citizen of New York, I often thought that was the way too many things got handled there: nice. Oh yes—Gilhooley, Fino, and Lefkowitz were resoundingly beaten. Even the magic of poetry cannot loosen the Democratic party's grip on New York City.

The point of all this is that light verse really needs no introduction because we have known it from the cradle and should be at ease with it. Most of us, indeed, probably are at ease with it and can even recite a limerick or two from memory. What is easily enjoyed, however, must often defend itself against charges of low aspirations.

The very term "light verse" suggests inferiority, for in the Anglo-Saxon world at least, lightness is considered contemptible, except in the female figure. Such terms as "light-headed," "lightweight," and "light entertainment" are little sneers meant to caution us against people and things that are, well, not quite . . . *worthy.*

We are dealing with the ancient prejudice against comedy, which is part of the residue of Puritanism, a doctrine defined by H.L. Mencken as the terrible suspicion that somebody somewhere may be having a good time. Thus the term "light verse" is universally accepted, even by poets who should know better, as poetry's equivalent to the surgeon-general's warning about cigarettes:

"Caution: These verses may be hazardous to your solemnity."

You will note that there are no collections of "heavy verse" or of "ponderous verse," though there is more than enough around to paste up a dozen volumes. Nor will you ever see an "Anthology of Serious Verse" or "A Compendium of Solemn Verse."

The explanation is that the public today expects poetry to be heavy, ponderous, serious, or solemn. Why confirm their worst fears? The public's position on this, let me hasten to say, is badly outdated. Anticipating that most poetry will be worse than carrying heavy luggage through O'Hare Airport, the public, to its loss, reads very little of it.

I speak here with some humility, because I gave up on new poetry myself thirty years ago when most of it began to read like coded messages passing between lonely aliens in a hostile world. Assembling this collection, though, introduced me to dozens of contemporary poets whose work is full of wonders. Most of them are not much read. That's a pity because it seems to me that, contrary to popular supposition, this is a good age for poetry in America.

Most of these contemporary poets do not write verse that asks to be classified as "serious" or "light." When doing their work they obviously find it unnecessary, perhaps impossible, to distinguish between light and heavy. Perhaps this is what makes them feel so in touch; the world we have made here at the end of the twentieth century is simultaneously light and serious, grave and absurd. Our terrible tragedy is also our low comedy, or vice versa.

Some of this new poetry is very serious indeed, yet makes me smile; some of it reads light enough, but turns weighty in the digestive system. I have included some of it here, though it lacks the rigid poetic discipline necessary for wit, and wit is usually vital to this sort of verse.

Even these poets whose work defies the old classification system, I suspect, may not be flattered to appear in a volume like this. Two to whom I spoke face to face seemed startled by the prospect of turning up in a book of light verse, as though they were worried about the possibility their reputations might lose weight.

I hope you're not waiting for me to define "light verse," because I am not the defining type. As soon as you define a thing it will show you a piece of itself you failed to notice while working out your definition. Then you either have to redefine it or start weaseling about "exceptions that prove the rule."

What's more, after you finish defining it as completely as it can possibly be defined, two or three or thirty other people who have also defined it are going to get angry because your definition disagrees wildly with their definitions.

Having studied the field, I am aware that some good people have had a whack at defining light verse. They include W.H. Auden and Kingsley Amis. I would be foolish to disagree with either on the subject of poetry, especially since they widely disagree with each other.

Auden's definition, curiously, was far more liberal than Amis's about admitting inferior verse to the hall. I say curiously because Auden is regarded as one of the high mandarins of twentieth-century poetry and might have been expected to be persnickety about excluding second-rate verse.

The evidence also suggests that Auden, whose own collection appeared in 1938, used it too for mischievous political purposes. The most famous clue: his inclusion of Rudyard Kipling's "Danny Deever," an unrelievedly bleak ballad about a military hanging.

Kipling ranked high on the list of aging imperial father figures whom the youth of Auden's generation despised as authors of World War I. Somebody has suggested that by classifying the immensely popular "Danny Deever" in the light-verse category, Auden was giving the old gentleman's poetry the raspberry. I don't profess to know, but you will not find "Danny Deever" around here. You will, however, find a couple of poems by Auden, whose light touch was as elegant as they come.

Amis insists that light verse must first qualify as good poetry. He seems rather short-tempered about beloved old chestnuts that have managed to stay beloved for generations despite a deplorable lack of poetic sparkle. I am afraid you will find some of these in the pages ahead. When you pay good money, you are entitled to a few old chestnuts, in my book. If you agree with Amis, however, let me suggest that you count your blessings whenever you find yourself stuck with nothing worse than an old chestnut in today's go-go marketplace, and be thankful it isn't a lemon.

Amis is not much for the free verse of contemporary poets, either. His view seems to accord with Robert Frost's, that writing poetry with no discernible rhyme or meter is like playing tennis with the net down.

I sympathize with this viewpoint but you will find some unrhymed stuff ahead, not to mention plenty that's poorly rhymed. As the Communists used to say before the thought was appropriated by the Democrats and Republicans, you have to break a few eggs to make an omelet. I am loose enough about principle to put up with free verse, bad rhyme, and even old chestnuts if they are necessary to create the kind of amusement park I have in mind.

An amusement park, in fact, is not a bad metaphor for what I wanted this book to be after Ms Kasia Baker, also known as my daughter, spoke to me sharply on the subject. She is the poet in our family and not only performed all the drudgery involved in a project like this, but also provided indispensable esthetic guidance. Such as? Well, for one thing, she saved me, and you too, from "The Shooting of Dan McGrew" and "Casey at the Bat" by pointing out that she would have to scream in boredom if forced to type them. Thus confronted, I realized that I would probably scream in boredom if forced to read them, and said, "To hell with them."

She is also the reason you will not get another chance here to feel guilty about not reading "The Wife of Bath's Tale." I am so devoted to "The Wife of Bath's Tale" that I promised to do the typing of it myself. My daughter said "The Wife of Bath's Tale" was marvelous, but so long that it would disfigure the shape of the book.

I agreed to cut it by omitting all of the Wife of Bath's husbands but Number Four. My daughter observed that this would mutilate it shamefully. I thought we owed it to Chaucer to put it in; she said we owed Chaucer the right to tell his story in its entirety.

I said even an amputated Chaucer was better than none, since Chaucer was beyond complaining, and professors would be shocked by a book of light verse that didn't include Chaucer, even amputated. Mention of professors unsettled her. She said something like, "Professors! I thought this was going to be a book for people who were looking for fun."

We let the Wife of Bath twist slowly in the wind for six months while I pondered how to organize the material. I have great respect for professors. Some of my best friends are professors, and all of them frequently read books that are fun; some read books that are salacious to boot. I was not sure, however, that they could afford public endorsements of a book that was fun, and I wanted this book to be praised by scholarly society.

"Why?" you may ask, as my daughter did. To which I could only reply that now that she asked, I didn't know why, except that somehow, in the primal recesses of my brain lay buried an irrational association between professors and anthologies.

My daughter finally raised her voice respectfully, but insistently. What I wanted to create, she pointed out, was a book that would be like an amusement park. There was no higher purpose in going to an amusement park than simply to ride the merry-go-round, the whip, and the roller coaster; to wander through the spook house, goggle at distortions created by ridiculous mirrors, eat spun candy, and watch boys put protective arms around girls terrified by the flight of the Ferris wheel.

All very fine, I agreed, except that nobody went to amusement parks anymore. I had the impression that the last amusement park died with the trolley car. Even if there was one left someplace, boys and girls didn't use the Ferris wheel ride as a pretext for necking. Boys and girls interested in carnal doings nowadays would certainly not waste time on Ferris wheels. They would check into a motel in the next county.

Still, I allowed, my daughter had the germ of an idea. What's more, she produced statistics proving that people do still go to amusement parks, some promotional literature from the Disney empire proving that they travel far distances to do so, and a newspaper report that there are more than a hundred roller coasters operating in the country at this very moment.

As a result, you will not find here the chronological arrangement of verses customary in books like this. The down-through-the-ages organization which starts with "Beowulf," gives you a little "Piers Plowman," followed by Chaucer, Spenser, Marlowe, Shakespeare, Jonson—this conventional textbook presentation evoking chalky memories of school survey courses is too likely to leave people with a heavy heart.

Well, you can't enjoy light verse with a heavy heart, so I have thrown away the calendar and set up a number of bins, each identified by a different theme title, and thrown the poems into what seemed like the appropriate bin for each. You wander around, as you might in an amusement park, and take things as they come, or, surfeited on too many spinning rides, drift to the quieter side of the park for a change of pace.

Don't bother looking for the Wife of Bath; she is a big, big woman, and deserves a grander spread than this book affords. I urge you to look her up in the *Canterbury Tales.* She is worth a detour.

On the theory that nobody wants a tour guide at the amusement park, I shall not harass you with explanations why this verse, so obviously a parody, was assigned to the section about death ("Departures"), while this one about death is placed among "Arts and Letters." There is compelling logic behind every placement here. Part of the pleasure ahead might be trying to guess what it was. In certain cases, I am still trying to guess myself.

When you get inside you will notice that light verse has some heavy preoccupations. Infanticide seems an endless source of titillation for some poets, and I have had to prune them severely to keep the flow of childish gore within bounds. The snoring of wives, husbands, and lovers is another favorite subject. The snoring poems at my disposal were all so superior that it was heartbreaking to abandon a single one, but there is such a thing as letting a book snore itself to death, I suppose, so I cut. Ruthlessly.

Few subjects produce more glee in the light versifier than death, including his own. There is an ancient tradition of suicide verse in which the poet decides to kill himself, then changes his mind after reflecting on the inconvenience of the grave and the discomfort involved in getting there.

There is another, quite different kind of poetry about suicide, which is certainly not light verse, and which is not represented here. We have recently come through a period in which suicide came to seem like the occupational disease of poets. It is worth noting that the poets who became suicides wrote almost nothing that can be construed as light verse, except by the most awkward distortion of the term.

I suppose it's possible for people who are temperamentally capable of composing light verse also to commit suicide, but I would bet they are, collectively, excellent insurance bets to see life through, if only to enjoy railing at the absurd spectacle it presents them and see how it will finally decide to dispose of them.

But I meander garrulously. Now I shall be quiet.

You may enter.

THE NORTON BOOK OF
LIGHT VERSE

Twentieth Century Blues 〰️

from CERTAIN
MAXIMS OF ARCHY

i once heard the survivors
of a colony of ants
that had been partially
obliterated by a cow s foot
seriously debating
the intention of the gods
towards their civilization

DON MARQUIS

THE UNKNOWN CITIZEN

(To JS/07/M/378
This Marble Monument
Is Erected by the State)

He was found by the Bureau of Statistics to be
One against whom there was no official complaint,
And all the reports on his conduct agree
That, in the modern sense of an old-fashioned word, he
    was a saint,
For in everything he did he served the Greater Community.
Except for the War till the day he retired

He worked in a factory and never got fired,
But satisfied his employers, Fudge Motors Inc.
Yet he wasn't a scab or odd in his views,
For his Union reports that he paid his dues,
(Our report on his Union shows it was sound)
And our Social Psychology workers found
That he was popular with his mates and liked a drink.
The Press are convinced that he bought a paper every day
And that his reactions to advertisements were normal in every way
Policies taken out in his name prove that he was fully insured,
And his Health-card shows he was once in hospital but left
    it cured.
Both Producers Research and High-Grade Living declare
He was fully sensible to the advantages of the Instalment Plan
And had everything necessary to the Modern Man,
A phonograph, a radio, a car and a frigidaire.
Our researchers into Public Opinion are content
That he held the proper opinions for the time of year;
When there was peace, he was for peace; when there was war,
    he went.
He was married and added five children to the population,
Which our Eugenist says was the right number for a parent of
    his generation,
And our teachers report that he never interfered with
    their education.
Was he free? Was he happy? The question is absurd:
Had anything been wrong, we should certainly have heard.

W. H. AUDEN

DOGGEREL BY A SENIOR CITIZEN

for Robert Lederer

Our earth in 1969
Is not the planet I call mine,
The world, I mean, that gives me strength
To hold off chaos at arm's length.

My Eden landscapes and their climes
Are constructs from Edwardian times,
When bath-rooms took up lots of space,
And, before eating, one said Grace.

The automobile, the aeroplane,
Are useful gadgets, but profane:
The enginry of which I dream
Is moved by water or by steam.

Reason requires that I approve
The light-bulb which I cannot love:
To me more reverence-commanding
A fish-tail burner on the landing.

My family ghosts I fought and routed,
Their values, though, I never doubted:
I thought their Protestant Work-Ethic
Both practical and sympathetic.

When couples played or sang duets,
It was immoral to have debts:
I shall continue till I die
To pay in cash for what I buy.

The Book of Common Prayer we knew
Was that of 1662:
Though with-it sermons may be well,
Liturgical reforms are hell.

Sex was, of course—it always is—
The most enticing of mysteries,
But news-stands did not yet supply
Manichaean pornography.

Then Speech was mannerly, an Art,
Like learning not to belch or fart:
I cannot settle which is worse,
The Anti-Novel or Free Verse.

Nor are those Ph.D's my kith,
Who dig the symbol and the myth:
I count myself a man of letters
Who writes, or hopes to, for his betters.

Dare any call Permissiveness
An educational success?
Saner those class-rooms which I sat in
Compelled to study Greek and Latin.

Though I suspect the term is crap,
If there *is* a Generation Gap,
Who is to blame? Those, old or young,
Who will not learn their Mother-Tongue.

But Love, at least, is not a state
Either *en vogue* or out-of-date,
And I've true friends, I will allow,
To talk and eat with here and now.

Me alienated? Bosh! It's just
As a sworn citizen who must
Skirmish with it that I feel
Most at home with what is Real.

W. H. AUDEN

BAGPIPE MUSIC

It's no go the merrygoround, it's no go the rickshaw,
All we want is a limousine and a ticket for the peepshow.
Their knickers are made of crêpe-de-chine, their shoes are
    made of python,
Their halls are lined with tiger rugs and their walls with
    heads of bison.

John MacDonald found a corpse, put it under the sofa,
Waited till it came to life and hit it with a poker,

Sold its eyes for souvenirs, sold its blood for whiskey,
Kept its bones for dumb-bells to use when he was fifty.

It's no go the Yogi-Man, it's no go Blavatsky,
All we want is a bank balance and a bit of skirt in a taxi.

Annie MacDougall went to milk, caught her foot in the heather,
Woke to hear a dance record playing of Old Vienna.
It's no go your maidenheads, it's no go your culture,
All we want is a Dunlop tyre and the devil mend the puncture.

The Laird o' Phelps spent Hogmanay declaring he was sober;
Counted his feet to prove the fact and found he had one foot over.
Mrs. Carmichael had her fifth, looked at the job with repulsion,
Said to the midwife 'Take it away; I'm through with
    overproduction'.

It's no go the gossip column, it's no go the ceilidh,
All we want is a mother's help and a sugar-stick for the baby.

Willie Murray cut his thumb, couldn't count the damage,
Took the hide of an Ayrshire cow and used it for a bandage.
His brother caught three hundred cran when the seas were lavish,
Threw the bleeders back in the sea and went upon the parish.

It's no go the Herring Board, it's no go the Bible,
All we want is a packet of fags when our hands are idle.

It's no go the picture palace, it's no go the stadium,
It's no go the country cot with a pot of pink geraniums,
It's no go the Government grants, it's no go the elections,
Sit on your arse for fifty years and hang your hat on a pension.

It's no go my honey love, it's no go my poppet;
Work your hands from day to day, the winds will blow the profit.
The glass is falling hour by hour, the glass will fall for ever,
But if you break the bloody glass you won't hold up the weather.

LOUIS MACNEICE

INSOMNIA THE GEM
OF THE OCEAN

When I lay me down to sleep
My waterbed says, "Gurgle gleep,"
And when I readjustment crave
It answers me with a tidal wave
That lifts me like a bark canoe
Adrift in breakers off Peru.

Neap to my spring, ebb to my flow,
It turns my pulse to undertow,
It turns my thoughts to bubbles, it
Still undulates when I would quit;
Two bags of water, it and I
In restless sympathy here lie.

JOHN UPDIKE

IN A PARLOR
CONTAINING A TABLE

In a parlor containing a table
And three chairs, three men confided
Their inmost thoughts to one another.
I, said the first, am miserable.
I am miserable, the second said.
I think that for me the correct word
Is miserable, asserted the third.
Well, they said at last, it's quarter to two.
Good night. Cheer up. Sleep well.
You too. You too. You too.

GALWAY KINNELL

THE DEVELOPMENT

The bulldozers come, they rip
a hole in the sand along
the new blacktop road with a tony name
(Trotting Park, Pamet Hills)
and up goes another glass-walled-
split-level-livingroom-vast-as-a-
roller-rink-$100,000
summer home for a psychiatrist
and family.

Nine months vacation homes
stand empty except for mice
and spiders, an occasional
bird with a broken back twitching
on the deck under a gape of glass.

I live in such a development
way at the end of a winding
road where the marsh begins
to close in: two houses,
the one next door a local
fisherman lost to the bank
last winter, ours a box
half buried in the sand.
This land is rendered
too expensive
to live on. We feed
four people off it,
a kind of organic tall corn
ornery joke at road's end.
We planted for the birds cover
and berries, we compost, we set out
trees and at night
the raccoons come shambling.
Yet the foxes left us,

shrinking into the marsh.
I found their new den.
I don't show it
to anyone.

Forgive us, grey fox, our stealing
your home, our loving
this land carved into lots
over a shrinking watertable
where the long sea wind that blows
the sand whispers to developers
money, money, money.

                                        MARGE PIERCY

SUBURBAN

Yesterday Mrs. Friar phoned. "Mr. Ciardi,
        how do you do?" she said. "I am sorry to say
this isn't exactly a social call. The fact is
        your dog has just deposited—forgive me—
a large repulsive object in my petunias."

I thought to ask, "Have you checked the rectal grooving
        for a positive I.D.?" My dog, as it happened,
was in Vermont with my son, who had gone fishing—
        if that's what one does with a girl, two cases of beer,
and a borrowed camper. I guessed I'd get no trout.

But why lose out on organic gold for a wise crack?
        "Yes, Mrs. Friar," I said, "I understand."
"Most kind of you," she said. "Not at all," I said.
        I went with a spade. She pointed, looking away.
"I always have loved dogs," she said, "but really!"

I scooped it up and bowed. "The animal of it.
        I hope this hasn't upset you, Mrs. Friar."
"Not really," she said, "but really!" I bore the turd

across the line to my own petunias
and buried it till the glorious resurrection

when even these suburbs shall give up their dead.

JOHN CIARDI

I AM A VICTIM OF TELEPHONE

When I lie down to sleep dream the Wishing Well it rings
"Have you a new play for the brokendown theater?"
When I write in my notebook poem it rings
"Buster Keaton is under the brooklyn bridge on Frankfurt and
      Pearl . . ."
When I unsheath my skin extend my cock toward someone's thighs
      fat or thin, boy or girl
Tingaling—"Please get him out of jail . . . the police are crashing
      down"
When I lift the soupspoon to my lips, the phone on the floor begins
      purring
"Hello it's me—I'm in the park two broads from Iowa . . . nowhere
      to sleep last night . . . hit 'em in the mouth"
When I muse at smoke crawling over the roof outside my street
      window
purifying Eternity with my eye observation of gray vaporous columns
      in the sky
ring ring "Hello this is Esquire be a dear and finish your political
      commitment manifesto"
When I listen to radio presidents roaring on the convention floor
the phone also chimes in "Rush up to Harlem with us and see the
      riots"
Always the telephone linked to all the hearts of the world beating at
      once
crying my husband's gone my boyfriend's busted forever my poetry
      was rejected
won't you come over for money and please won't you write me a
      piece of bullshit
How are you dear can you come to Easthampton we're all here
      bathing in the ocean we're all so lonely

and I lie back on my pallet contemplating $50 phone bill,
    broke, drowsy, anxious, my heart
    fearful of the fingers dialing, the deaths, the
    singing of telephone bells
ringing at dawn ringing all afternoon ringing up midnight
    ringing now forever.

ALLEN GINSBERG

IN ANSWER TO YOUR QUERY

We are sorry to inform you
the item you ordered
is no longer being produced.
It has not gone out of style
nor have people lost interest in it.
In fact, it has become
one of our most desired products.
Its popularity is still growing.
Orders for it come in
at an ever increasing rate.
However, a top-level decision
has caused this product
to be discontinued forever.

Instead of the item you ordered
we are sending you something else.
It is not the same thing,
nor is it a reasonable facsimile.
It is what we have in stock,
the very best we can offer.

If you are not happy
with this substitution
let us know as soon as possible.
    As you can imagine

we already have quite an accumulation
of letters such as the one
you may or may not write.
To be totally fair
We respond to these complaints
as they come in.
Yours will be filed accordingly,
answered in its turn.

NAOMI LAZARD

CLOTHES MAKE THE MAN

Clothes make the man, Jack,
and that's a fact.
They make coats for blokes,
what's got maids,
and got it made too,
you chump.

They make hats for cats like us, Jack
Shoes for dudes,
what's feeling in the mood for being cool.
Rags for fags and hags,
what watches soap operas all the time.
And they got pants what dance all by themselves, Jack,
that is if you ain't got no rhythm.

Got clothes made in Milan,
Japan, Iran,
even got designer sheets for "de Klan,"
you got that man?

They got avant-garde leotards,
debonair underwear,
even got some risque, sashays.
Got them high heels for Lucille,

And obscene jeans for Geraldine,
You know what I mean, Jack,
the kind she likes to wear.

They got it all,
from Presidents to malcontents;
hip,
slick,
double-knits.
Get that in your head.
Ain't no cop a cop,
No priest a priest,
nun a nun,
or bum a bum,
without his threads.

Clothes make the man, Jack,
until your dead,
and then we all just naked again.

JACK CONWAY

[MISERICORDIA!]

Misericordia!
College of Cardinals,
Nervously rising to
Whisper its will:

'Rather than being so
Unecumenical,
Can't we just quietly
Swallow The Pill?'

JAMES LIPTON

Annus Mirabilis

Sexual intercourse began
In nineteen sixty-three
(Which was rather late for me)—
Between the end of the *Chatterley* ban
And the Beatles' first LP.

Up till then there'd only been
A sort of bargaining,
A wrangle for a ring,
A shame that started at sixteen
And spread to everything.

Then all at once the quarrel sank:
Everyone felt the same,
And every life became
A brilliant breaking of the bank,
A quite unlosable game.

So life was never better than
In nineteen sixty-three
(Though just too late for me)—
Between the end of the *Chatterley* ban
And the Beatles' first LP.

PHILIP LARKIN

Guess Who

1.
I got a one-eyed wife, a headless child
I was born to be defiled

2.
I live on Elm St. with my adequate wife,
3 children, raunchy dears,

aet. 27, haven't seen an Elm
in thirteen American Years.

FRED CHAPPELL

[BABIES HAVEN'T ANY HAIR]

Babies haven't any hair;
Old men's heads are just as bare;—
Between the cradle and the grave
Lies a haircut and a shave.

SAMUEL HOFFENSTEIN

A MAN CAN COMPLAIN, CAN'T HE?
(A LAMENT FOR THOSE WHO THINK OLD)

Pallid and moonlike in the smog,
Now feeble Phoebus 'gins arise;
The upper floors of Empire State
Have vanished into sooty skies.
Half missing, like the shrouded tower,
Lackluster, like the paten solar,
I draw reluctant waking breath;
Another day, another dolor.

That breath I draw was first exhaled
By diesel and incinerator;
I should have wakened not at all,
Or, were it feasible, even later.
Walls of the world close in on me,
Threats equatorial and polar;
Twixt pit and pendulum I lie;
Another day, another dolor.

Here's news about the current strike,
The latest, greatest test of fission,

A fatal mugging in the park,
An obit of the Geneva mission.
One envelope yields a baffling form
Submitted by the tax comptroller;
A jury summons completes my mail;
Another day, another dolor.

Once eager for, I've come to dread,
The nimble fingers of my barber;
He's training strands across my scalp
Like skimpy vines across an arbor.
The conversation at the club
Is all intestinal or molar;
What dogs the Class of '24?
Another day, another dolor.

Between the dotard and the brat
My disaffection veers and varies;
Sometimes I'm sick of clamoring youth,
Sometimes of my contemporaries.
I'm old too soon, yet young too long;
Could Swift himself have planned it droller?
Timor vitae conturbat me;
Another day, another dolor.

OGDEN NASH

WHAT'S GOING TO HAPPEN TO THE TOTS?

Verse 1   Life today is hectic,
           Our world is running away,
           Only the wise
           Can recognize
           The process of decay,
           Unhappily all our dialectic
           Is quite unable to say
           Whether we're on the beam or not
           Whether we'll rise supreme or not

Whether this new régime or not
Is leading us astray.
We all have Frigidaires, radios,
Television and movie shows
To shield us from the ultimate abyss,
We have our daily bread neatly cut,
Every modern convenience, but
The question that confronts us all is this:

Refrain 1   What's going to happen to the children
When there aren't any more grown-ups?
Having been injected with some rather peculiar glands
Darling Mum's gone platinum and dances to all the
        rhumba bands,
The songs that she sings at twilight
Would certainly be the highlight
For some of those claques
That Elsa Maxwell takes around in yachts.
Rock-a-bye, rock-a-bye, rock-a-bye, my darlings,
Mother requires a few more shots,
Does it amuse the tiny mites
To see their parents high as kites?
What's, what's, what's going to happen to the tots?

Verse 2   Life today's neurotic,
A ceaseless battle we wage,
Millions are spent
To circumvent
The march of middle-age,
The fact that we grab each new narcotic
Can only prove in the end
Whether our hormones jell or not
Whether our cells rebel or not
Whether we're blown to hell or not
We'll all be round the bend
From taking Benzedrine, Dexamil,
Every possible sleeping pill
To knock us out or knock us into shape,
We all have shots for this, shots for that,

Shots for making us thin or fat,
But there's one problem that we can't escape:

Refrain 2   What's going to happen to the children
When there aren't any more grown-ups?
Thanks to plastic surgery and Uncle's abrupt demise
Dear Aunt Rose has changed her nose but doesn't
    appear
    to realize
That pleasures that once were heaven
Look silly at sixty-seven
And youthful allure you can't procure
In terms of perms and pots—so
Lullaby, lullaby, lullaby, my darlings,
Try not to scratch those large red spots.
Think of the shock when Mummy's face
Is lifted from its proper place,
What's, what's, what's going to happen to
    the tots?

Refrain 3   What's going to happen to the children
When there aren't any more grown-ups?
It's bizarre when Grandmamma, without getting out
    of breath,
Starts to jive at eighty-five
And frightens the little ones to death,
The police had to send a squad car
When Daddy got fried on Vodka
And tied a tweed coat round Mummy's throat
In several sailor's knots.
Hush-a-bye, hush-a-bye, hush-a-bye, my darlings,
Try not to fret and wet your cots
One day you'll clench your tiny fists
And murder your psychiatrists,
What's, what's, what's going to happen to the tots?

NOEL COWARD

PIPPA PASSES,
BUT I CAN'T GET AROUND THIS
TRUCK

Morning's at seven,
The plane's at the airport
God's in his Heaven,
But I'm still in Fairport.

MARGARET BLAKER

MINIVER CHEEVY

Miniver Cheevy, child of scorn,
    Grew lean while he assailed the seasons;
He wept that he was ever born,
    And he had reasons.

Miniver loved the days of old
    When swords were bright and steeds were prancing;
The vision of a warrior bold
    Would set him dancing.

Miniver sighed for what was not,
    And dreamed, and rested from his labors;
He dreamed of Thebes and Camelot,
    And Priam's neighbors.

Miniver mourned the ripe renown
    That made so many a name so fragrant;
He mourned Romance, now on the town,
    And Art, a vagrant.

Miniver loved the Medici,
    Albeit he had never seen one;
He would have sinned incessantly
    Could he have been one.

Miniver cursed the commonplace
   And eyed a khaki suit with loathing;
He missed the medieval grace
   Of iron clothing.

Miniver scorned the gold he sought,
   But sore annoyed was he without it;
Miniver thought and thought and thought
   And thought about it.

Miniver Cheevy, born too late,
   Scratched his head and kept on thinking;
Miniver coughed and called it fate,
   And kept on drinking.

EDWIN ARLINGTON ROBINSON

MINIVER CHEEVY, JR.

Miniver Cheevy, Jr., child
   Of Robinson's renowned creation,
Also lamented and reviled
   His generation.

Miniver similarly spurned
   The present that so irked his pater,
But that langsyne for which he yearned
   Came somewhat later.

Miniver wished he were alive
   When dividends came due each quarter,
When Goldman Sachs was 205,
   And skirts were shorter.

Miniver gave no hoot in hell
   For Camelot or Troy's proud pillage;
He would have much preferred to dwell
   In Greenwich Village.

Miniver cherished fond regrets
    For days when benefits were boundless;
When radios were crystal sets,
    And films were soundless.

Miniver missed the iron grills,
    The whispered word, the swift admission,
The bath-tub gin, and other thrills
    Of Prohibition.

Miniver longed, as all men long,
    To turn back time (his eyes would moisten),
To dance the Charleston, play mah jong,
    And smuggle Joyce in.

Miniver Cheevy, Jr. swore,
    Drank till his health was quite imperiled;
Miniver sighed, and read some more
    F. Scott Fitzgerald.

DAVID FISHER PARRY

Arts and Letters

~~~~~~~~~~~~

The Prisoner of Zenda

At the end a
"The Prisoner of Zenda,"
The King being out of danger,
Stewart Granger
(As Rudolph Rassendyll)
Must swallow a bitter pill
By renouncing his co-star,
Deborah Kerr.

It would be poor behavia
In him and in Princess Flavia
Were they to put their own
Concerns before those of the Throne.
Deborah Kerr must wed
The King instead.

Rassendyll turns to go.
Must it be so?
Why can't they have their cake
And eat it, for heaven's sake?
Please let them have it both ways,
The audience prays.
And yet it is hard to quarrel
With a plot so moral.

One redeeming factor,
However, is that the actor
Who plays the once-dissolute King
(Who has learned through suffering
Not to drink or be mean
To his future Queen),
Far from being a stranger,
Is *also* Stewart Granger.

RICHARD WILBUR

[WHAT FRENZY HAS OF LATE POSSESS'D THE BRAIN!]

What frenzy has of late possess'd the brain!
Though few can write, yet fewer can refrain.

SAMUEL GARTH

TRIANGULAR LEGS

I should not presume to express any view
    On the Modernist Movement in Art,
But I've studied the work of Elizabeth Glue,
    And this I can say from the heart—
        She can do what she please
        With her houses and trees
And I shall not attempt to advise,
        But I do not believe
        That the daughters of Eve
Have such *very* triangular thighs.

No doubt there are women with indigo necks
    And heliotrope hips to be found,
But I should have said that the shape of the sex
    Was not so much oblong as round;
        Paint peonies green

And I see what you mean,
Paint eyes like an ostrich's eggs,
But *is* it the case
That the girls of our race
Have such *very* triangular legs?

I do not know much of the feminine tribe,
But I've watched one or two in the Tube,
And I've seen very few you could fairly describe
As a couple of squares and a cube;
But that is the view
Of Elizabeth Glue,
And my vision with sympathy swims
When I think of the boobs
Who are married to cubes
With a set of triangular limbs.

Was Sheba the Queen, who made Solomon gape,
A collection of parallel lines?
Was Juliet just an elliptical shape
With a few geometrical signs?
Elizabeth Glue,
Give me anything new,
And I'll swallow it down to the dregs,
But *did* Helen of Troy
Run away with the boy
On such *very* triangular legs?

A. P. HERBERT

I PAINT WHAT I SEE

(A Ballad of Artistic Integrity, on the Occasion of the Removal of Some Rather Expensive Murals from the RCA Building in the Year 1933)

"What do you paint, when you paint on a wall?"
Said John D.'s grandson Nelson.

"Do you paint just anything there at all?
"Will there be doves, or a tree in fall?
"Or a hunting scene, like an English hall?"

"I paint what I see," said Rivera.

"What are the colors you use when you paint?"
Said John D.'s grandson Nelson.
"Do you use any red in the beard of a saint?
"If you do, is it terribly red, or faint?
"Do you use any blue? Is it Prussian?"

"I paint what I paint," said Rivera.

"Whose is that head that I see on my wall?"
Said John D.'s grandson Nelson.
"Is it anyone's head whom we know, at all?
"A Rensselaer, or a Saltonstall?
"Is it Franklin D.? Is it Mordaunt Hall?
"Or is it the head of a Russian?"

"I paint what I think," said Rivera.

"I paint what I paint, I paint what I see,
"I paint what I think," said Rivera,
"And the thing that is dearest in life to me
"In a bourgeois hall is Integrity;
"However . . .
"I'll take out a couple of people drinkin'
"And put in a picture of Abraham Lincoln;
"I could even give you McCormick's reaper
"And still not make my art much cheaper.
"But the head of Lenin has got to stay
"Or my friends will give me the bird today,
"The bird, the bird, forever."

"It's not good taste in a man like me,"
Said John D.'s grandson Nelson,
"To question an artist's integrity

"Or mention a practical thing like a fee,
"But I know what I like to a large degree,
    "Though art I hate to hamper;
"For twenty-one thousand conservative bucks
"You painted a radical. I say shucks,
    "I never could rent the offices—
    "The capitalistic offices.
"For this, as you know, is a public hall
"And the people want doves, or a tree in fall,
"And though your art I dislike to hamper,
"I owe a *little* to God and Gramper,
    "And after all,
    "It's *my* wall . . ."

"We'll see if it is," said Rivera.

E. B. WHITE

THE RUSSIAN SOUL II

Higgledy-piggledy
Anna Karenina
Went off her feed and just
Couldn't relax,

Then, quite ignoring the
Unsuitability,
Threw in the sponge and was
Scraped off the tracks.

JOHN HOLLANDER

WHAT HIAWATHA PROBABLY DID

He slew the noble Mudjekeewis,
With his skin he made him mittens;
Made them with the fur side inside;
Made them with the skin-side outside;

He, to keep the warm side inside,
Put the cold side, skin-side outside;
He, to keep the cold side outside,
Put the warm side, fur-side, inside:—
That's why he put the cold side outside,
Why he put the warm side inside,
Why he turned them inside outside.

ANONYMOUS

ROBINSON CRUSOE
DANIEL DEFOE

Wrecked castaway
　　On lonely strand
Works hard all day
　　To tame the land,
Takes time to pray;
　　Makes clothes by hand.

For eighteen years
　　His skill he plies,
Then lo! A footprint
　　He espies—
"Thank God it's Friday!"
　　Crusoe cries.

Take heart from his
　　Example, chums:
Work hard, produce;
　　Complete your sums;
Eventually,
　　Friday comes.

MAURICE SAGOFF

Preface ShrinkLit: Elements of Style
William Strunk, Jr. and E.B. White

"Omit needless words!"
Said Strunk to White.

"You're right,"
Said White,
"That's nice
Advice,
But Strunk,
You're drunk
With words—
Two-thirds
Of those
You chose
For that
Fiat
Would fill
The bill!

Would not
The thought
—The core—
Be more
Succinct
If shrinked
(Or shrunk)?"

Said Strunk:
"Good grief!
I'm brief
(I thought)
P'raps not . . .
Dear me!
Let's see . . .
Okay!
Just say
'Write tight!'
No fat
in that!"

"Quite right!"
Said White,
"Er—I mean 'Quite!'
Or, simply, 'Right!' "

MAURICE SAGOFF

Earning a Dinner

Full oft doth Mat. with Topaz dine,
Eateth baked meats, drinketh Greek wine;
But Topaz his own werke rehearseth;
And Mat. mote praise what Topaz verseth.

Now sure as priest did e'er shrive sinner,
Full hardly earneth Mat. his dinner.

MATTHEW PRIOR

THE DOVER BITCH

A Criticism of Life:
for Andrews Wanning

So there stood Matthew Arnold and this girl
With the cliffs of England crumbling away behind them,
And he said to her, 'Try to be true to me,
And I'll do the same for you, for things are bad
All over, etc., etc.'
Well now, I knew this girl. It's true she had read
Sophocles in a fairly good translation
And caught that bitter allusion to the sea,
But all the time he was talking she had in mind
The notion of what his whiskers would feel like
On the back of her neck. She told me later on
That after a while she got to looking out
At the lights across the channel, and really felt sad,
Thinking of all the wine and enormous beds
And blandishments in French and the perfumes.
And then she got really angry. To have been brought
All the way down from London, and then be addressed
As a sort of mournful cosmic last resort
Is really tough on a girl, and she was pretty.
Anyway, she watched him pace the room
And finger his watch-chain and seem to sweat a bit,
And then she said one or two unprintable things.
But you mustn't judge her by that. What I mean to say is,
She's really all right. I still see her once in a while
And she always treats me right. We have a drink
And I give her a good time, and perhaps it's a year
Before I see her again, but there she is,
Running to fat, but dependable as they come.
And sometimes I bring her a bottle of *Nuit d'Amour*.

ANTHONY HECHT

Simplicity

Odes of Horace I, 38

Boy, I hate their empty shows,
   Persian garlands I detest,
Bring me not the late-blown rose
   Lingering after all the rest:

Plainer myrtle pleases me
   Thus outstretched beneath my vine,
Myrtle more becoming thee,
   Waiting with thy master's wine.

WILLIAM COWPER

Fie on Eastern Luxury!

Odes of Horace I, 38

Nay, nay, my boy—'tis not for me,
This studious pomp of Eastern luxury;
Give me no various garlands—fine
   With linden twine,
Nor seek, where latest lingering blows,
   The solitary rose.

Earnest I beg—add not with toilsome pain,
One far-sought blossom to the myrtle plain,
For sure, the fragrant myrtle bough
   Looks seemliest on thy brow;
Nor me mis-seems, while, underneath the vine,
Close interweaved, I quaff the rosy wine.

HARTLEY COLERIDGE

A VICTORIAN PARAPHRASE

Odes of Horace I, 38

Dear Lucy, you know what my wish is,—
    I hate all your Frenchified fuss:
Your silly entrees and made dishes
    Were never intended for us.
No footman in lace and in ruffles
    Need dangle behind my arm-chair;
And never mind seeking for truffles,
    Although they be ever so rare.

But a plain leg of mutton, my Lucy,
    I prithee get ready at three:
Have it smoking, and tender and juicy,
    And what better meat can there be?
And when it has feasted the master
    'Twill amply suffice for the maid;
Meanwhile I will smoke my canaster
    And tipple my ale in the shade.

WILLIAM MAKEPEACE THACKERAY

THE PREFERENCE DECLARED

Odes of Horace I, 38

Boy, I detest the Persian pomp;
    I hate those linden-bark devices;
And as for roses, holy Moses!
    They can't be got at living prices!
Myrtle is good enough for us,—
    For *you,* as bearer of my flagon;
For *me,* supine beneath this vine,
    Doing my best to get a jag on!

EUGENE FIELD

Persicos Odi: Pocket Version

Odes of Horace I, 38

Davus, I detest
Persian decoration;
Roses and the rest,
Davus, I detest.

Simple myrtle best
    Suits our modest station;—
Davus, I detest
    Persian decoration.

Austin Dobson

Myrtle for Two

Odes of Horace I, 38

Persian flummery—
Boy, how I hate it!
Not with linden bark
Let our wreaths be plaited;
And no roses, hark!
Late and last-of-summery.

Simple myrtle gather.
Myrtle, boy, is fitting
For a head like thine;
And while I drink, sitting
Shaded by the vine,
Myrtle suits me, rather.

George F. Whicher

Chicago Analogue

Odes of Horace I, 38

I do not share the common craze
    For food with jazzy singers;
Boy, tell me not of cabarets,
    Where the late Loophound lingers.

A glass of home brew cool and clear
    Wets down my home-cooked victuals;
So long as I can have my beer,
    I'll gladly miss the skittles.

KEITH PRESTON

The Sycophantic Fox and the Gullible Raven

A raven sat upon a tree,
    and not a word he spoke, for
His beak contained a piece of Brie,
    Or, maybe, it was Roquefort:
        We'll make it any kind you please—
        At all events, it was a cheese.

Beneath the tree's umbrageous limb
    A hungry fox sat smiling;
He saw the raven watching him,
    And spoke in words beguiling.
        "J'admire," said he, "ton beau plumage."
        (The which was simply persiflage.)

Two things there are, no doubt you know,
    To which a fox is used:
A rooster that is bound to crow,
    A crow that's bound to roost,

And whichsoever he espies,
He tells the most unblushing lies.

"Sweet fowl," he said, "I understand
    You're more than merely natty,
I hear you sing to beat the band
    And Adelina Patti.
        Pray render with your liquid tongue
        A bit from 'Götterdämmerung.' "

This subtle speech was aimed to please
    The crow, and it succeeded:
He thought no bird in all the trees
    Could sing as well as he did.
        In flattery completely doused,
        He gave the "Jewel Song" from "Faust."

But gravitation's law, of course,
    As Isaac Newton showed it,
Exerted on the cheese its force,
    And elsewhere soon bestowed it.
        In fact, there is no need to tell
        What happened when to earth it fell.

I blush to add that when the bird
    Took in the situation
He said one brief, emphatic word,
    Unfit for publication.
        The fox was greatly startled, but
        He only sighed and answered "Tut."

The moral is: A fox is bound
    To be a shameless sinner.
And also: When the cheese comes round
    You know it's after dinner.
        But (what is only known to few)
        The fox is after dinner, too.

GUY WETMORE CARRYL

HE NEVER DID THAT TO ME

Verse 1   I have been a Movie fan
               Since the cinemas first began;
               My young brother's a cameraman,
               And when I start
               Meeting heroes of romance,
               I shall firmly take my chance.
               Though I find the hero charming,
               I prefer the more alarming
               Man who plays the villain's part.
               The things he does to nice young girls
               Aren't easy to forget;
               He never minces matters,
               When he traps them in his net.

Refrain 1   He never did that to me;
               He never did that to me;
               Though I must admit
               He wasn't a bit
               Like what I'd supposed he'd be.
               The way that he uses
               Ingénues is
               Really a sight to see;
               He binds them across his saddle tight,
               Regardless of all their shrieks of fright,
               And carries them upside down all night,
               He never did that to me.

Refrain 2   He never did that to me;
               He never did that to me;
               Though I must admit
               He wasn't a bit
               Like what I'd supposed he'd be.
               I once saw him save
               A Christian slave,
               And gallantly set her free.

She knelt at his feet with downcast head;
'God will reward you, sir', she said.
He gave her a look and shot her dead,
He never did that to me.

Verse 2

Though my disappointment's great,
I shall never procrastinate,
I'm determined to watch and wait,
And then you'll see;
He'll revert to type, perhaps,
Have a violent moral lapse,
When the moment's quite propitious,
He'll do something really vicious.
Think how lovely that will be.
His reputation's terrible,
Which comforts me a lot;
If any girl is seen with him,
She's branded on the spot.

Refrain 3

He never did that to me;
He never did that to me;
Though I must admit
He wasn't a bit
Like what I'd supposed he'd be.
He went in his car
But not too far,
Some mutual friends to see;
The car gave a lurch and then a skid,
We didn't turn over—God forbid!
Whatever you may have *thought* he did,
He never did that to me.

Refrain 4

He never did that to me;
He never did that to me;
Though I must admit
He wasn't a bit
Like what I'd supposed he'd be.
I once saw him fish
The Sisters Gish

From out of a stormy sea;
He locked them in his refined Rolls Royce,
And said in a most determined voice,
'It's death or dishonour—take your choice!'
He never did that to me.

NOEL COWARD

THE PURPLE COW

I never saw a Purple Cow,
    I never hope to see one;
But I can tell you, anyhow,
    I'd rather see than be one.

GELETT BURGESS

CONFESSION

Ah, yes! I wrote the "Purple Cow"—
    I'm Sorry, now, I Wrote it,
But I can Tell you Anyhow,
    I'll Kill you if you Quote it.

GELETT BURGESS

HAMLET

Prince Hamlet thought Uncle a traitor
For having it off with his Mater;
    Revenge Dad or not?
    That's the gist of the plot,
And he did—nine soliloquies later.

STANLEY J. SHARPLESS

You're the Top

You're the top!
You're Miss Pinkham's tonic.
You're the top!
You're a high colonic.
You're the burning heat of a bridal suite in use,
You're the breasts of Venus,
You're King Kong's penis,
You're self-abuse.
You're an arch
In the Rome collection.
You're the starch
In a groom's erection.
I'm a eunuch who
Has just been through an op,
But if, Baby, I'm the bottom
You're the top.

> ANONYMOUS (Erotic lyrics are anonymous and not by
> Cole Porter. They are printed with apologies to him.)

Brush Up Your Shakespeare

The girls today in society
Go for classical poetry,
So to win their hearts one must quote with ease
Aeschylus and Euripides.
One must know Homer and, b'lieve me, bo,
Sophocles, also Sappho-ho.
Unless you know Shelley and Keats and Pope,
Dainty debbies will call you a dope.
But the poet of them all
Who will start 'em simply ravin'
Is the poet people call
"The bard of Stratford-on-Avon."

Brush up your Shakespeare,
Start quoting him now,

Brush up your Shakespeare
And the women you will wow.
Just declaim a few lines from "Othella"
And they'll think you're a helluva fella,
If your blonde won't respond when you flatter 'er
Tell her what Tony told Cleopaterer,
If she fights when her clothes you are mussing,
What are clothes? "Much Ado About Nussing."
Brush up your Shakespeare
And they'll all kowtow.

Brush up your Shakespeare,
Start quoting him now,
Brush up your Shakespeare
And the women you will wow.
With the wife of the British embessida
Try a crack out of "Troilus and Cressida,"
If she says she won't buy it or tike it
Make her tike it, what's more, "As You Like It."
If she says your behavior is heinous
Kick her right in the "Coriolanus,"
Brush up your Shakespeare
And they'll all kowtow.

Brush up your Shakespeare,
Start quoting him now,
Brush up your Shakespeare
And the women you will wow.
If you can't be a ham and do "Hamlet"
They will not give a damn or a damnlet,
Just recite an occasional sonnet
And your lap'll have "Honey" upon it,
When your baby is pleading for pleasure
Let her sample you "Measure for Measure,"
Brush up your Shakespeare
And they'll all kowtow.

Brush up your Shakespeare,
Start quoting him now,

Brush up your Shakespeare
And the women you will wow.
Better mention "The Merchant of Venice"
When her sweet pound o' flesh you would menace,
If her virtue, at first, she defends—well,
Just remind her that "All's Well That Ends Well,"
And if still she won't give you a bonus
You know what Venus got from Adonis!
Brush up your Shakespeare
And they'll all kowtow.

Brush up your Shakespeare
Start quoting him now,
Brush up your Shakespeare
And the women you will wow.
If your goil is a Washington Heights dream
Treat the kid to "A Midsummer Night's Dream,"
If she then wants an all-by-herself night
Let her rest ev'ry 'leventh or "Twelfth Night,"
If because of your heat she gets huffy
Simply play on and "Lay on, Macduffy!"
Brush up your Shakespeare
And they'll all kowtow,
We trow, and they'll all kowtow.

Brush up your Shakespeare,
Start quoting him now,
Brush up your Shakespeare
And the women you will wow.
So tonight just recite to your matey,
"Kiss me, Kate, kiss me, Kate, kiss me, Katey,"
Brush up your Shakespeare
And they'll all kowtow.

COLE PORTER

To Minerva

My temples throb, my pulses boil,
    I'm sick of Song and Ode and Ballad—
So Thyrsis, take the Midnight Oil,
    And pour it on a lobster salad.

My brain is dull, my sight is foul,
    I cannot write a verse, or read,—
Then Pallas, take away thine Owl,
    And let us have a lark instead.

THOMAS HOOD

[The Limerick Is Furtive And Mean]

The limerick is furtive and mean;
You must keep her in close quarantine,
    Or she sneaks to the slums
    And promptly becomes
Disorderly, drunk and obscene.

MORRIS BISHOP

Song (*from* "Patience")

If you're anxious for to shine in the high esthetic line as a man
    of culture rare,
You must get up all the germs of the transcendental terms, and
    plant them everywhere.
You must lie upon the daisies and discourse in novel phrases
    of your complicated state of mind,
The meaning doesn't matter if it's only idle chatter of a tran-
    scendental kind.
            And every one will say
            As you walk your mystic way,
"If this young man expresses himself in terms too deep for *me*,

Why, what a very singularly deep young man this deep young
    man must be!"

Be eloquent in praise of the very dull old days which have
    long since passed away,
And convince 'em, if you can, that the reign of good Queen
    Anne was Culture's palmiest day.
Of course you will pooh-pooh whatever's fresh and new, and
    declare it's crude and mean;
For art stopped short in the cultivated court of the Empress
    Josephine.
        And every one will say
        As you walk your mystic way,
"If that's not good enough for him which is good enough for
    me,
Why, what a very cultivated kind of youth this kind of youth
    must be!"

Then a sentimental passion of a vegetable fashion must excite
    your languid spleen,
An attachment *à la Plato* for a bashful young potato, or a not-
    too-French French bean!
Though the Philistines may jostle, you will rank as an apostle
    in the high esthetic band,
If you walk down Piccadilly, with a poppy or a lily in your
    medieval hand.
        And every one will say,
        As you walk your flowery way,
"If he's content with a vegetable love which would certainly
    not suit *me,*
Why, what a particularly pure young man this pure young
    man must be!"

W. S. GILBERT

Cacoëthes Scribendi

If all the trees in all the woods were men,
And each and every blade of grass a pen;
If every leaf on every shrub and tree
Turned to a sheet of foolscap; every sea
Were changed to ink, and all earth's living tribes
Had nothing else to do but act as scribes,
And for ten thousand ages, day and night,
The human race should write, and write, and write,
Till all the pens and paper were used up,
And the huge inkstand was an empty cup,
Still would the scribblers clustered round its brink
Call for more pens, more paper, and more ink.

                                    Oliver Wendell Holmes

The Good Old Days

When love was structured, so was verse—both fit
Reflections of those times severe and proud
When rituals informed the sonnet's wit
And rhyme described such bliss the law allowed.

Now? None of the above
Few norms
No forms
Little reason
Less rhyme
The only sequence
A careless mumble
Of
        one
            night
        Stands

                                    Barbara Fried

To a Thesaurus

O precious code, volume, tome,
    Book, writing, compilation, work
Attend the while I pen a pome,
    A jest, a jape, a quip, a quirk.

For I would pen, engross, indite,
    Transcribe, set forth, compose, address,
Record, submit—yea, even write
    An ode, an elegy to bless—

To bless, set store by, celebrate,
    Approve, esteem, endow with soul,
Commend, acclaim, appreciate,
    Immortalize, laud, praise, extol,

Thy merit, goodness, value, worth,
    Experience, utility—
O mana, honey, salt of earth,
    I sing, I chant, I worship thee!

How could I manage, live, exist,
    Obtain, produce, be real, prevail,
Be present in the flesh, subsist,
    Have place, become, breathe or inhale,

Without thy help, recruit, support,
    Opitulation, furtherance,
Assistance, rescue, aid, resort,
    Favour, sustention and advance?

Alack! Alack! and well-a-day!
    My case would then be dour and sad,
Likewise distressing, dismal, gray,
    Pathetic, mournful, dreary, bad.

Though I could keep this up all day,
    This lyric, elegiac, song,
Meseems hath come the time to say
    Farewell! Adieu! Good-by! So long!

                    FRANKLIN P. ADAMS ("F.P.A.")

THE PARENTAL CRITIC

We cannot bear to roast a book
    Nor brutally attack it;
We lay it gently on our lap
    And dust its little jacket.

                    KEITH PRESTON

ON HIS BOOKS

When I am dead, I hope it may be said:
'His sins were scarlet, but his books were read.'

                    HILAIRE BELLOC

TO A LIVING AUTHOR

Your comedy I've read, my friend,
    And like the half you pilfer'd best;
But sure the piece you yet may mend:
    Take courage, man! and steal the rest.

                    ANONYMOUS

WHAT'S GOOD FOR THE SOUL
IS GOOD FOR SALES

If fictive music fails your lyre, confess—
Though not, of course, to any happiness.

So it be tristful, tell us what you choose:
Hangover, Nixon on the TV news,
God's death, the memory of your rocking-horse,
Entropy, housework, Buchenwald, divorce,
Those damned flamingoes in your neighbor's yard . . .
All hangs together if you take it hard.

RICHARD WILBUR

TO AN AMERICAN POET JUST DEAD

In the *Boston Sunday Herald* just three lines
Of no-point type for you who used to sing
The praises of imaginary wines,
And died, or so I'm told, of the real thing.

Also gone, but a lot less forgotten,
Are an eminent cut-rate druggist, a lover of Giving,
A lender, and various brokers: gone from this rotten
Taxable world to a higher standard of living.

It is out in the comfy suburbs I read you are dead,
And the soupy summer is settling, full of the yawns
Of Sunday fathers loitering late in bed,
And the ssshh of sprays on all the little lawns.

Will the sprays weep wide for you their chaplet tears?
For you will the deep-freeze units melt and mourn?
For you will Studebakers shred their gears
And sound from each garage a muted horn?

They won't. In summer sunk and stupefied
The suburbs deepen in their sleep of death.
And though they sleep the sounder since you died
It's just as well that now you save your breath.

RICHARD WILBUR

The Sorrows of Werther

Werther had a love for Charlotte
    Such as words could never utter;
Would you know how first he met her?
    She was cutting bread and butter.

Charlotte was a married lady,
    And a moral man was Werther,
And for all the wealth of Indies,
    Would do nothing for to hurt her.

So he sighed and pined and ogled,
    And his passion boiled and bubbled,
Till he blew his silly brains out,
    And no more was by it troubled.

Charlotte, having seen his body
    Borne before her on a shutter,
Like a well-conducted person,
    Went on cutting bread and butter.

                    WILLIAM MAKEPEACE THACKERAY

Thomas Hardy and A. E. Housman

How compare either of this grim twain?
    Each has an equal knack,
Hardy prefers the pill that's blue,
    Housman the draught that's black.

                    MAX BEERBOHM

On English Monsieur

Would you believe, when you this mónsieur see,
That his whole body, should speak French, not he?

That so much scarf of France, and hat, and feather,
And shoe, and tie, and garter should come hether,
And land on one whose face durst never be
Toward the sea farther then Half-Way Tree?
That he, untraveled, should be French so much
As Frenchmen in his company should seem Dutch?
Or had his father, when he did him get,
The French disease, with which he labors yet?
Or hung some mónsieur's picture on the wall,
By which his dam conceived him, clothes and all?
Or is it some French statue? No: 'T doth move,
And stoop, and cringe, O then, it needs must prove
The new French tailor's motion monthly made,
Daily to turn in Paul's, and help the trade.

BEN JONSON

(*from* JONSONIAN POEM IN PROGRESS)

I put my hat upon my head,
And walked into the Strand,
And there I met another man
Whose hat was in his hand.

'Pray, sir,' I said, 'why don't you place
Your hat upon your head?'
He cried, 'Be silent, meddling fool,
And may God strike you dead!'

I turned astonished and distressed
By words so fierce and rude.
Then, on a sudden, lightning flashed
And killed him where he stood.

From the dark clouds that glowered above
There came a mighty roar:
'I missed you, Johnson—damn it all,
I ought to practise more.'

Much shaken, I resumed my stroll,
Pondering what I'd heard,
And even Boswell, when we met,
Would not believe a word.

                                        PETER VEALE

SURVEY OF LITERATURE

In all the good Greek of Plato
I lack my roast beef and potato.

A better man was Aristotle,
Pulling steady on the bottle.

I dip my hat to Chaucer,
Swilling soup from his saucer,

And to Master Shakespeare
Who wrote big on small beer.

The abstemious Wordsworth
Subsisted on a curd's-worth,

But a slick one was Tennyson,
Putting gravy on his venison.

What these men had to eat and drink
Is what we say and what we think.

The influence of Milton
Came wry out of Stilton.

Sing a song for Percy Shelley,
Drowned in pale lemon jelly,

And for precious John Keats,
Dripping blood of pickled beets.

Then there was poor Willie Blake,
He foundered on sweet cake.

God have mercy on the sinner
Who must write with no dinner,

No gravy and no grub,
No pewter and no pub,

No belly and no bowels,
Only consonants and vowels.

JOHN CROWE RANSOM

MYSTERY STORY

Formal as a minuet or sonnet,
It zeroes in on the guilty one;
But by the time I'm told who done it,
I can't remember what he done.

HOWARD NEMEROV

THE PROBATIOUN OFFICERES TALE

The lede guiterriste was a craftie ladde,
Wel koude he luren chickes to his padde
To dyg the sownes of Clapton or The Stones
And share a joynte and turn on for the nones,
Till met he wyth a drogge squadde maiden fayre
Who yaf him think she was a Frenssche au pair,
That whan at last he caused hir sens to feynte
And subtilly to frote hir at the queynte,
And whyspere sucred words and strook her sore,
'Lay on!' she cried, 'my rammysh prikasour!'
For she was nothing loth to amorous sport
So be she got hir Pusheres into court.

GERARD BENSON

On Scott's "The Field of Waterloo"

On Waterloo's ensanguined plain
Lie tens of thousands of the slain;
But none, by sabre or by shot,
Fell half so flat as Walter Scott.

THOMAS, LORD ERSKINE

Oboe

Hard to pronounce and play, the OBOE—
(With cultured folk it rhymes with
        "doughboy"
Though many an intellectual hobo
Insists that we should call it oboe)
However, be that as it may,
Whene'er the oboe sounds its A
All of the others start their tuning
And there is fiddling and bassooning.
Its plaintive note presaging gloom
Brings anguish to the concert room,
Even the player holds his breath
And scares the audience to death
For fear he may get off the key,
Which happens not infrequently.
This makes the saying understood:
"It's an ill wood wind no one blows good."

LAURENCE McKINNEY

A Ballad

In the Manner of R-dy-rd K-pl-ng

As I was walkin' the jungle round, a-killin' of tigers an' time;
I seed a kind of an author man a-writin' a rousin' rhyme;

'E was writin' a mile a minute an' more, an' I sez to 'im,
   " 'Oo are you?"
Sez 'e, "I'm a poet—'er majesty's poet—soldier an' sailor, too!"
An' 'is poem began in Ispahan an' ended in Kalamazoo,
It 'ad army in it, an' navy in it, an' jungle sprinkled through,
For 'e was a poet—'er majesty's poet—soldier an' sailor, too!

An' after, I met 'im all over the world, a doin' of things a host;
'E 'ad one foot planted in Burmah, an' one on the Gloucester coast;
'E's 'alf a sailor an' 'alf a whaler, 'e's captain, cook, and crew,
But most a poet—'er majesty's poet—soldier an' sailor too!
'E's often Scot an' 'e's often not, but 'is work is never through
For 'e laughs at blame, an' 'e writes for fame, an' a bit for
   revenoo,—
Bein' a poet—'er majesty's poet—soldier an' sailor too!

'E'll take you up to the Ar'tic zone, 'e'll take you down to the Nile,
'E'll give you a barrack ballad in the Tommy Atkins style,
Or 'e'll sing you a Dipsy Chantey, as the bloomin' bo'suns do,
For 'e is a poet—'er majesty's poet—soldier an' sailor too.
An' there isn't no room for others, an' there's nothin' left to do;
'E 'as sailed the main from the 'Orn to Spain, 'e 'as tramped the
   jungle through,
An' written up all there is to write—soldier an' sailor, too!

There are manners an' manners of writin', but 'is is the *proper* way,
An' it ain't so hard to be a bard if you'll imitate Rudyard K.;
But sea an' shore an' peace an' war, an' everything else in view—
'E 'as gobbled the lot!—'er majesty's poet—soldier an' sailor,
   too.
'E's not content with 'is Indian 'ome, 'e's looking for regions new,
In another year 'e'll 'ave swept 'em clear, an' what'll the rest of
   us do?
'E's crowdin' us out!—'er majesty's poet—soldier an' sailor too!

GUY WETMORE CARRYL

('ALL THE WORLD'S A STAGE . . .')

Seven ages, first puking and mewling,
Then very pissed off with one's schooling,
   Then fucks, and then fights,
   Then judging chaps' rights;
Then sitting in slippers; then drooling.

                                        VICTOR GRAY

BIRDIE McREYNOLDS

I kept the house on the corner of Linden and Pineapple Streets,
Down in the district.
And a lively house it was, too,
For a burg like Fork River.
I liked the business,
And that's why I went in it.
Nobody has to do anything he doesn't want to.
How else could I have stuck it out in that hick town?
Imagine me a Fork River housewife,
With a Fork River husband,
The kind that used to come down to my house—
Me, Birdie McReynolds!
Don't make me swallow some dirt.
I never lost my virtue.
Don't think it!
I gave it away for a while,
And then I sold it,
And I had a good time both ways.
I knew everybody,
And everybody liked me.
I kept the judge in his place,
The Mayor, the Sheriff, and the Councilmen,
Or the town couldn't have held them.
They needed somebody like me to tone them down,
The poor, swell-headed, small-town fish,

And it's usually a Birdie McReynolds that does it.
I could read a man's character
By the kind of suspenders he wore;
The old sports went in for white silk ones
With "Fireman" or "Policeman" engraved on the buckles.
It made them feel virile,
The poor saps!
Don't think you'll get a sob-story out of me, Eddie Masters;
I wasn't that kind of a jezebel.
There ain't any, anyhow.
It's the good women must weep
While the men work.
We like them to work—
They spend more.
Now go away and let me sleep;
That's one thing I never got enough of
In my business,
Or I wouldn't be here.

SAMUEL HOFFENSTEIN

MISS MILLAY SAYS SOMETHING TOO

I want to drown in good-salt water,
I want my body to bump the pier;
Neptune is calling his wayward daughter,
Crying, "Edna, come over here!"

I hate the town and I hate the people;
I hate the dryness of floor and pave;
The spar of a ship is my tall church-steeple;
My soul is wet as the wettest wave.

I'm seven-eighths salt and I want to roister
Deep in the brine with the submarine;
I speak the speech of the whale and oyster;
I know the ways of the wild sardine.

I'm tired of standing still and staring
Across the sea with my heels in dust:
I want to live like the sober herring,
And die as pickled when die I must.

SAMUEL HOFFENSTEIN

PUBLIC JOURNAL

VERSES INSPIRED BY A DAY SPENT IN
COMMUNION WITH THE BRIGHT YOUNG
MEN OF ENGLISH VERSE

Christopher Isherwood, Stephen Spender,
  Auden and L. MacNeice—
I can't come along on an all-night bender,
  But I'll have a quick one with you.

It is four in the afternoon. Time still for a poem,
A poem not topical, wholly, or romantic, or metaphysic,
But fetched from the grab-bag of my mind and gaudy with
Symbol, slogan, quotation, and even music.
And many a Marxian maxim and many allusions
To a daft system and a world-disorder.
I will mention machines and the eight hour day and
Czecho-Slovakia and the invaded border.

I will speak of love and I will do it slyly,
Unloosing the sacred girdle with a tired air,
Taking particular pains to notice the elastic garters
And the literal underwear.

I will put learning into my poem, for I acquired learning
At Cambridge or Oxford, it does not matter which.
But I'll freshen it up with slang which I got by ear,
Though it may sound a little off pitch.
And I'll be casual with rhymes for that is the trend,
Fashionable as the black hat of Anthony Eden.
I may put them at the middle of the stanza instead of the end,
For really amazing effect.

Or perhaps I'll find that assonance heightens the meaning better.
Yes, definitely, I prefer the latter.

Well, it will be sport, writing my privates hates
And my personal credo.
I must bring in how I went to Spain on a holiday,
And how cold it was in Toledo.
There was a bootblack, too, in Madrid,
Who gave my shoes a burnish.
He told me something important which I cannot repeat,
For though I understand Spain, I do not understand Spanish.

I'll recall autumn weather in Birmingham,
Drearier than Boston.
And the pump-attendant there who sold me stormy petrol
For my thirsting Austin.

I will put tarts into my poem, and tenement people,
The poor but not the meek;
And pieces of popular songs for a hint of nostalgia,
And bits of Greek.

I shall be tough and ardent and angry-eyed,
Aware that the world is dying, gasping, its face grown pallid;
But quick to embalm it in language as an aspic
Enfolds the chicken salad.

Now it is five o'clock. The poem is finished
Like Poland, like the upper classes, like Sunday's roast.
I must straighten my waistcoat and see that it goes straight out
By the evening post.

For what is left for us? Only
The stanza a day,
And the American royalties, and an inherited income,
To keep the wolf at bay.

PHYLLIS McGINLEY

Upon Julia's Arctics

Whenas galoshed my Julia goes,
Unbuckled all from top to toes,
How swift the poem becometh prose!
And when I cast mine eyes and see
Those arctics flopping each way free,
Oh, how that flopping floppeth me!

BERT LESTON TAYLOR ("B.L.T.")

What, Still Alive

What, still alive at twenty-two,
A clean upstanding chap like you?
Sure, if your throat 'tis hard to slit,
Slit your girl's, and swing for it.

Like enough, you won't be glad,
When they come to hang you, lad:
But bacon's not the only thing
That's cured by hanging from a string.

So, when the spilt ink of the night
Spreads o'er the blotting pad of light,
Lads whose job is still to do
Shall whet their knives, and think of you.

HUGH KINGSMILL

Variations on a Theme by William Carlos Williams

1

I chopped down the house that you had been saving to live in next
summer.

I am sorry, but it was morning, and I had nothing to do
and its wooden beams were so inviting.
     2
We laughed at the hollyhocks together
and then sprayed them with lye.
Forgive me. I simply do not know what I am doing.
     3
I gave away the money that you had been saving to live on for
     the next ten years.
The man who asked for it was shabby
and the firm March wind on the porch was so juicy and cold.
     4
Last evening we went dancing and I broke your leg.
Forgive me. I was clumsy, and
I wanted you here in the wards, where I am a doctor.

Kenneth Koch

Chard Whitlow

(Mr. Eliot's Sunday Evening Postscript)

As we get older we do not get any younger.
Seasons return, and today I am fifty-five,
And this time last year I was fifty-four,
And this time next year I shall be sixty-two.
And I cannot say I should care (to speak for myself)
To see my time over again—if you can call it time,
Fidgeting uneasily under a draughty stair,
Or counting sleepless nights in the crowded Tube.

There are certain precautions—though none of them very reliable—
Against the blast from bombs, or the flying splinter,
But not against the blast from Heaven, *vento dei venti*,
The wind within a wind, unable to speak for wind;
And the frigid burnings of purgatory will not be touched
By any emollient.
                    I think you find this put,
Far better than I could ever hope to express it,

In the words of Kharma: 'It is, we believe,
Idle to hope that the simple stirrup-pump
Can extinguish hell.'
                    Oh, listeners,
And you especially who have switched off the wireless,
And sit in Stoke or Basingstoke, listening appreciatively to the
    silence
(Which is also the silence of hell), pray not for yourselves but
    your souls.

And pray for me also under the draughty stair.
As we get older we do not get any younger.

And pray for Kharma under the holy mountain.

HENRY REED

FROM EMILY DICKINSON
IN SOUTHERN CALIFORNIA

I called one day—on Eden's strand
But did not find her—Home—
Surfboarders triumphed in—in Waves—
Archangels of the Foam—

I walked a pace—I tripped across
Browned couples—in cahoots—
No more than Tides need shells to fill
Did they need—bathing suits—

From low boughs—that the Sun kist—hung
A Fruit to taste—at will—
October rustled but—Mankind
Seemed elsewhere gone—to Fall—

X. J. KENNEDY

JUSTICE TO SCOTLAND

An Unpublished poem by Burns

O mickle yeuks the keckle doup,
 An' a' unsicker girns the graith,
For wae and wae! the crowdies loup
 O'er jouk an' hallan, braw an' baith
Where ance the coggie hirpled fair,
 And blithesome poortith toomed the loof,
There's nae a burnie giglet rare
 But blaws in ilka jinking coof.

The routhie bield that gars the gear
 Is gone where glint the pawky een.
And aye the stound is birkin lear
 Where sconnered yowies wheeped yestreen,
The creeshie rax wi' skelpin' kaes
 Nae mair the howdie bicker whangs,
Nor weanies in their wee bit claes
 Glour light as lammies wi' their sangs.

Yet leeze me on my bonny byke!
 My drappie aiblins blinks the noo,
An' leesome luve has lapt the dyke
 Forgatherin' just a wee bit fou.
And Scotia! while thy rantin' lunt
 Is mirk and moop with gowans fine,
I'll stowlins pit my unco brunt,
 An' cleek my duds for auld lang syne.

ANONYMOUS

Variations on an Air Composed on Having to Appear in a Pageant as Old King Cole

After Walt Whitman

Me clairvoyant,
Me conscious of you, old camarado,
Needing no telescope, lorgnette, field-glass, opera-glass,
    pince-nez,
Me piercing two thousand years with eye naked and not
    ashamed;
The crown cannot hide you from me;
Musty old feudal-heraldic trappings cannot hide you from me,
I perceive that you drink.
(I am drinking with you. I am as drunk as you are.)
I see you are inhaling tobacco, puffing, smoking, spitting
(I do not object to your spitting),
You prophetic of American largeness,
You anticipating the broad masculine manners of these States;
I see in you also there are movements, tremors, tears, desire for
    the melodious,
I salute your three violinists, endlessly making vibrations,
Rigid, relentless, capable of going on for ever;
They play my accompaniment; but I shall take no notice of any
    accompaniment;
I myself am a complete orchestra.
So long

                                                    G. K. Chesterton

Some Fun with the Mother Tongue ~

Ascot Waistcoat

Prescott, press my Ascot waistcoat—
Let's not risk it
Just to whisk it:
Yes, my Ascot waistcoat, Prescott.
Worn subfusc, it's
Cool and dusk: it
Might be grass-cut
But it's Ascot,
And it fits me like a gasket—
Ascot is *the* waistcoat, Prescott!
Please get
Off the spot of grease. Get
Going, Prescott—
Where's that waistcoat?
It's no task at
All, an Ascot:
Easy to clean a musket
Or to dust an ivory tusk. It
Doesn't take a lot of fuss. Get
To it, Prescott,
Since I ask it:
We can't risk it—

Let's not whisk it.
That's the waistcoat;
Thank *you*, Prescott.

DAVID McCORD

ON THE MOTOR BUS

What is this that roareth thus?
Can it be a Motor Bus?
Yes, the smell and hideous hum
Indicant Motorem Bum!
Implet in the Corn and High
Terror me Motoris Bi:
Bo Motori clamitabo
Ne Motore caedar a Bo—
Dative be or Ablative
So thou only let us live:—
Whither shall thy victims flee?
Spare us, spare us, Motor Be!
Thus I sang; and still anigh
Came in hordes Motores Bi,
Et complebat omne forum
Copia Motorum Borum.
How shall wretches live like us
Cincti Bis Motoribus?
Domine, defende nos
Contra hos Motores Bos!

A. D. GODLEY

THE AMERICAN INDIAN

There once were some people called Sioux
Who spent all their time making shioux
Which they colored in various hioux;

Don't think that they made them to ioux
Oh, no! they just sold them for bioux.

Anonymous

'Twixt Cup and Lip

The introduction of a refrain
(With a Taisez-vous and a Vive le Roi)
In a foreign language now and again
Gives a poem a *je ne sais quoi.*

And a *je ne sais quoi* is what I need
(With an a, ab, absque, coram, de)
To tell of Uncle John's good deed
(With a bene, melius, optime).

For what do you think that Uncle did?
(With Sitzen Sie and a Komm herein)
He gave me a cheque for fifty quid
(With a Kraft durch Freude and Wacht am Rhein).

I flung my arms round Uncle's neck
(With a Far niente and Nada hoy)
But the bank have just dishonoured the cheque
(With a Mene Tekel and ὀτοτοτοῖ).

Mark Hollis

Everything in Its Place

The skeleton is hiding in the closet as it should,
The needle's in the haystack and the trees are in the wood,
The fly is in the ointment and the froth is on the beer,
The bee is in the bonnet and the flea is in the ear.

The meat is in the coconut, the cat is in the bag,
The dog is in the manger and the goat is on the crag,
The worm is in the apple and the clam is on the shore,
The birds are in the bushes and the wolf is at the door.

ARTHUR GUITERMAN

CARMEN POSSUM

The nox was lit by lux of Luna,
And 'twas a nox most opportuna
To catch a possum or a coona;
For nix was scattered o'er this mundus,
A shallow nix, et non profundus.
On sic a nox with canis unus,
Two boys went out to hunt for coonus.
The corpus of this bonus canis
Was full as long as octo span is,
But brevior legs had canis never
Quam had hic dog; et bonus clever,
Some used to say, in stultum jocum
Quod a field was too small locum
For sic a dog to make a turnus
Circum self from stem to sternus.
Unis canis, duo puer,
Nunquam braver, nunquam truer,
Quam hoc trio nunquam fuit,
If there was I never knew it.
This bonus dog had one bad habit,
Amabat much to tree a rabbit,
Amabat plus to chase a rattus,
Amabat bene tree a cattus.
But on this nixy moonlight night
This old canis did just right.
Nunquam treed a starving rattus,
Nunquam chased a starving cattus.
But sucurrit on, intentus
On the track and on the scentus,

Till he trees a possum strongum,
In a hollow trunkem longum.
Loud he barked in horrid bellum,
Seemed on terra vehit pellum.
Quickly ran the duo puer
Mors of possum to secure.
Quam venerit, one began
To chop away like quisque man.
Soon the axe went through the truncum
Soon he hit it all kerchunkum;
Combat deepens, on ye braves!
Canis, pueri et staves;
As his powers on longius tarry,
Possum potest, non pugnare.
On the nix his corpus lieth.
Down to Hades spirit flieth,
Joyful pueri, canis bonus,
Think him dead as any stonus.

Now they seek their pater's domo
Feeling proud as any homo,
Knowing, certe, they will blossom
Into heroes, when with possum
They arrive, narrabunt story,
Plenus blood et plenior glory.
Pompey, David, Samson, Caeser,
Cyrus, Black Hawk, Shalmanezer!
Tell me where est now the gloria,
Where the honors of victoria?
Nunc a domum narrent story,
Plenus sanguine, tragic, gory.
Pater praiseth, likewise mater,
Wonders greatly younger frater.
Possum leave they on the mundus,
Go themselves to sleep profundus,
Somniunt possums slain in battle,
Strong as ursae, large as cattle.
When nox gives way to lux of morning,
Albam terram much adorning,

Up they jump to see the varmen,
Of the which this is the carmen.
Lo! possum est resurrectum!
Ecce pueri dejectum,
Ne relinquit track behind him,
Et the pueri never find him.
Cruel possum! bestia vilest,
How the pueros thou beguilest!
Pueri think non plus of Caesar,
Go ad Orcum, Shalmanezer,
Take your laurels, cum the honor,
Since ista possum is a goner!

Anonymous

The Naughty Preposition

I lately lost a preposition:
    It hid, I thought, beneath my chair.
And angrily I cried: 'Perdition!
    Up from out of in under there!'

Correctness is my vade mecum,
    And straggling phrases I abhor;
And yet I wondered: 'What should he come
    Up from out of in under for?'

Morris Bishop

O-U-G-H

A Fresh Hack at an Old Knot

I'm taught P-l-o-u-g-h
    S'all be pronounce "plow."
"Zat's easy w'en you know," I say,
    "Mon Anglais, I'll get through!"

My teacher say zat in zat case,
    O-u-g-h is "oo."
An zen I laugh and say to him,
    "Zees Anglais make me cough."

He say "Not 'coo,' but in zat word,
    O-u-g-h is 'off,' "
Oh, *Sacre bleu!* such varied sounds
    Of words makes my hiccough!

He say, "Again mon frien' ees wrong;
    O-u-g-h is 'up'
In hiccough." Zen I cry, "No more,
    You make my t'roat feel rough."

"Non, non!" he cry, "you are not right;
    O-u-g-h is 'uff.' "
I say, "I try to spik your words,
    I cannot spik zem though!"

"In time you'll learn, but now you're wrong!
    O-u-g-h is 'owe.' "
"I'll try no more, I s'all go mad,
    I'll drown me in ze lough!"

"But ere you drown yourself," said he,
    "O-u-g-h is 'ock' "
He taught no more, I held him fast,
    And killed him wiz a rough.

CHARLES BATTELL LOOMIS

IDYLL

He was a selfish shellfish,
    A sylphish shellfish she,
She flirted with a jellfish
    One day, beside the sea.

And, in a manner elfish,
    Yet lacking greed for pelf,
She told the selfish shellfish
    His place was on the shelf.

Then he, in rage, cried: "*Well*, fish,
    Your flirting makes me wroth!"
He fell upon the jellfish
    And beat him to a froth.

To-day, the folk who sell fish
    The touching story tell
Of a sylphish shellfish weeping
    By a selfish shellfish' cell.

                    STODDARD KING

LOCAL NOTE

In Sparkhill buried lies that man of mark
    Who brought the Obelisk to Central Park,
Redoubtable Commander H. H. Gorringe,
    Whose name supplies the long-sought rhyme
    for 'orange'.

                    ARTHUR GUITERMAN

OH, NOA, NOA!

In Aku Aku is there double
The happiness, and half the trouble?
And far away in Bali Bali,
Should not it all be twice as jolly?

Does sunset out in Bora Bora
Reveal a repetitious aura?
And surely every joke would be a
Double entendre in Fia Fia?

Do residents of Pago Pago
Get twice the juice from every mango?
Do people out in Walla Walla
Get twofold value for their dollah?

Don't men in Sing Sing, who for crime go,
Hate like the deuce to see their time go?
And over there in Baden Baden,
I'm sure that life's not half so sodden?

* * * *

Alas! I'm told in *no* vicinity
Is such a thing as blessed twinnity!

WILLIAM COLE

WOOLLY WORDS

The spine has been tingled; the horn has been swoggled.
The blood has been curdled; the polly's been woggled.
    The mind has been bent, and the heart has been rent;
    The pan has been handled; the ambi is ent.
The polysyllabics have got the mind boggled.

So fiddle the faddle while whimming the wham
And cater the corner while flimming the flam.
    The ki has been boshed, the hog has been washed,
    The gast has been flabbered, the buckles are swashed,
And here is a boozle in search of its bam.

The tara's been diddled; the kum has been quat.
The fili's been bustered by Hotten the tot.
    The horn has been piped, and the tin has been typed;
    The knick has been knacked, and the gutter's been sniped,
So hiero the glyphics and poly the glot!

ROBERT N. FEINSTEIN

AN ARAB AND HIS DONKEY

An Arab came to the river side,
  With a donkey bearing an obelisk;
But he would not try to ford the tide,
  For he had too good an *.
    Boston Globe

* * *

So he camped all night by the river side,
  And he remained till the tide ceased to swell,
For he knew should the donkey from life subside,
  He never would find its ||.
    Salem Sunbeam

* * *

When the morning dawned, and tide was out,
  The pair crossed over 'neath Allah's protection;
And the Arab was happy, we have no doubt,
  For he had the best donkey in all that §.
    Somerville Journal

* * *

You are wrong, they were drowned in crossing over,
  Though the donkey was bravest of all his race;
He luxuriates now in horse-heaven clover,
  And his master has gone to the Prophet's #.
    Elevated Railway Journal

* * *

These asinine poets deserved to be "blowed,"
  Their rhymes being faulty and frothy and beery;
What really befell the ass and its load

Will ever remain a desolate ?.
    Paper and Print

* * *

Our Yankee friends, with all their ——
    For once, we guess, their mark have missed;
And with poetry Paper and Print is rash
    In damming its flow with its editor's ☞.

In parable and moral leave a   between,
    For reflection, or your wits fall out of joint;
The "Arab," ye see, is a printing machine,
    And the donkey is he who can't see the .

BRITISH AND COLONIAL PRINTER

LAPSUS LINGUAE

We wanted Li Wing
    But we winged Willie Wong.
A sad but excusable
    Slip of the tong.

KEITH PRESTON

Only Human

Life Cycle of Common Man

Roughly figured, this man of moderate habits,
This average consumer of the middle class,
Consumed in the course of his average life span
Just under half a million cigarettes,
Four thousand fifths of gin and about
A quarter as much vermouth; he drank
Maybe a hundred thousand cups of coffee,
And counting his parents' share it cost
Something like half a million dollars
To put him through life. How many beasts
Died to provide him with meat, belt and shoes
Cannot be certainly said.
                              But anyhow,
It is in this way that a man travels through time,
Leaving behind him a lengthening trail
Of empty bottles and bones, of broken shoes,
Frayed collars and worn out or outgrown
Diapers and dinnerjackets, silk ties and slickers.

Given the energy and security thus achieved,
He did . . .? What? The usual things, of course,
The eating, dreaming, drinking and begetting,
And he worked for the money which was to pay
For the eating, et cetera, which were necessary

If he were to go on working for the money, et cetera,
But chiefly he talked. As the bottles and bones
Accumulated behind him, the words proceeded
Steadily from the front of his face as he
Advanced into the silence and made it verbal.
Who can tally the tale of his words? A lifetime
Would barely suffice for their repetition;
If you merely printed all his commas the result
Would be a very large volume, and the number of times
He said "thank you" or "very little sugar, please,"
Would stagger the imagination. There were also
Witticisms, platitudes, and statements beginning
"It seems to me" or "As I always say."

Consider the courage in all that, and behold the man
Walking into deep silence, with the ectoplastic
Cartoon's balloon of speech proceeding
Steadily out of the front of his face, the words
Borne along on the breath which is his spirit
Telling the numberless tale of his untold Word
Which makes the world his apple, and forces him to eat.

HOWARD NEMEROV

I'M NOBODY! WHO ARE YOU?

I'm nobody! Who are you?
Are you nobody, too?
Then there's a pair of us—don't tell!
They'd banish us, you know.

How dreary to be somebody!
How public, like a frog,
To tell your name the livelong day
To an admiring bog!

EMILY DICKINSON

Brian O'Linn

Brian O'Linn was a gentleman born,
His hair it was long and his beard unshorn,
His teeth were out and his eyes far in—
"I'm a wonderful beauty," says Brian O'Linn!

Brian O'Linn was hard up for a coat,
He borrowed the skin of a neighbouring goat,
He buckled the horns right under his chin—
"They'll answer for pistols," says Brian O'Linn!

Brian O'Linn had no breeches to wear,
He got him a sheepskin to make him a pair,
With the fleshy side out and the woolly side in—
"They are pleasant and cool," says Brian O'Linn!

Brian O'Linn had no hat to his head,
He stuck on a pot that was under the shed,
He murdered a cod for the sake of his fin—
" 'T will pass for a feather," says Brian O'Linn!

Brian O'Linn had no shirt to his back,
He went to a neighbour and borrowed a sack,
He puckered a meal-bag under his chin—
"They'll take it for ruffles," said Brian O'Linn!

Brian O'Linn had no shoes at all,
He bought an old pair at a cobbler's stall,
The uppers were broke and the soles were thin—
"They'll do me for dancing," says Brian O'Linn!

Brian O'Linn had no watch for to wear,
He bought a fine turnip and scooped it out fair,
He slipped a live cricket right under the skin—
"They'll think it is ticking," says Brian O'Linn!

Brian O'Linn was in want of a brooch,
He stuck a brass pin in a big cockroach,
The breast of his shirt he fixed it straight in—
"They'll think it's a diamond," says Brian O'Linn!

Brian O'Linn went a-courting one night,
He set both the mother and daughter to fight—
"Stop, stop," he exclaimed, "if you have but the tin,
I'll marry you both," says Brian O'Linn!

Brian O'Linn went to bring his wife home,
He had but one horse, that was all skin and bone—
"I'll put her behind me, as nate as a pin,
And her mother before me," says Brian O'Linn!

Brian O'Linn and his wife and wife's mother,
They all crossed over the bridge together,
The bridge broke down and they all tumbled in—
"We'll go home by water," says Brian O'Linn!

ANONYMOUS

THE JOLLY BEGGARS

See! the smoking bowl before us,
Mark our jovial ragged ring!
Round and round take up the chorus,
And in raptures let us sing:
A fig for those by law protected!
Liberty's a glorious feast!
Courts for cowards were erected,
Churches built to please the priest.

What is title? what is treasure?
What is reputation's care?
If we lead a life of pleasure,
'Tis no matter when or where.
Life is all a variorum,

We regard not how it goes;
Let them cant about decorum
Who have characters to lose.

ROBERT BURNS

THE DIGNITY OF LABOR

Labor raises honest sweat;
Leisure puts you into debt.

Labor gives you rye and wheat;
Leisure gives you naught to eat.

Labor makes your riches last;
Leisure gets you nowhere fast.

Labor makes you bed at eight;
Leisure lets you stay up late.

Labor makes you swell with pride;
Leisure makes you shrink inside.

Labor keeps you fit and prime,
But give me leisure every time.

ROBERT BERSOHN

WHEN A MAN HATH NO FREEDOM TO FIGHT FOR AT HOME

When a man hath no freedom to fight for at home,
    Let him combat for that of his neighbors;
Let him think of the glories of Greece and of Rome,
    And get knocked on his head for his labors.

To do good to mankind is the chivalrous plan,
    And is always as nobly requited;
Then battle for freedom wherever you can,
    And, if not shot or hanged, you'll get knighted.

GEORGE GORDON, LORD BYRON

CARROUSEL TUNE

Turn again, turn again, turn once again;
the freaks of the cosmic circus are men.

We are the gooks and the geeks of creation;
Believe-It-Or-Not is the name of our star.
Each of us here thinks the other is queer
and no one's mistaken since all of us are!

Turn again, turn again, turn once again;
the freaks of the cosmic circus are men.

We sweat and we fume in a four-cornered room
and love is the reason. But what does love do?
It gives willy-nilly to poor silly Billy
the chance to discover what daddy went through.

Turn again, turn again, turn once again;
the freaks of the cosmic circus are men.

We may hum and hop like a musical top
or stop like a clock that's run down,
but why be downhearted, the season's just started,
and new shows are coming to town!

Turn again, turn again, turn once again;
the freaks of the cosmic circus are men.

TENNESSEE WILLIAMS

from MY MOTHER SHOOTS THE BREEZE

First time I met your Pa he took my slip
Off. "Miss Davis, I want your pretty slip,
If you've got one loose about, for my Science class."
He was going to fly them Benjamin Franklin's kite.
I went to the women's room and squirmed it down
And sneaked it to him in a paper bag.
Under the table at lunch he grinned like a hound.
That afternoon he patched the kite together
And taught them about Electricity.
"Touch that, boys," he said, "if you want a shock.
We've got Miz Silverside's silk panties here."
(Jake Silverside was our Acting Principal.)

But I knew better what I couldn't say
And giggled like a chicken when that kite
Sailed up past my fifth period Spanish window.
I don't know what to tell you how I mean,
But I felt it was me, seeing my slip
Flying up there. It was a childish folly
But it made me warm. I know there's pictures now
Of people doing anything, whatever
Only a doctor could think of, but my slip,
Scented the way that I alone could know,
Flying past the windows made me warm.
J.T.'s the man I want, I thought, *because*
He'd do anything . . . And so he would.

But wouldn't stop . . . Everyday two weeks
In a row he ran that kite up past my window,
Long after he had worn Ben Franklin out.
It's time to show that man that I mean business,
I thought, it's time we both came down to earth.
The very next day I borrowed my daddy's 12 gauge
And smuggled it to school under a raincoat,

And when that kite came past me one more time
I propped and took my time and lagged and sighted
And blew the fool out of it, both barrels.
It floated up and down in a silky snow
Till there was nothing left. I can still remember
Your Pa's mouth open like the arch of a bridge.
"Quit troubling us maiden girls with your silly Science,"
I said, "While we're learning to talk to Mexico."

And one month later, after we were married,
He still called me Annie Mexico.

FRED CHAPPELL

from THREE EPIGRAMS

2. *The Mistake*

He left his pants upon a chair:
She was a widow, so she said:
But he was apprehended, bare,
By one who rose up from the dead.

THEODORE ROETHKE

TO A LADY ACROSS THE WAY

Dear, I do not count it flighty
Thus to frolic in your nightie;
You who have such mirthful ways
Need not fear my curious gaze.
Prettily dance and sweetly carol,
Garbed, 'tis true, in scant apparel;
Blithesome heart and levity
Counteract that brevity.
Bold you are and unafraid,
Ignorant of undrawn shade.

Prithee know, my dear, that I've a
Scorn for him who watched Godiva.

E. B. WHITE

HA! ORIGINAL SIN!

Vanity, vanity, all is vanity
That's any fun at all for humanity.
Food is vanity, so is drink,
And undergarments of gossamer pink.
P. G. Wodehouse and long vacations,
Going abroad, and rich relations,
The kind of engagements you want to keep,
A hundred honours, and twelve hours' sleep.
Vanities all—Oh Worra, worra!
Rooted in Sodom and Gomorrah.

Vanity, vanity, all is vanity
That's any fun at all for humanity.
This is the gist of the prophet's case,
From Bishop Cannon to Canon Chase.
The prophets chant and the prophets chatter,
But somehow it never seems to matter,
For the world hangs on to its ancient sanity
And orders another round of vanity.
Then Hey! for Gomorrah! and Nonny! for Sodom!
Marie! the Chanel model for Modom!

OGDEN NASH

REPENTANCE

"Now that poor, wayward Jane is big with child,
She has repented and is reconciled
To lead a virtuous life in thought and deed."
So spoke her aunt, and all the girls agreed.

Then one of them, an artless, large-eyed one,
Murmured, "Repentance we would never shun—
But first let's learn to do what Jane has done."

Louis Untermeyer

Translation from Jean De La Fontaine

THE SONG OF MEHITABEL

this is the song of mehitabel
of mehitabel the alley cat
as i wrote you before boss
mehitabel is a believer
in the pythagorean
theory of the transmigration
of the soul and she claims
that formerly her spirit
was incarnated in the body
of cleopatra
that was a long time ago
and one must not be
surprised if mehitabel
has forgotten some of her
more regal manners

i have had my ups and downs
but wotthehell wotthehell
yesterday sceptres and crowns
fried oysters and velvet gowns
and today i herd with bums
but wotthehell wotthehell
i wake the world from sleep
as i caper and sing and leap
when i sing my wild free tune
wotthehell wotthehell
under the blear eyed moon
i am pelted with cast off shoon
but wotthehell wotthehell

do you think that i would change
my present freedom to range
for a castle or moated grange
wotthehell wotthehell
cage me and i d go frantic
my life is so romantic
capricious and corybantic
and i m toujours gai toujours gai

i know that i am bound
for a journey down the sound
in the midst of a refuse mound
but wotthehell wotthehell
oh i should worry and fret
death and i will coquette
there s a dance in the old dame yet
toujours gai toujours gai

i once was an innocent kit
wotthehell wotthehell
with a ribbon my neck to fit
and bells tied onto it
o wotthehell wotthehell
but a maltese cat came by
with a come hither look in his eye
and a song that soared to the sky
and wotthehell wotthehell
and i followed adown the street
the pad of his rhythmical feet
o permit me again to repeat
wotthehell wotthehell

my youth i shall never forget
but there s nothing i really regret
wotthehell wotthehell
there s a dance in the old dame yet
toujours gai toujours gai

the things that i had not ought to
i do because i ve gotto
wotthehell wotthehell
and i end with my favorite motto
toujours gai toujours gai

boss sometimes i think
that our friend mehitabel
is a trifle too gay

DON MARQUIS

MOTLEY

Hairband, homespun, opera-hat, afghan,
turtleneck, sheepskin, catskin, buckskin,
denim, dimity, beadwork, braidwork,
rags ripped off from old six-reelers—

all serve as signals to allies and enemies
that Whatintheworld may be taking the air.
Could he be banker, butcher, broker,
madman, marauder, masquerader?

Men who wear ascots, waistcoats, cheviots
are ostracized as doctors, lawyers, palaverers,
rich men and thieves—uncurious costumes!
Young men, beggar men, brawny men saunter

in pigskin, lambskin, desert boots, sandalslippers,
hairshirts and hiphuggers. Others lay footbones
bare to the broken glass, dogshit, chewing gum,
sleep in the park with guitar cases, rucksacks,
stretched on the sidewalk, curbside, fenderwise.

Whether they're indoors, outcast, uptight,
grant them their groin bulges, hairlines, hiplines,
toenails, kneecaps, beardstubble, sticknipples,

grant them their armpits, cockpits, spitballs,
precious possessions, all body-portable.

Better go dogsbody, jackanapes, bareass
than strut through Necropolis unrecognizable,
sexless, seducible, deeply disguisable!

PETER DAVISON

REFLECTIONS AT DAWN

I wish I owned a Dior dress
    Made to my order out of satin.
I wish I weighed a little less
    And could read Latin,
Had perfect pitch or matching pearls,
    A better head for street directions,
And seven daughters, all with curls
    And fair complexions.
I wish I'd tan instead of burn.
    But most, on all the stars that glisten,
I wish at parties I could learn
    to sit and listen.

I wish I didn't talk so much at parties.
It isn't that I want to hear
My voice assaulting every ear,
Uprising loud and firm and clear
    Above the cocktail clatter.
It's simply, once a doorbell's rung,
(I've been like this since I was young)
Some madness overtakes my tongue
    And I begin to chatter.

Buffet, ball, banquet, quilting bee,
    Wherever conversation's flowing,
Why must I feel it falls on me
    To keep things going?

Though ladies cleverer than I
    Can loll in silence, soft and idle,
Whatever topic gallops by,
    I seize its bridle,
Hold forth on art, dissect the stage,
    Or babble like a kindergart'ner
Of politics till I enrage
    My dinner partner.

I wish I didn't talk so much at parties.
When hotly boil the arguments,
Ah! would I had the common sense
To sit demurely on a fence
    And let who will be vocal,
Instead of plunging in the fray
With my opinions on display
Till all the gentlemen edge away
    To catch an early local.

Oh! there is many a likely boon
    That fate might flip me from her griddle.
I wish that I could sleep till noon
    And play the fiddle,
Or dance a *tour jeté* so light
    It would not shake a single straw down.
But when I ponder how last night
    I laid the law down,
More than to have the Midas touch
    Or critics' praise, however hearty,
I wish I didn't talk so much,
I wish I didn't talk *so much,*
I wish *I didn't talk so much,*
    When I am at a party.

PHYLLIS McGINLEY

THIS SMOKING WORLD

Tobacco is a dirty weed:
  I like it.
It satisfies no normal need:
  I like it.
It makes you thin, it makes you lean,
It takes the hair right off your bean,
It's the worst darn stuff I've ever seen:
  I like it.

GRAHAM LEE HEMMINGER

SATURDAY NIGHT

It's Saturday night, and I'm feeling reckless;
I'll stand you a cider, I'll buy you a necklace;
We'll go to the pictures and settle down snugly;
You be my MARY and I'll be your DOUGLY.

        I feel so bright
       On a Saturday night,
  I want to jump over the moon;
      I want to change hats
      With a lady, and that's
  A sign there'll be trouble quite soon.
        Douggie, my boy!
        Mary, ahoy!
Come to the pictures and register joy,
     For it's jolly old Saturday,
     Mad-as-a-Hatter-day,
     Nothing-much-matter-day-night!

It's Saturday night, I could fight the whole town—
Just say the word and I'll knock a man down.
Monday won't happen again till next week;
You be my soul-mate and I'll be your Sheikh.

Saturday night!
Saturday night!
I'm a rash irresponsible spark;
Let's get a box
Of the two-shilling chocs,
And gobble them up in the dark.
Soul-mate, hullo!
Sheikhy, what-ho!
Come to the pictures and let yourself go,
For it's jolly old Saturday,
Mad-as-a-Hatter-day,
Nothing-much-matter-day-night!

It's Saturday night and I like your new hat;
I'm ready to pop with emotion and that;
I'm fizzy and fiery and fruity and tense,
So let's have a sundae and hang the expense!

Saturday night!
Saturday night!
I want to make Hammersmith hum;
I'm longing to thump
A piano, or jump
Up and down on the top of a drum.
Harriet, Hi!
Light of my eye!
Come to the pictures and have a good cry,
For it's jolly old Saturday,
Mad-as-a-Hatter-day,
Nothing-much-matter-day-night!

A. P. HERBERT

DARWINISM IN
THE KITCHEN

I was takin' off my bonnet
One arternoon at three,

When a hinseck jumped upon it
    As proved to be a flea.

Then I takes it to the grate,
    Between the bars to stick it,
But I hadn't long to wait
    Ere it changed into a cricket.

Says I, "Surelie my senses
    Is a-gettin' in a fog!"
So to drown it I commences,
    When it halters to a frog.

Here my heart began to thump,
    And no wonder I felt funky;
For the frog, with one big jump,
    Leaped hisself into a monkey.

Then I opened wide my eyes,
    His features for to scan,
And observed, with great surprise,
    That that monkey was a man.

But he vanished from my sight,
    And I sunk upon the floor,
Just as missus with a light
    Come inside the kitching door.

Then, beginnin' to abuse me,
    She says, "Sarah, you've been drinkin'!"
I says, "No, mum, you'll excuse me,
    But I've merely been a-thinkin'.

"But as sure as I'm a cinder,
    That party what you see
A-gettin' out the winder
    Have developed from a flea!"

Anonymous

SONG FOR THE SQUEEZE-BOX

It wasn't Ernest; it wasn't Scott—
The boys I knew when I went to pot;
They didn't boast; they didn't snivel,
But stepped right up and swung at the Devil;
And after exchanging a punch or two,
They all sat down like me and you
—And began to drink up the money.

It wasn't the Colony; it wasn't the Stork;
It wasn't the joints in New York, New York;
But me and a girl friend learned a lot
In Ecorse, Toledo, and Wyandotte
—About getting rid of our money.

It was jump-in-the-hedge; it was wait-in-the-hall;
It was "Would you believe it—*fawther's* tall!"
(It turned out she hadn't a father at all)
—But how she could burn up the money!

A place I surely did like to go
Was the underbelly of Cicero;
And East St. Louis and Monongahela
Had the red-hot spots where you feel a
—Lot like losing some money.

Oh, the Synco Septet played for us then,
And even the boys turned out to be men
As we sat there drinking that bathtub gin
—And loosened up with our money.

It was Samoots Matuna and Bugs Moran;
It was Fade me another and Stick out your can;
It was Place and Show and Also Ran
—For you never won with that money.

Oh, it wasn't a crime, it wasn't a sin,
And nobody slipped me a Mickey Finn,
For whenever I could, I dealt them all in
—On that chunk of Grandpa's money.

It was Dead Man's Corner, it was Kelly's Stable;
It was Stand on your feet as long as you're able,
But many a man rolled under the table
—When he tried to drink up the money.

To some it may seem a sad thing to relate,
The dough I spent on Chippewa Kate,
For she finally left town on the Bay City freight
—When she thought I'd run out of the money.

The doctors, the lawyers, the cops are all paid—
So I've got to get me a rich ugly old maid
Who isn't unwilling, who isn't afraid
—To help me eat up her money.

Theodore Roethke

In Westminster Abbey

Let me take this other glove off
    As the *vox humana* swells,
And the beauteous fields of Eden
    Bask beneath the Abbey bells.
Here, where England's statesmen lie,
Listen to a lady's cry.

Gracious Lord, oh bomb the Germans.
    Spare their women for Thy Sake,
And if that is not too easy
    We will pardon Thy Mistake.
But, gracious Lord, whate'er shall be,
Don't let anyone bomb me.

Keep our Empire undismembered
    Guide our Forces by Thy Hand,
Gallant blacks from far Jamaica,
    Honduras and Togoland;
Protect them Lord in all their fights,
And, even more, protect the whites.

Think of what our Nation stands for,
    Books from Boots' and country lanes,
Free speech, free passes, class distinction,
    Democracy and proper drains.
Lord, put beneath Thy special care
One-eighty-nine Cadogan Square.

Although dear Lord I am a sinner,
    I have done no major crime;
Now I'll come to Evening Service
    Whensoever I have time.
So, Lord, reserve for me a crown,
And do not let my shares go down.

I will labour for Thy Kingdom,
    Help our lads to win the war,
Send white feathers to the cowards,
    Join the Women's Army Corps,
Then wash the Steps around Thy Throne
In the Eternal Safety Zone.

Now I feel a little better,
    What a treat to hear Thy Word,
Where the bones of leading statesmen,
    Have so often been interred.
And now, dear Lord, I cannot wait
Because I have a luncheon date.

JOHN BETJEMAN

TROMBONE SOLO

I like people
Who strut their stuff;
Any kind of people,
Nice ones or tough.
I like people
With swagger in their step,
Hot-air people, full
Of popcorn and pep,
Four-flushing people
Whose gestures are free—
Strut your stuff, people,
Don't
      mind
         me!

I like people
Who feel their oats,
High-stepping people
With ego in their throats,
Telling tall stories,
Taller than the steeple,
Getting away with it—
That kind of people.
If it's done properly,
Carried with an air,
Strut your stuff, people—
I
    won't
      care!

STODDARD KING

I've Been to a Marvellous Party

Verse 1   Quite for no reason
I'm here for the Season
And high as a kite,
Living in error
With Maud at Cap Ferrat
Which couldn't be right.
Everyone's here and frightfully gay,
Nobody cares what people say,
Though the Riviera
Seems really much queerer
Than Rome at its height,
Yesterday night—

Refrain 1   I've been to a marvellous party
With Nounou and Nada and Nell,
It was in the fresh air
And we went as we were
And we stayed as we were
Which was Hell.
Poor Grace started singing at midnight
And didn't stop singing till four;
We knew the excitement was bound to begin
When Laura got blind on Dubonnet and gin
And scratched her veneer with a Cartier pin,
I couldn't have liked it more.

Refrain 2   I've been to a marvellous party,
I must say the fun was intense,
We all had to do
What the people we knew
Would be doing a hundred years hence.
Dear Cecil arrived wearing armour,
Some shells and a black feather boa,
Poor Millicent wore a surrealist comb
Made of bits of mosaic from St. Peter's in Rome,

But the weight was so great that she had to go home,
I couldn't have liked it more!

Verse 2   People's behaviour
Away from Belgravia
Would make you aghast,
So much variety
Watching Society
Scampering past,
If you have any mind at all
Gibbon's divine *Decline and Fall*
Seems pretty flimsy,
No more than a whimsy,
By way of contrast
On Saturday last—

Refrain 3   I've been to a marvellous party,
We didn't start dinner till ten
And young Bobbie Carr
Did a stunt at the bar
With a lot of extraordinary men;
Dear Baba arrived with a turtle
Which shattered us all to the core,
The Grand Duke was dancing a foxtrot with me
When suddenly Cyril screamed Fiddledidee
And ripped off his trousers and jumped in the sea,
I couldn't have liked it more.

Refrain 4   I've been to a marvellous party,
Elise made an entrance with May,
You'd never have guessed
From her fisherman's vest
That her bust had been whittled away.
Poor Lulu got fried on Chianti
And talked about esprit de corps.
Maurice made a couple of passes at Gus
And Freddie, who hates any kind of a fuss,
Did half the Big Apple and twisted his truss,
I couldn't have liked it more.

Refrain 5   I've been to a marvellous party,
We played the most wonderful game,
Maureen disappeared
And came back in a beard
And we all had to guess at her name!
We talked about growing old gracefully
And Elsie who's seventy-four
Said, 'A, it's a question of being sincere,
And B, if you're supple you've nothing to fear.'
Then she swung upside down from a glass chandelier,
I couldn't have liked it more.

NOEL COWARD

Life's Losers

The Pessimist

Nothing to do but work,
   Nothing to eat but food,
Nothing to wear but clothes
   To keep one from going nude.

Nothing to breathe but air
Quick as a flash 'tis gone;
Nowhere to fall but off,
   Nowhere to stand but on.

Nothing to comb but hair,
   Nowhere to sleep but in bed,
Nothing to weep but tears,
   Nothing to bury but dead.

Nothing to sing but songs,
   Ah, well, alas! alack!
Nowhere to go but out,
   Nowhere to come but back.

BEN KING

BRATS

1

John while swimming in the ocean
Rubbed sharks' backs with suntan lotion.
Now those sharks have skin of bronze
In their bellies—namely, John's.

2

Stealing eggs, Fritz ran afoul
Of an angry great horned owl.
Now she has him—what a catch!—
Seeing if his head will hatch.

3

Doris Drummond sneaked a look
In a locked and cobwebbed book,
Found some secret words you said
That could summon up the dead.
Sad to say, the dead she summoned
Had it in for Doris Drummond.

5

At the market Philbert Spicer
Peered into the cold-cut slicer—
Whiz! the wicked slicer sped
Back and forth across his head
Quickly shaving—what a shock!—
Fifty chips off Phil's old block,
Stopping just above the eyebrows.
Phil's not one of them there highbrows.

X. J. KENNEDY

THE FLAW IN PAGANISM

Drink and dance and laugh and lie,
　　Love, the reeling midnight through,
For tomorrow we shall die!
　　(But, alas, we never do.)

DOROTHY PARKER

THE OBJECTION TO BEING
STEPPED ON

At the end of the row
I stepped on the toe
Of an unemployed hoe.
It rose in offense
And struck me a blow
In the seat of my sense.
It wasn't to blame
But I called it a name.
And I must say it dealt
Me a blow that I felt
Like malice prepense.
You may call me a fool,
But *was* there a rule
The weapon should be
Turned into a tool?
And what do we see?
The first tool I step on
Turned into a weapon.

ROBERT FROST

On the Vanity of Earthly Greatness

The tusks that clashed in mighty brawls
Of mastodons, are billiard balls.

The sword of Charlemagne the Just
Is ferric oxide, known as rust.

The grizzly bear whose potent hug
Was feared by all, is now a rug.

Great Caesar's dead and on the shelf,
And I don't feel so well myself!

Arthur Guiterman

Mr. Artesian's Conscientiousness

Once there was a man named Mr. Artesian and his activity
was tremendous,
And he grudged every minute away from his desk because the
importance of his work was so stupendous;
And he had one object all sublime,
Which was to save simply oodles of time.
He figured that sleeping eight hours a night meant that if he
lived to be seventy-five he would have spent twenty-
five years not at his desk but in bed,
So he cut his slumber to six hours which meant he only lost
eighteen years and nine months instead,
And he figured that taking ten minutes for breakfast and
twenty minutes for luncheon and half an hour for
dinner meant that he spent three years, one month and
fifteen days at the table,
So that by subsisting solely on bouillon cubes which he
swallowed at his desk to save this entire period he was
able,

And he figured that at ten minutes a day he spent a little over
    six months and ten days shaving,
So he grew a beard, which gave him a considerable saving,
And you might think that now he might have been satisfied,
    but no, he wore a thoughtful frown,
Because he figured that at two minutes a day he would spend
    thirty-eight days and a few minutes in elevators just
    traveling up and down,
So as a final timesaving device he stepped out the window of
    his office, which happened to be on the fiftieth floor,
And one of his partners asked "Has he vertigo?" and the other
    glanced out and down and said "Oh no, only about ten
    feet more."

OGDEN NASH

LAST LAUCH

The Minister said it wad dee,
the cypress bush I plantit.
But the bush grew til a tree,
naething dauntit.

Hit's growin, stark and heich,
derk and straucht and sinister,
kirkyairdie-like and dreich.
But whaur's the Minister?

DOUGLAS YOUNG

HALLELUJAH!

"Hallelujah!" was the only observation
That escaped Lieutenant-Colonel Mary Jane,
When she tumbled off the platform in the station,
And was cut in little pieces by the train.
    Mary Jane, the train is through yer:

Hallelujah, Hallelujah!
We will gather up the fragments that remain.

A. E. HOUSMAN

REQUIEM

There was a young belle of old Natchez
Whose garments were always in patchez.
When comment arose
On the state of her clothes,
She drawled, When Ah itchez, Ah scratchez!

OGDEN NASH

SANCTUARY

My land is bare of chattering folk;
    The clouds are low along the ridges,
And sweet's the air with curly smoke
    From all my burning bridges.

DOROTHY PARKER

DE SADE

There once was a Marquis de Sade
From whose novels we seem to be barred,
For he said that one's leisure
Should be given to pleasure,
A belief against which we must guard.

He said you must treat number one
As the one most entitled to fun,
But if you are weak

Then the outlook is bleak,
And not very much can be done.

It will work for a Count or a Monk
Who can cut up a corpse in a trunk
Or hire a spruce valet
With whom he can dally,
But if you're a peasant you're sunk.

It's the man with most power and craft
Who can see that his château's well-staffed
With housemaids and hordes
Of terrified wards:
But what if the victims just laughed?

If they chatted they'd lessen their trial.
Such behaviour would cripple his style,
For the sexual invention
Supplies the intention
But action's dismayed at a smile.

Yes, he almost convinced us but I'm
Afraid that it's certainly time
To cast final doubts
On the cruel ins and outs
Of his logical theory of crime.

The rich men are ruled by the poor,
And the way that they do it is Law,
And it's Law that comes after
That primitive laughter
That stifled the cave-man's roar.

De Sade went inside for a season
For his dubious sexual treason.
It was groaningly tame,
But he's known all the same
As the dark *ne plus ultra* of Reason.

JOHN FULLER

[THE NIGHT WAS GROWING OLD]

The night was growing old
　　As she trudged through snow and sleet;
And her nose was long and cold,
　　And her shoes were full of feet.

ANONYMOUS

DETERMINISM

There was a young man who said, 'Damn!'
It appears to me now that I am
　　Just a being that moves
　　In predestinate grooves,
Not a taxi or bus, but a tram.

ANONYMOUS

FOR THE POET WHO SAID POETS ARE STRUCK BY LIGHTNING ONLY TWO OR THREE TIMES

One is so seldom struck by
lightning, so seldom struck by
everything beautiful.

Oh, sometimes a butane fuel
truck intercepts you enroute
to a new supermarket;
if you even get a toot
out of that, you're lucky
to find a place to park it.

Or some guy stops, his car key
still plugged in his ignition,

hits you with a tire iron
(not even a fire arm) and
—what kind of inspiration
is that?

And the impression
I get on occasions when
I am struck by the sidewalk
is something I will not talk
about. How pedestrian
can you get. (Though each upset
makes me considerably more
concrete than I was before.)

PETER KLAPPERT

NOBODY LOSES ALL THE TIME

i had an uncle named
Sol who was a born failure and
nearly everybody said he should have gone
into vaudeville perhaps because my Uncle Sol could
sing McCann He Was A Diver on Xmas Eve like Hell itself which
may or may not account for the fact that my Uncle

Sol indulged in that possibly most inexcusable
of all to use a highfalootin phrase
luxuries that is or to
wit farming and be
it needlessly
added

my Uncle Sol's farm
failed because the chickens
ate the vegetables so
my Uncle Sol had a
chicken farm till the
skunks ate the chickens when

my Uncle Sol
had a skunk farm but
the skunks caught cold and
died and so
my Uncle Sol imitated the
skunks in a subtle manner

or by drowning himself in the watertank
but somebody who'd given my Uncle Sol a Victor
Victrola and records while he lived presented to
him upon the auspicious occasion of his decease a
scrumptious not to mention splendiferous funeral with
tall boys in black gloves and flowers and everything and

i remember we all cried like the Missouri
when my Uncle Sol's coffin lurched because
somebody pressed a button
(and down went
my Uncle
Sol

and started a worm farm)

E. E. CUMMINGS

MY ANGELINE

She kept her secret well, oh, yes,
   Her hideous secret well.
We together were cast, I knew not her past;
   For how was I to tell?
I married her, guileless lamb I was;
   I'd have died for her sweet sake.
How could I have known that my Angeline
   Had been a Human Snake?
Ah, we have been wed but a week or two
   When I found her quite a wreck:
   Her limbs were tied in a double bow-knot

At the back of her swan-like neck.
No curse there sprang to my pallid lips,
    Nor did I reproach her then;
I calmly untied my bonny bride
    And straightened her out again.

REFRAIN

My Angeline! My Angeline!
Why didst disturb my mind serene?
My well-belovèd circus queen,
My Human Snake, my Angeline!

At night I'd wake at the midnight hour,
    With a weird and haunted feeling,
And there she'd be, in her *robe de nuit,*
    A-walking upon the ceiling.
She said she was being "the human fly,"
    And she'd lift me up from beneath
By a section slight of my garb of night,
    Which she held in her pearly teeth.
For the sweet, sweet sake of the Human Snake
    I'd have stood this conduct shady;
But she skipped in the end with an old, old friend,
    An eminent bearded lady.
But, oh, at night, when my slumber's light,
    Regret comes o'er me stealing;
For I miss the sound of those little feet,
    As they pattered along the ceiling.

REFRAIN

My Angeline! My Angeline!
Why didst disturb my mind serene?
My well-belovèd circus queen,
My Human Snake, my Angeline!

HARRY B. SMITH

Poor but Honest

She was poor, but she was honest,
    Victim of the squire's whim:
First he loved her, then he left her,
    And she lost her honest name.

Then she ran away to London,
    For to hide her grief and shame;
There she met another squire,
    And she lost her name again.

See her riding in her carriage,
    In the Park and all so gay:
All the nibs and nobby persons
    Come to pass the time of day.

See the little old-world village
    Where her aged parents live,
Drinking the champagne she sends them;
    But they never can forgive.

In the rich man's arms she flutters,
    Like a bird with broken wing:
First he loved her, then he left her,
    And she hasn't got a ring.

See him in the splendid mansion,
    Entertaining with the best,
While the girl that he has ruined,
    Entertains a sordid guest.

See him in the House of Commons,
    Making laws to put down crime,
While the victim of his passions
    Trails her way through mud and slime.

Standing on the bridge at midnight,
　　She says: 'Farewell, blighted Love.'
There's a scream, a splash—Good Heavens!
　　What is she a-doing of?

Then they drag her from the river,
　　Water from her clothes they wrang,
For they thought that she was drownded;
　　But the corpse got up and sang:

'It's the same the whole world over;
　　It's the poor that gets the blame,
It's the rich that get the pleasure.
　　Isn't it a blooming shame?'

ANONYMOUS

DISILLUSIONMENT

Shyness and modesty, they said,
　　Will bring love to your side,
Seek not to gild the gingerbread;
　　Dear heavens, how they lied!

The ointment pots are full of flies,
　　And bitter is the cup
For those of us who drop our eyes
　　And no one picks them up.

VIRGINIA GRAHAM

HELLO UP THERE

Are you You or Me or It?
I go littering you over the furniture
and picking you out of the stew.
Often I've wished you otherwise: sleek,
docile, decorative and inert.

Yet even in daydreams I cannot imagine myself
otherwise thatched: coarse, black and abundant
like weeds burst from the slagheaps of abandoned mines.

In the '50's children used to point and shout Witch.
Later they learned to say Beatnik and later yet, Hippie,
but old grandmamas with Thessaloniki or Kiev in their throats
thought I must be nice because I looked like a peasant.
In college my mother tried to change my life
by bribing me to cut it off and have it "done."
Afterwards the hairdresser chased me waving my hair in a
    paper bag.
The next man who happened was a doctor's son
who quoted the Lord Freud in bed and on the pot,
thought I wrote poems because I lacked a penis
and beat me when he felt ugly.
I grew my hair back just as quick as I could.

Cloud of animal vibrations
tangle of hides and dark places
you keep off the tidy and the overly clean and the wango upright.
You proclaim the sharp limits of my patience
with trying to look like somebody's wet dream.
Though I can trim you and throw you out with the coffee grounds,
when I am dead and beginning to smell worse than my shoes
presumably you will continue out of my skull
as if there were inside no brains at all
but only a huge bobbin of black wire unwinding.

MARGE PIERCY

IN A PROMINENT BAR IN
SECAUCUS ONE DAY

In a prominent bar in Secaucus one day
Rose a lady in skunk with a topheavy sway,
Raised a knobby red finger—all turned from their beer—
While with eyes bright as snowcrust she sang high and clear:

"Now who of you'd think from an eyeload of me
That I once was a lady as proud as could be?
Oh I'd never sit down by a tumbledown drunk
If it wasn't, my dears, for the high cost of junk.

"All the gents used to swear that the white of my calf
Beat the down of the swan by a length and a half.
In the kerchief of linen I caught to my nose
Ah, there never fell snot, but a little gold rose.

"I had seven gold teeth and a toothpick of gold,
My Virginia cheroot was a leaf of it rolled
And I'd light it each time with a thousand in cash—
Why the bums used to fight if I flicked them an ash.

"Once the toast of the Biltmore, the belle of the Taft,
I would drink bottle beer at the Drake, never draft,
And dine at the Astor on Salisbury steak
With a clean tablecloth for each bite I did take.

"In a car like the Roxy I'd roll to the track,
A steel-guitar trio, a bar in the back,
And the wheels made no noise, they turned over so fast,
Still it took you ten minutes to see me go past.

"When the horses bowed down to me that I might choose,
I bet on them all, for I hated to lose.
Now I'm saddled each night for my butter and eggs
And the broken threads race down the backs of my legs.

"Let you hold in mind, girls, that your beauty must pass
Like a lovely white clover that rusts with its grass.
Keep your bottoms off barstools and marry you young
Or be left—an old barrel with many a bung.

"For when time takes you out for a spin in his car
You'll be hard-pressed to stop him from going too far
And be left by the roadside, for all your good deeds,
Two toadstools for tits and a face full of weeds."

All the house raised a cheer, but the man at the bar
Made a phonecall and up pulled a red patrol car
And she blew us a kiss as they copped her away
From that prominent bar in Secaucus, N.J.

X. J. KENNEDY

A PIAZZA TRAGEDY

The beauteous Ethel's father has a
Newly painted front piazza,
    He has a
    Piazza;
When with tobacco juice 'twas tainted,
They had the front piazza painted,
    That tainted
    Piazza painted.

Algernon called that night, perchance,
Arrayed in comely sealskin pants,
    That night, perchance,
    In gorgeous pants;
Engaging Ethel in a chat
On the piazza down he sat,
    In chat,
    They sat.

And when an hour or two had passed,
He tried to rise, but oh, stuck fast,
    At last
    Stuck fast!
Fair Ethel shrieked, "It is the paint!"
And fainted in a deadly faint,
    This saint
    Did faint.

Algernon sits there till this day,
He cannot tear himself away;

Away?
Nay, nay,
His pants are firm, the paint is dry,
He's nothing else to do but die;
    To die!
    Oh my!

                                        Eugene Field

To the Terrestrial Globe
(by a miserable wretch)

Roll on, thou ball, roll on!
Through pathless realms of Space
        Roll on!
What though I'm in a sorry case?
What though I cannot meet my bills?
What though I suffer toothache's ills?
What though I swallow countless pills?
        Never *you* mind!
        Roll on!

Roll on, thou ball, roll on!
Through seas of inky air
        Roll on!
It's true I've got no shirts to wear;
It's true my butcher's bill is due;
It's true my prospects all look blue—
But don't let that unsettle you:
        Never *you* mind!
        Roll on!
        It rolls on.

                                        W. S. Gilbert

Personalities

By Way of Preface

'How pleasant to know Mr. Lear!'
   Who has written such volumes of stuff!
Some think him ill-tempered and queer,
   But a few think him pleasant enough.

His mind is concrete and fastidious,
   His nose is remarkably big;
His visage is more or less hideous,
   His beard it resembles a wig.

He has ears, and two eyes, and ten fingers,
   Leastways if you reckon two thumbs;
Long ago he was one of the singers,
   But now he is one of the dumbs.

He sits in a beautiful parlour,
   With hundreds of books on the wall;
He drinks a great deal of Marsala,
   But never gets tipsy at all.

He has many friends, laymen and clerical,
   Old Foss is the name of his cat:
His body is perfectly spherical,
   He weareth a runcible hat.

When he walks in a waterproof white,
    The children run after him so!
Calling out, 'He's come out in his night-
    gown, that crazy old Englishman, oh!'

He weeps by the side of the ocean,
    He weeps on the top of the hill;
He purchases pancakes and lotion,
    And chocolate shrimps from the mill.

He reads but he cannot speak Spanish,
    He cannot abide ginger-beer:
Ere the days of his pilgrimage vanish,
    How pleasant to know Mr. Lear!

EDWARD LEAR

LINES TO RALPH HODGSON, ESQRE.

How delightful to meet Mr. Hodgson!
            (Everyone wants to know *him*)—
With his musical sound
And his Baskerville Hound
Which, just at a word from his master
Will follow you faster and faster
And tear you limb from limb.
How delightful to meet Mr. Hodgson!
Who is worshipped by all waitresses
(They regard him as something apart)
While on his palate fine he presses
The juice of the gooseberry tart.

How delightful to meet Mr. Hodgson!
            (Everyone wants to know *him*).
He has 999 canaries
And round his head finches and fairies
In jubilant rapture skim.
How delightful to meet Mr. Hodgson!
            (Everyone wants to meet *him*).

T. S. ELIOT

LINES FOR CUSCUSCARAWAY
AND MIRZA MURAD ALI BEG

How unpleasant to meet Mr. Eliot!
With his features of clerical cut,
And his brow so grim
And his mouth so prim
And his conversation, so nicely
Restricted to What Precisely
And If and Perhaps and But.
How unpleasant to meet Mr. Eliot!
With a bobtail cur
In a coat of fur
And a porpentine cat
And a wopsical hat:
How unpleasant to meet Mr. Eliot!
               (Whether his mouth be open or shut).

                           T. S. ELIOT

THE GOSPEL OF MR. PEPYS

"Among the others pretty Mrs. Margaret;
who indeed is a very pretty lady;
and though by my vow it costs me 12*d.* a
kiss yet I did adventure
upon a couple."
              Pepys's Diary, Feb. 8, 1665

Good Mr. Peeps or Peps or Pips
    (However he should be yclept),
Clerk of the King's Bureau of Ships,
    A snappy, spicy journal kept.
He knew a Lemon from a Peach,
    And, witting that, he also knew
When kisses are a shilling each
    We should adventure on a few.

He was a connoisseur of lips,
    And though I cannot quite accept

Some of his rather shady tips
    (I grant he often overstepped
The bounds of taste)—still he can teach
    Misogynists a thing or two—
When kisses are a shilling each
    We should adventure on a few.

He drank the wine of life by sips;
    He roundly ate and soundly slept;
His spirits suffered no eclipse;
    But Lord! How sore he would have wept
To see his private linen bleach
    And flutter in the public view . . .
For kisses were a shilling each
    And he adventured on a few!

I love to read about his trips
    With Nell or Knipp; how home he crept
And told his wife a lot of quips,
    Albeit many were inept.
And yet, although he loved to preach,
    Than this he never spake more true:
When kisses are a shilling each
    We should adventure on a few.

CHRISTOPHER MORLEY

[SIR CHRISTOPHER WREN]

Sir Christopher Wren
Said, 'I am going to dine with some men.
'If anyone calls
'Say I am designing St. Paul's.'

Sir Humphry Davy
Detested gravy.
He lived in the odium
Of having discovered sodium.

'Dear me!' exclaimed Homer
'What a delicious aroma!
'It smells as if a town
'Was being burnt down.'

Sir James Jeans
Always says what he means:
He is really perfectly serious
About the universe being mysterious.

The meaning of the poet Gay
Was always as clear as day,
While that of the poet Blake
Was often practically opaque.

Professor Dewar
Is a better man than you are.
None of you ases
Can condense gases.

When they told Cimabue
He didn't know how to cooeee
He replied, 'Perhaps I mayn't,
'But I do know how to paint.'

The digestion of Milton
Was unequal to Stilton.
He was only feeling so-so
When he wrote *Il Penseroso.*

Dante Alighieri
Seldom troubled a dairy.
He wrote the *Inferno*
On a bottle of Pernod.

EDMUND CLERIHEW BENTLEY

ALMA

(Alma Schindler was married at various
times to Gustav Mahler, Walter Gropius,
and Franz Werfel)

The loveliest girl in Vienna
Was Alma—the smartest as well;
Once you picked her up on your antenna
You'd never be free of her spell.

Her loves were many and varied
From the day she began her beguine;
There were three famous ones whom she married,
And God knows how many between.

　　　Alma, tell us—
　　　All modern women are jealous—
　　　Which of your magical wands
　　　Got you Gustav and Walter and Franz?

The first one she married was Mahler,
Whose buddies all knew him as Gustav,
And each time he saw her he'd holler,
"Ach, that is the *fraulein* I must have!"

Their marriage, however, was murder.
He'd scream to the heavens above,
"I'm writing *Das Lied von der Erde*,
And she only wants to make love."

　　　Alma, tell us—
　　　All modern women are jealous—
　　　You should have a statue in bronze
　　　For bagging Gustav and Walter and Franz.

While married to Gus she met Gropius,
And soon she was swinging with Walter.

Gus died, and her tears were copious;
She cried all the way to the altar.

But he would work late at the Bauhaus
And only came home now and then.
She said, "What am I running—a chowhouse?
It's time to change partners again."

Alma, tell us—
All modern women are jealous—
Though you didn't even use Pond's,
You got Gustav and Walter and Franz.

While married to Walt she'd met Werfel,
And he, too, was caught in her net.
He married her, but he was careful,
'Cause Alma was no Bernadette.

And that is the story of Alma,
Who knew how to receive and to give.
The body that reached her embalma
Was one that had known how to live.

Alma, tell us—
How can they help being jealous?
Ducks always envy the swans
Who get Gustav and Walter
You never can falter
With Gustav
   And Walter
     And Franz.

Tom Lehrer

SOME FRENCHMEN

Monsieur Etienne de Silhouette
  Was slim and uniformly black;

His profile was superb, and yet
He vanished when he turned his back.

Humane and gaunt, precise and tall
    Was Docteur J. I. Guillotin;
He had one tooth, diagonal
    And loose, which, when it fell, spelled *fin.*

André Marie Ampere, a spark,
    Would visit other people's homes
And gobble volts until the dark
    Was lit by his resisting ohms.

Another type, Daguerre (Louis),
    In silver salts would soak his head,
Expose himself to light, and be
    Developed just in time for bed.

JOHN UPDIKE

FABLE

Franklin sailed a key-hung kite
And watched the storm-stung flight of it.
Everyone seemed much impressed—
But Edison made light of it.

JAMES FACOS

GRAFFITI

Nietzsche is pietsche
But Sartre is smartre.

ANONYMOUS

PARADISE LOST, BOOK V
AN EPITOME

Higgledy-piggledy
Archangel Raphael,
Speaking of Satan's re-
Bellion from God:

"Chap was decidedly
Tergiversational,
Given to lewdness and
Rodomontade."

ANTHONY HECHT

HELIOGABALUS

Higgledy-piggledy
Heliogabalus
Lurched through the Forum, his
Bottom a-wag,

Vainly pretending to
Gynaecological
Problems beneath his Im-
Perial drag.

JOHN HOLLANDER

DANISH WIT

Higgledy-piggledy
Franklin D. Roosevelt
High over Jutland flew
In from the East;

"Well," quipped a Minister
Plenipotentiary,

"Something is Groton in
Denmark, at least!"

JOHN HOLLANDER

AUTHORSHIP

King David and King Solomon
    Led merry, merry lives,
With many, many lady friends
    And many, many wives;
But when old age crept over them,
    With many, many qualms,
King Solomon wrote the Proverbs
    And King David wrote the Psalms.

JAMES B(ALL) NAYLOR

HERNANDO DE SOTO
1499?–1542

Hernando De Soto was Spanish,
An iron-clad *conquistador.*
Adventure he knew in the sack of Peru,
But it just made him anxious for more.

Hernando De Soto was knightly,
Hernando De Soto was bold,
But like most of his lot, he'd be off like a shot
Wherever he heard there was gold.

So, with priest and physician and army,
Not to speak of a number of swine,
At Tampa he started a quest, fiery-hearted,
For the gold of a fabulous mine.

And from Florida way out to Texas,
This Don of the single-track mind,

Went chasing his dream over prairie and stream,
And the pigs kept on trotting behind.

He discovered the great Mississippi,
He faced perils and hardships untold,
And his soldiers ate bacon, if I'm not mistaken,
But nobody found any gold.

They buried De Soto at midnight,
Where the wide Mississippi still jigs.
He was greedy for gain but a soldier of Spain.
(I hope someone looked after the pigs.)

ROSEMARY AND STEPHEN VINCENT BENÉT

HIGH RENAISSANCE

"Nomine Domini
Theotocopoulos,
None of these prelates can
Manage your name.

Change it. Appeal to their
Hellenophilia.
Sign it 'El Greco.' I'll
Slap on a frame."

GEORGE STARBUCK

THE BABY HILARY, SIR EDMUND

Small fists waving
clenched in the air
to strike at all the universe
just because it's there.

KATHLEEN LELAND BAKER

Food and Drink

A Thousand Hairy Savages

A thousand hairy savages
Sitting down to lunch
Gobble gobble glup glup
Munch munch munch.

Spike Milligan

G. K. Chesterton on His Birth

When I was born in a world of sin,
Praise be God it was raining gin;
Gin on the house, gin on the walls,
Gin on the bun-shops and copy-book stalls.

A. E. Housman

Miss Foggerty's Cake

As I sat by my window last evening,
   The letterman brought unto me
A little gilt-edged invitation
   Saying, "Gilhooley, come over to tea."

Sure I knew 'twas the Foggertys sent it,
　So I went for old friendship's sake,
And the first thing they gave me to tackle
　Was a slice of Miss Foggerty's cake.

Miss Martin wanted to taste it,
　But really there weren't no use,
For they worked at it over an hour
　And couldn't get none of it loose.

Till Foggerty went for a hatchet
　And Killey came in with a saw;
The cake was enough, by the powers,
　To paralyze any man's jaw.

In it were cloves, nutmegs and berries,
　Raisins, citron and cinnamon, too;
There were sugar, pepper and cherries,
　And the crust of it nailed on with glue.

Miss Foggerty, proud as a preacher,
　Kept winking and blinking away,
Till she fell over Flanigan's brogans
　And spilt a whole brewing of tay.

"O, Gilhooley," she cried, "you're not eating,
　Just take another piece for my sake."
"No thanks, Miss Foggerty," says I,
　"But I'd like the recipe for that cake."

McNulley was took with the colic,
　McFadden complained of his head,
McDoodle fell down on the sofa
　And swore that he wished he was dead.

Miss Martin fell down in hysterics,
　And there she did wriggle and shake,

While every man swore he was poisoned
By eating Miss Foggerty's cake.

ANONYMOUS

LINES ON THE MERMAID TAVERN

Souls of Poets dead and gone,
What Elysium have ye known,
Happy field or mossy cavern,
Choicer than the Mermaid Tavern?
Have ye tippled drink more fine
Than mine host's Canary wine?
Or are fruits of Paradise
Sweeter than those dainty pies
Of venison? O generous food!
Dressed as though bold Robin Hood
Would, with his maid Marian,
Sup and browse from horn and can.

I have heard that on a day
Mine host's sign-board flew away
Nobody knew whither, till
An Astrologer's old quill
To a sheepskin gave the story,—
Said he saw you in your glory,
Underneath a new-old sign
Sipping beverage divine,
And pledging with contented smack
The Mermaid in the Zodiac.

Souls of Poets dead and gone,
What Elysium have ye known—
Happy field or mossy cavern—
Choicer than the Mermaid Tavern?

JOHN KEATS

XIII
(*from* AS THE CROW FLIES, LET HIM FLY)

The early bird may catch the worm;
I do not care for foods that squirm;
I'll wait till noon to make my rounds,
And catch some coffee off the grounds.

SAMUEL HOFFENSTEIN

from THE CYNIC

Once at a merry wedding feast
A cynic chanced to be a guest;
Rich was the father of the bride
And hospitality his pride.
The guests were numerous and the board
With dainties plentifully stored.
There mutton, beef, and vermicelli,
Here venison stewed with currant jelly,
Here turkeys robbed of bones and lungs
Are crammed with oysters and with tongues.
There pickled lobsters, prawn, and salmon
And there a stuffed Virginia gammon.
Here custards, tarts, and apple pies
There syllabubs and jellies rise,
Ice creams, and ripe and candied fruits
With comfits and eryngo roots.
Now entered every hungry guest
And all prepared to taste the feast.
Our cynic cries—"How damned absurd
To take such pains to make a—!"

ST. GEORGE TUCKER

THE SAGINAW SONG

In Saginaw, in Saginaw,
   The wind blows up your feet,
When the ladies' guild puts on a feed,
   There's beans on every plate,
And if you eat more than you should,
   Destruction is complete.

Out Hemlock Way there is a stream
   That some have called Swan Creek;
The turtles have bloodsucker sores,
   And mossy filthy feet;
The bottoms of migrating ducks
   Come off it much less neat.

In Saginaw, in Saginaw,
   Bartenders think no ill;
But they've ways of indicating when
   You are not acting well:
They throw you through the front plate glass
   And then send you the bill.

The Morleys and the Burrows are
   The aristocracy;
A likely thing for they're no worse
   Than the likes of you or me,—
A picture window's one you can't
   Raise up when you would pee.

In Shaginaw, in Shaginaw
   I went to Shunday Shule;
The only thing I ever learned
   Was called the Golden Rhule,—
But that's enough for any man
   What's not a proper fool.

I took the pledge cards on my bike;
   I helped out with the books;

The stingy members when they signed
    Made with their stingy looks,—
The largest contributions came
    From the town's biggest crooks.

In Saginaw, in Saginaw,
    There's never a household fart,
For if it did occur,
    It would blow the place apart,—
I met a woman who could break wind
    And she is my sweet-heart.

O, I'm the genius of the world,—
    Of that you can be sure,
But alas, alack, and me achin' back,
    I'm often a drunken boor;
But when I die—and that won't be soon—
    I'll sing with dear Tom Moore,
    With that lovely man, Tom Moore.

Coda:
    My father never used a stick,
        He slapped me with his hand;
    He was a Prussian through and through
        And knew how to command;
    I ran behind him every day
        He walked our greenhouse land.

I saw a figure in a cloud,
    A child upon her breast,
And it was O, my mother O,
    And she was half-undressed,
All women, O, are beautiful
    When they are half-undressed.

THEODORE ROETHKE

ATTACK OF THE SQUASH PEOPLE

And thus the people every year
in the valley of humid July
did sacrifice themselves
to the long green phallic god
and eat and eat and eat.

They're coming, they're on us,
the long striped gourds, the silky
babies, the hairy adolescents,
the lumpy vast adults
like the trunks of green elphants.
Recite fifty zucchini recipes!

Zucchini tempura; creamed soup;
saute with olive oil and cumin,
tomatoes, onion; frittata;
casserole of lamb; baked
topped with cheese; marinated;
stuffed; stewed; driven
through the heart like a stake.

Get rid of old friends: they too
have gardens and full trunks.
Look for newcomers: befriend
them in the post office, unload
on them and run. Stop tourists
in the street. Take truckloads
to Boston. Give to your Red Cross.
Beg on the highway: please
take my zucchini, I have a crippled
mother at home with heartburn.

Sneak out before dawn to drop
them in other people's gardens,
in baby buggies at churchdoors.

Shot, smuggling zucchini into
mailboxes, a federal offense.

With a suave reptilian glitter
you bask among your raspy
fronds sudden and huge as
alligators. You give and give
too much, like summer days
limp with heat, thunderstorms
bursting their bags on our heads,
as we salt and freeze and pickle
for the too little to come.

MARGE PIERCY

WAITER, PLEASE

An epicure, dining at Crewe,
Found quite a large mouse in his stew.
   Said the waiter, "Don't shout,
   And wave it about,
Or the rest will be wanting one, too!"

ANONYMOUS

THE STORY OF AUGUSTUS
WHO WOULD NOT HAVE ANY SOUP

Augustus was a chubby lad;
Fat, ruddy cheeks Augustus had;
And everybody saw with joy
The plump and hearty, healthy boy.
He ate and drank as he was told,
And never let his soup get cold.
But one day, one cold winter's day,
He scream'd out—'Take the soup away!
O take the nasty soup away!
I won't have any soup to-day.'

Next day begins his tale of woes,
Quite lank and lean Augustus grows.
Yet though he feels so weak and ill,
The naughty fellow cries out still—
'Not any soup for me, I say:
O take the nasty soup away!
I won't have any soup to-day.'

The third day comes; O what a sin!
To make himself so pale and thin.
Yet, when the soup is put on table,
He screams, as loud as he is able,—
'Not any soup for me, I say:
O take the nasty soup away!
I won't have any soup to-day.'

Look at him, now the fourth day's come!
He scarcely weighs a sugar-plum;
He's like a little bit of thread,
And on the fifth day, he was—dead!

HEINRICH HOFFMANN
(translated anonymously)

SALAD

To make this condiment, your poet begs
The pounded yellow of two hard-boiled eggs;
Two boiled potatoes, passed through kitchen-sieve,
Smoothness and softness to the salad give;
Let onion atoms lurk within the bowl,
And, half-suspected, animate the whole.
Of mordant mustard add a single spoon,
Distrust the condiment that bites so soon;
But deem it not, thou man of herbs, a fault,
To add a double quantity of salt.
And, lastly, o'er the flavored compound toss
A magic soup-spoon of anchovy sauce.

Oh, green and glorious! Oh, herbaceous treat!
'T would tempt the dying anchorite to eat;
Back to the world he'd turn his fleeting soul,
And plunge his fingers in the salad bowl!
Serenely full, the epicure would say,
Fate can not harm me, I have dined to-day!

SYDNEY SMITH

THE UNIVERSAL FAVORITE

Salad of greens! Salad of greens!
What's that? You like it? Go tell the Marines!
Greenery yellery, Lettuce and celery,
How I abominate salad of greens!
Romaine and escarole, cress, and tomatoes,
Radishes, chicory, beets, and potatoes;
Apples and cabbages, seeded white grapes,
Peppers and onions and chervil and cepes.
Yes, in the best of our modern cuisines,
They serve you that terrible salad of greens!
Capers and olives, mustard, and chili,
Cucumbers, artichokes, chives, piccalilli,
Pickles, paprika, pimentos, and cheese,
Tips of asparagus, carrots and peas.
Cantaloupe, cherries, grapefruit, nectarines,
Dock, avocado, and haricot beans;
Oh, Fate, let me fly to some far distant scenes,
In villages, hamlets, or deserts or denes,
I care not if peopled by peasants or queens
If they never have heard of a Salad of Greens!
That very detestable
Horrid Comestible,
    Incredible,
        Inedible,
Salad of Greens!

CAROLYN WELLS

Notes for a Southern Road Map

Carry me back to old Virginny,
   Land of cotton and the Williamsburg Plan,
Where the banjo calls to the pickaninny
   And the sun never sets on the Ku Klux Klan.
Carry me anywhere south of the line, there,
   To old Kentucky or Fla. or Tenn.,
But when I hear that it's time to dine, there,
   You can carry me North again.
For Dixie's myth is a myth I dote on;
   The South's my mammy is what I mean.
But never, ah never, they'll get my vote on

   Their pet cuisine.
For it's ham,
Ham,
Frizzled or fried,
Baked or toasted,
Or on the side.
Ham for breakfast
And ham for luncheon,
Nothing but ham to sup or munch on.
Ham for dinner and ham for tea,
Ham from Atlanta
To the sea,
With world-worn chicken for change of venue,
But ham immutable on the menu.

Dear to my heart are the Southland's bounties,
   Where honeysuckle is sweet in May,
Where warble the Byrds from important counties
   And everything runs by the TVA.
I love the mint that they spice the cup with,
   Their women fair and their horses fast;
An accent, even, can I put up with,
   And stories, suh, from a Noble Past.
So carry me back to an old plantation

In North Carolina or Alabam',
But succor me still from a steadfast ration
Of ham.

Ham,
Ham,
Not lamb or bacon
But ham in Raleigh
And ham in Macon.
Ham for plutocrats,
Ham for pore folk,
Ham in Paducah and ham in Norfolk;
In Memphis, ham, and in Chapel Hill,
Chattanooga,
And Charlottesville.
Ham for the Missy,
Ham for the Colonel,
And for the traveler, Ham Eternal.

Oh, patriotically, I implore,
Look away, Dixieland, from the smokehouse door.

PHYLLIS McGINLEY

ANY PART OF PIGGY

Any part of piggy
Is quite all right with me
Ham from Westphalia, ham from Parma
Ham as lean as the Dalai Lama
Ham from Virginia, ham from York,
Trotters, sausages, hot roast pork.
Crackling crisp for my teeth to grind on
Bacon with or without the rind on
Though humanitarian
I'm not a vegetarian.
I'm neither crank nor prude nor prig
And through it may sound infra dig

Any part of darling pig
Is perfectly fine with me.

NOEL COWARD

OH, FOR A BOWL OF FAT CANARY

Oh, for a bowl of fat Canary,
Rich Palermo, sparkling Sherry,
Some nectar else, from Juno's dairy;
Oh, these draughts would make us merry!

Oh, for a wench (I deal in faces,
And in other daintier things);
Tickled am I with her embraces,
Fine dancing in such fairy rings.

Oh, for a plump fat leg of mutton,
Veal, lamb, capon, pig, and coney;
None is happy but a glutton,
None an ass but who wants money.

Wines indeed and girls are good,
But brave victuals feast the blood;
For wenches, wine, and lusty cheer,
Jove would leap down to surfeit here.

JOHN LYLY

TURTLE SOUP

Beautiful Soup, so rich and green,
Waiting in a hot tureen!
Who for such dainties would not stoop?
Soup of the evening, beautiful Soup!
Soup of the evening, beautiful Soup!
    Beau—ootiful Soo—oop!
    Beau—ootiful Soo—oop!

Soo—oop of the e—e—evening,
　　Beautiful, beautiful Soup!

Beautiful Soup! Who cares for fish,
Game, or any other dish?
Who would not give all else for two
pennyworth only of beautiful soup?
Pennyworth only of beautiful Soup?
　　Beau—ootiful Soo—oop!
　　Beau—ootiful Soo—oop!
Soo—oop of the e—e—evening,
　　Beautiful, beauti—FUL SOUP!

LEWIS CARROLL

AGAINST BROCCOLI

The local groceries are all out of broccoli,
Loccoli.

ROY BLOUNT, JR.

GIVING POTATOES

STRONG MAN:　　Mashed potatoes cannot hurt you, darling
　　　　　　　　Mashed potatoes mean no harm
　　　　　　　　I have brought you mashed potatoes
　　　　　　　　From my mashed potato farm.

LADY:　　　　　Take away your mashed potatoes
　　　　　　　　Leave them in the desert to dry
　　　　　　　　Take away your mashed potatoes—
　　　　　　　　You look like shepherd's pie.

BRASH MAN:　　A packet of chips, a packet of chips,
　　　　　　　　Wrapped in the *Daily Mail,*
　　　　　　　　Golden juicy and fried for a week
　　　　　　　　In the blubber of the Great White Whale.

LADY: Take away your fried potatoes
                 Use them to clean your ears
                 You can eat your fried potatoes
                 With birds-eye frozen tears.

OLD MAN: I have borne this baked potato
                 O'er the Generation Gap,
                 Pray accept this baked potato
                 Let me lay it in your heated lap.

LADY: Take away your baked potato
                 In your fusty musty van
                 Take away your baked potato
                 You potato-skinned old man.

FRENCHMAN: She rejected all potatoes
                 For a thousand nights and days
                 Till a Frenchman wooed and won her
                 With pommes de terre Lyonnaise.

LADY: Oh my corrugated lover

                 So creamy and so brown

                 Let us fly across to Lyons

                 And lay our tubers down.

                                        ADRIAN MITCHELL

A COUNTERBLAST AGAINST GARLIC

Horace's Epode 3

May the man who has cruelly murdered his sire—
    A crime to be punished with death—
Be condemned to eat garlic till he shall expire
    Of his own foul and venomous breath!

What stomachs these rustics must have who can eat
  This dish that Canidia made,
Which imparts to my colon a torturous heat,
  And a poisonous look, I'm afraid.

They say that ere Jason attempted to yoke
  The fire-breathing bulls to the plough
He smeared his whole body with garlic,—a joke
  Which I fully appreciate now.
When Medea gave Glauce her beautiful dress,
  In which garlic was scattered about,
It was cruel and rather low-down, I confess,
  But it settled the point beyond doubt.

On thirsty Apulia ne'er has the sun
  Inflicted such terrible heat;
As for Hercules' robe, although poisoned, 't was fun
  When compared with this garlic we eat!
Maecenas, if ever on garbage like this
  You express a desire to be fed,
May Mrs. Maecenas object to your kiss,
  And lie at the foot of the bed!

ROSWELL MARTIN FIELD

CAUTIONARY LIMERICK

When you think of the hosts without No.
Who are slain by the deadly cuco.,
    It's quite a mistake
    Of such food to partake,
It results in a permanent slo.

ANONYMOUS

THE LITTLE VAGABOND

Dear Mother, dear Mother, the Church is cold,
But the Ale-house is healthy & pleasant & warm;
Besides I can tell where I am used well,
Such usage in Heaven will never do well.

But if at the Church they would give us some Ale,
And a pleasant fire our souls to regale,
We'd sing and we'd pray all the live-long day,
Nor ever once wish from the Church to stray.

Then the Parson might preach, & drink, & sing,
And we'd be as happy as birds in the spring;
And modest Dame Lurch, who is always at Church,
Would not have bandy children, nor fasting, nor birch.

And God, like a father rejoicing to see
His children as pleasant and happy as he,
Would have no more quarrel with the Devil or the
        Barrel,
But kiss him, & give him both drink and apparel.

WILLIAM BLAKE

"HERMIT HOAR . ."

Hermit hoar, in solemn cell,
    Wearing out life's evening gray,
Smite thy bosom, Sage, and tell,
    What is bliss? And which the way?

Thus I spoke; and speaking sigh'd;
    Scarce repress'd the starting tear;
When the hoary sage reply'd:
    "Come, my lad, and drink some beer."

SAMUEL JOHNSON

ON JAM

I write of Jam, a subject stiff
With interest to the reader if
He is (or she is), as am I,
From youth of Jam a votary.

Jam should be only eaten spread
By Nurse—or some one else—on bread.
A decent child would just as soon
Have none as eat it with a spoon.
And if you take it with your fingers,
There's always something sticks and lingers,
And visitors go muttering "D . . . (Oh! look!)
The little brute's been eating Jam!"

Jam is of various sorts and kinds,
As—Apple (made of apple-rinds);
And Strawberry—of which the fruit
Recalls the luscious Turnip root;
And Cherry Jam—extremely rich;
And Currant and Banana (which
The Germans oddly love to eat
With Boiled and Baked and Roasted Meat);
And Quince (which is of Quinces, since
It otherwise could not be Quince);
And Marmalade—but that expression
Compels me to a short digression.

The haughty Nobles of Seville
Could make no use of Orange Peel
Until the Merchants of Dundee
Came sailing thither oversea,
And, steering up the noble river
Called, in their tongue, the Guadalquiver,
Took back the skins with them and made
The mixture known as Marmalade,

As popular as it can be
From Dingwall on the Northern Sea
To Cherrajuinji in Assam—
But certainly is never Jam!

What is there more that I can say
Of Jam? Why, nothing more to-day.
The Jam's before me, thick and sweet:
What's writing, when a man can eat?
And as Erigena has said
(An author far too little read),
Jam hora adest ut mangiam.
And that is all I know of Jam.

HILAIRE BELLOC

LIPS THAT TOUCH LIQUOR

You are coming to woo me, but not as of yore,
When I hastened to welcome your ring at the door;
For I trusted that he who stood waiting me then,
Was the brightest, the truest, the noblest of men,
Your lips, on my own, when they printed "Farewell,"
Had never been soiled by the "beverage of hell;"
But they come to me now with the bacchanal sign,
And the lips that touch liquor must never touch mine.

GEORGE W. YOUNG

JUDGED BY THE COMPANY ONE KEEPS

One night in late October,
When I was far from sober,
Returning with my load with manly pride,
My feet began to stutter,
So I lay down in the gutter,
And a pig came near and lay down by my side;

A lady passing by was heard to say:
"You can tell a man who boozes,
By the company he chooses,"
And the pig got up and slowly walked away.

Anonymous

Chorus (*from* Crotchet Castle)

If I drink water while this doth last,
May I never again drink wine:
For how can a man, in his life of a span,
Do anything better than dine?
We'll dine and drink, and say if we think
That anything better can be;
And when we have dined, wish all mankind
May dine as well as we.
And though a good wish will fill no dish,
And brim no cup with sack,
Yet thoughts will spring, as the glasses ring,
To illume our studious track.
On the brilliant dreams of our hopeful schemes
The light of the flask shall shine;
And we'll sit till day, but we'll find the way
To drench the world with wine.

Thomas Love Peacock

R-E-M-O-R-S-E

The cocktail is a pleasant drink;
It's mild and harmless—I don't think.
When you've had one, you call for two,
And then you don't care what you do.
Last night I hoisted twenty-three
Of those arrangements into me.
My wealth increased, I swelled with pride,
I was pickled, primed and ossified.

R-E-M-O-R-S-E!
Those dry martinis did the work for me;
Last night at twelve I felt immense;
Today I feel like thirty cents.
At four I sought my whirling bed,
At eight I woke with such a head!
It is no time for mirth or laughter—
The cold, gray dawn of the morning after.

If ever I want to sign the pledge,
It's the morning after I've had an edge;
When I've been full of the oil of joy
And fancied I was a sporty boy.
This world was one kaleidoscope
Of purple bliss, transcendent hope.
But now I'm feeling mighty blue—
Three cheers for the W.C.T.U.!

R-E-M-O-R-S-E!
The water wagon is the place for me;
I think that somewhere in the game,
I wept and told my maiden name.
My eyes are bleared, my coppers hot;
I try to eat, but I can not;
It is no time for mirth or laughter—
The cold, gray dawn of the morning after

GEORGE ADE

OF DRUNKENNESS

At night when ale is in,
    Like friends we part to bed;
In morrow gray, when ale is out,
    Then hatred is in head.

GEORGE TURBERVILLE

OCCUPATIONS AND PREOCCUPATIONS ⌣

ANTHOLOGISTICS

Since one anthologist put in his book
Sweet things by Morse, Bone, Potter, Bliss and Brook,
All subsequent anthologists, of course,
Have quoted Bliss, Brook, Potter, Bone and Morse.
For, should some rash anthologist make free
To print selections, say, from you and me,
Omitting with a judgment all his own
The classic Brook, Morse, Potter, Bliss and Bone,
Contemptuous reviewers, passing by
Our verses, would unanimously cry,
"What manner of anthology is this
That leaves out Bone, Brook, Potter, Morse and Bliss!"

ARTHUR GUITERMAN

THE ANATOMY OF HUMOR

"What is funny?" you ask, my child,
    Crinkling your bright-blue eye.
"Ah, that is a curious question indeed,"
    Musing, I make reply.

"Contusions are funny, not open wounds,
    And automobiles that go

Crash into trees by the highwayside;
   Industrial accidents, no.

"The habit of drink is a hundred per cent,
   But drug addiction is nil.
A nervous breakdown will get no laughs;
   Insanity surely will.

"Humor, aloof from the cigarette,
   Inhabits the droll cigar;
The middle-aged are not very funny;
   The young and the old, they are.

"So the funniest thing in the world should be
   A grandsire, drunk, insane,
Maimed in a motor accident,
   And enduring moderate pain.

"But why do you scream and yell, my child?
   Here comes your mother, my honey,
To comfort you and to lecture me
   For trying, she'll say, to be funny."

MORRIS BISHOP

1. PIPLING (*from* THREE EPIGRAMS)

Behold the critic, pitched like the *castrati*,
Imperious youngling, though approaching forty;
He heaps few honors on a living head;
He loves himself, and the illustrious dead;
He pipes, he squeaks, he quivers through his nose,—
Some cannot praise him: *I* am one of those.

THEODORE ROETHKE

CRITIC (*from* DEFINITIONS)

The critic leaves at curtain fall
    To find, in starting to review it,
He scarcely saw the play at all
    For watching his reaction to it.

E. B. WHITE

CYNICAL PORTRAITS

Eggleston was a taxi-driver.
He wasn't the madman and sadic destroyer
Who secretly held a degree as a lawyer,
He didn't paint pictures for salon or foyer,
But drove his cab safely.

Ruddymore was a poet.
He wasn't the pale little poet of fashion
Whose lucently frail little ghost recalled passion,
The world and its daughter was Ruddymore's ration.
He some times wrote verse.

Rummick was a politician.
He wasn't the cheap little orating slicker
Who spent his spare time at a stock broker's ticker;
He never took orders, consented to dicker,
But kept his convictions.

Frawley was an editor.
He wasn't a man with a vaunting ambition
Who envied the gifted their skill and position;
He didn't blue pencil to prove erudition.
He died years ago.

LOUIS PAUL

THE PURIST

I give you now Professor Twist,
A conscientious scientist.
Trustees exclaimed, "He never bungles!"
And sent him off to distant jungles.
Camped on a tropic riverside,
One day he missed his loving bride.
She had, the guide informed him later,
Been eaten by an alligator.
Professor Twist could not but smile.
"You mean," he said, "a crocodile."

OGDEN NASH

THE FIDDLER OF DOONEY

When I play on my fiddle in Dooney,
Folk dance like a wave of the sea;
My cousin is priest in Kilvarnet,
My brother in Mocharabuiee.

I passed my brother and cousin:
They read in their books of prayer;
I read in my book of songs
I bought at the Sligo fair.

When we come at the end of time
To Peter sitting in state,
He will smile on the three old spirits,
But call me first through the gate;

For the good are always the merry,
Save by an evil chance,
And the merry love the fiddle,
And the merry love to dance:

And when the folk there spy me,
They will all come up to me,
With "Here is the fiddler of Dooney!"
And dance like a wave of the sea.

WILLIAM BUTLER YEATS

BOHEMIA

Authors and actors and artists and such
Never know nothing, and never know much.
Sculptors and singers and those of their kidney
Tell their affairs from Seattle to Sydney.
Playwrights and poets and such horses' necks
Start off from anywhere, end up at sex.
Diarists, critics, and similar roe
Never say nothing, and never say no.
People Who Do Things exceed my endurance;
God, for a man that solicits insurance!

DOROTHY PARKER

THE NEWS

The *News*, Indeed!—pray do you call it news
When shallow noddles publish shallow views?
Pray, is it news that turnips should be bred
As large and hollow as the owner's head?
News, that a clerk should rob his master's hoard,
Whose meagre salary scarcely pays his board?
News, that two knaves, their spurious friendship o'er,
Should tell the truths which they concealed before?
News, that a maniac, weary of his life,
Should end his sorrows with a rope or knife?
News, that a wife should violate the vows
That bind her, loveless, to a tyrant spouse?
News, that a daughter cheats paternal rule,

And weds a scoundrel to escape a fool?—
The news, indeed!—Such matters are as old
As sin and folly, rust and must and mould!

JOHN GODFREY SAXE

THE FARMER AND
THE FARMER'S WIFE

The farmer and the farmer's wife
Lead frolicsome and carefree lives,
And all their work is but in play,
Their labors only exercise.

The farmer leaps from bed to board,
And board to binder on the land;
His wife awakes with shouts of joy,
And milks a cow with either hand.

Then all in fun they feed the pigs,
And plough the soil in reckless glee,
And play the quaint old-fashion game
Of mortgagor and mortgagee.

And all day long they dash about,
In barn and pasture, field and heath;
He sings a merry roundelay,
She whistles gaily through her teeth.

And when at night the chores are done,
And hand and hand they sit and beam,
He helps himself to applejack,
And she to Paris Green.

P. G. HIEBERT

LORD LUCKY

Lord Lucky, by a curious fluke,
Became a most important duke.
From living in a vile Hotel
A long way east of Camberwell
He rose, in less than half an hour,
To riches, dignity and power.
It happened in the following way:—
The Real Duke went out one day
To shoot with several people, one
Of whom had never used a gun.
This gentleman (a Mr. Meyer
Of Rabley Abbey, Rutlandshire),
As he was scrambling through the brake,
Discharged his weapon by mistake,
And plugged about an ounce of lead
Piff-bang into his Grace's Head—
Who naturally fell down dead.
His Heir, Lord Ugly, roared, "You Brute!
Take that to teach you how to shoot!"
Whereat he volleyed, left and right;
But being somewhat short of sight,
His right-hand Barrel only got
The second heir, Lord Poddleplot;
The while the left-hand charge (or choke)
Accounted for another bloke,
Who stood with an astounded air
Bewildered by the whole affair
—And was the third remaining heir.
After the Execution (which
Is something rare among the Rich)
Lord Lucky, while of course he needed
Some help to prove his claim, succeeded.
—But after his succession, though
All this was over years ago,

He only once indulged the whim
Of asking Meyer to lunch with him.

HILAIRE BELLOC

THE MODERN MAJOR-GENERAL

I am the very pattern of a modern Major-Gineral,
I've information vegetable, animal, and mineral;
I know the kings of England, and I quote the fights historical,
From Marathon to Waterloo, in order categorical;
I'm very well acquainted, too, with matters mathematical,
I understand equations, both the simple and quadratical;
About binomial theorem I'm teeming with a lot o' news,
With interesting facts about the square of the hypotenuse.
I'm very good at integral and differential calculus,
I know the scientific names of beings animalculous.
In short, in matters vegetable, animal, and mineral,
I am the very model of a modern Major-Gineral.

I know our mythic history—King Arthur's and Sir Caradoc's,
I answer hard acrostics, I've a pretty taste for paradox;
I quote in elegiacs all the crimes of Heliogabalus,
In conics I can floor peculiarities parabolous.
I tell undoubted Raphaels from Gerard Dows and Zoffanies,
I know the croaking chorus from the "Frogs" of Aristophanes;
Then I can hum a fugue, of which I've heard the music's din afore,
And whistle all the airs from that confounded nonsense "Pinafore."
Then I can write a washing-bill in Babylonic cuneiform,
And tell you every detail of Caractacus's uniform.
In short, in matters vegetable, animal, and mineral,
I am the very model of a modern Major-Gineral.

In fact, when I know what is meant by "mamelon" and "ravelin,"
When I can tell at sight a Chassepôt rifle from a javelin,
When such affairs as *sorties* and surprises I'm more wary at,
And when I know precisely what is meant by Commissariat,

When I have learnt what progress has been made in modern
  gunnery,
When I know more of tactics than a novice in a nunnery,
In short, when I've a smattering of elementary strategy,
You'll say a better Major-Gine*ral* has never *sat* a gee—
For my military knowledge, though I'm plucky and adventury,
Has only been brought down to the beginning of the century.
But still in learning vegetable, animal, and mineral,
I am the very model of a modern Major-Gineral!

W. S. GILBERT

THE FAMILY FOOL

Oh! a private buffoon is a light-hearted loon,
  If you listen to popular rumour;
From morning to night he's so joyous and bright,
  And he bubbles with wit and good humour!
He's so quaint and so terse, both in prose and in verse;
  Yet though people forgive his transgression,
There are one or two rules that all Family Fools
  Must observe, if they love their profession.
      There are one or two rules,
        Half-a-dozen, maybe,
      That all family fools,
        Of whatever degree,
    Must observe if they love their profession.

If you wish to succeed as a jester, you'll need
  To consider each person's auricular:
What is all right for B would quite scandalise C
  (For C is so very particular);
And D may be dull, and E's very thick skull
  Is as empty of brains as a ladle;
While F is F sharp, and will cry with a carp,
  That he's known your best joke from his cradle!
      When your humour they flout,

You can't let yourself go;
And it *does* put you out
When a person says, "Oh!
I have known that old joke from my cradle!"

If your master is surly, from getting up early
    (And tempers are short in the morning),
An inopportune joke is enough to provoke
    Him to give you, at once, a month's warning.
Then if you refrain, he is at you again,
    For he likes to get value for money:
He'll ask then and there, with an insolent stare,
    "If you know that you're paid to be funny?"
        It adds to the tasks
            Of a merryman's place,
        When your principal asks,
            With a scowl on his face,
    If you know that you're paid to be funny?

Comes a Bishop, maybe, or a solemn D. D.—
    Oh, beware of his anger provoking!
Better not pull his hair—don't stick pins in his chair;
    He won't understand practical joking.
If the jests that you crack have an orthodox smack,
    You may get a bland smile from these sages;
But should it, by chance, be imported from France,
    Half-a-crown is stopped out of your wages!
        It's a general rule,
            Though your zeal it may quench,
        If the Family Fool
            Makes a joke that's *too* French,
    Half-a-crown is stopped out of his wages!

Though your head it may rack with a bilious attack,
    And your senses with toothache you're losing,
And you're mopy and flat—they don't fine you for that
    If you're properly quaint and amusing!
Though your wife ran away with a soldier that day,
    And took with her your trifle of money;

Bless your heart, they don't mind—they're exceedingly
   kind—
They don't blame you—as long as you're funny!
      It's a comfort to feel
         If your partner should flit,
      Though *you* suffer a deal,
         They don't mind it a bit—
They don't blame you—so long as you're funny!

W. S. GILBERT

THE LAW

The law can take a purse in open court
While it condemns a less delinquent for 't.

SAMUEL BUTLER

POLL STAR

    Politicians, heart and soul,
    Pay obeisance to the poll
As the holy scroll controlling every trick.
It condenses the conglomerate consensus
    To the force that makes the body politick.

    If the survey ratings show
    That a policy ranks low,
It's *de trop* and must be promptly sacrificed.
For collectors of opinion hold dominion:
    They're the spirit of our times—the pollstergeist.

FELICIA LAMPORT

THE OLD HOKUM BUNCOMBE

How dear to my heart are the grand politicians
   Who constantly strive for the popular votes,

Indulging in platitudes, trite repetitions,
    And time-honored bromides surrounded with quotes;
Though equally verbose opponents assail them
    With bitter invective, they never can quell
The force of the buncombe, which never will fail them—
    The old hokum buncombe we all know so well.
The old hokum buncombe,
The iron-clad buncombe,
    The moss-covered buncombe we all know so well.

They aim to make friends of the laboring classes—
    The trust of the people is sacred with them—
They swear that they're slaves to the will of the masses,
    They hem and they haw, and they haw and they hem;
They rave with a vehemence almost terrific,
    There isn't a doubt which they cannot dispel,
They revel in orgies of hope beatific—
    And serve us the buncombe we all know so well.
The old hokum buncombe,
The iron-clad buncombe,
    The moss-covered buncombe we all know so well.

Their torrents of words are a sure paregoric
    For all of the ills to which mankind is prey.
They pose as a Hamlet lamenting the Yorick
    Who typifies that which their rivals betray.
They picture perfection in every effusion;
    We gaze at Utopia under their spell,
And though it is only an optic illusion—
    We fall for the buncombe we all know so well.
The old hokum buncombe,
The iron-clad buncombe,
    The moss-covered buncombe we all love so well.

ROBERT E. SHERWOOD

The Orator's Epitaph

"Here, reader, turn your weeping eyes,
    My fate a useful moral teaches;
The hole in which my body lies
    Would not contain one-half my speeches."

LORD BROUGHAM

[A POLITICAN IS AN ARSE UPON]

a politician is an arse upon
which everyone has sat except a man

E. E. CUMMINGS

Election Reflection

Each day into the upper air
Ascends the politician's prayer—
"Grant me the gift of swift retort
And keep the public memory short."

M. KEEL JONES

[NEXT TO OF COURSE GOD]

"next to of course god america i
love you land of the pilgrims' and so forth oh
say can you see by the dawn's early my
country 'tis of centuries come and go
and are no more what of it we should worry
in every language even deafanddumb
thy sons acclaim your glorious name by gorry
by jingo by gee by gosh by gum
why talk of beauty what could be more beaut-

iful than these heroic happy dead
who rushed like lions to the roaring slaughter
they did not stop to think they died instead
then shall the voice of liberty be mute?"

He spoke. And drank rapidly a glass of water

E. E. CUMMINGS

WHAT?

Some pimps wear summer hats
Into late fall
Since the money that comes in
Won't cover it all—
Suit, overcoat, shoes—
And hat, too!

Got to neglect something,
So what would you do?

LANGSTON HUGHES

THE RUINED MAID

'O 'Melia, my dear, this does everything crown!
Who could have supposed I should meet you in Town?
And whence such fair garments, such prosperi-ty?'—
'O didn't you know I'd been ruined?' said she.

—'You left us in tatters, without shoes or socks,
Tired of digging potatoes, and spudding up docks;
And now you've gay bracelets and bright feathers three!'—
'Yes: that's how we dress when we're ruined,' said she.

—'At home in the barton you said "thee" and "thou",
And "thik oon", and "theäs oon", and "t'other"; but now
Your talking quite fits 'ee for high compa-ny!'—
'Some polish is gained with one's ruin,' said she.

—'Your hands were like paws then, your face blue and bleak
But now I'm bewitched by your delicate cheek,
And your little gloves fit as on any la-dy!'—
'We never do work when we're ruined,' said she.

—'You used to call home-life a hag-ridden dream,
And you'd sigh, and you'd sock; but at present you seem
To know not of megrims or melancho-ly!'—
'True. One's pretty lively when ruined,' said she.

—'I wish I had feathers, a fine sweeping gown,
And a delicate face, and could strut about Town!'—
'My dear—a raw country girl, such as you be,
Cannot quite expect that. You ain't ruined,' said she.

THOMAS HARDY

CRIME AT ITS BEST

Disgusted with crimes that are piffling and messy,
We think of the James brothers, Frankie and Jesse,
Who never degraded the clan of the James
By writing "confessions" and signing their names.

When poverty hovered o'er Jesse and Frank,
They saddled their horses and held up a bank,
(A calling in which it is wrong to engage)
But they never appeared on the vaudeville stage.

Though Jesse was tough and his brother was tougher,
They never made readers of newspapers suffer
By reading the sob sisters' sorrowful sobbing
Of how they read Browning before going robbing.

The gang that they worked with was surely a bad one,
But as for smart lawyers, I doubt that they had one;
Insanity dodges they never were pleading,
And that's why their life makes such excellent reading.

A movie rights offer they'd both have resented,
(Provided that movies had then been invented).
So in spite of our virtue, it's hard to suppress
A sneaking affection for Frank and for Jess.

STODDARD KING

ON A CLERGYMAN'S
HORSE BITING HIM

The steed bit his master;
    How came this to pass?
He heard the good pastor
    Cry, 'All flesh is grass'.

ANONYMOUS

COMMUTER

Commuter—one who spends his life
    In riding to and from his wife;
A man who shaves and takes a train
    And then rides back to shave again.

E. B. WHITE

MONEY, MONEY, MONEY ~~~~

REFLEXIONS ON THE SEIZURE OF THE SUEZ,
AND ON A PROPOSAL TO LINE THE BANKS
OF THAT CANAL WITH BILLBOARD
ADVERTISEMENTS

From Molepolole and Morogoro,
Dongola, Dungun, Dush,
From Kongor and Gojjam and Juba,
Gagag and Segag and Geba Geba,
The bracelets of brass and the calico hankies
Come back a thousandfold.

Smoke Pyramids for Appearances' Sake

From Kanker and Kurnool and Bhor,
Bellary, Trivandrum, Nellore,
From Gooty and Owsa, Hubh and Alur,
Adoni and Chik- and Dod-Ballapur,
The glass beads and obsolete Lee Enfields
Return upon the makers.

Drink Pyramids the World's Premier Aperient

In Hebron, Jabal, Zebara,
In Jebel Tathlith and Wafi Harid,

Asterabad, Washraf, Miskin, Sham,
In Jask and Ras Nus, Beni Auf, Jauf,
It is the same. Everywhere the givers
Are in the hands of the receivers.

For That Serious Fear, Take a Pyramid

So also in Bumpass and Mauch Chunk,
Tallulah, Wabuska, Markle and Lair,
The burden of Tupelo, Tunica, Nampa, Dufur,
Of Grundy and Presho and Stackhouse and Bland.
Though oil cast upon the troubled waters
May be returned as capital gains.

Pyramids Are Silent, Speedy, Safe.
—Next Time, Go by Pyramid.

HOWARD NEMEROV

DIOGENES

Diogenes lived in a tub,
Eating the plainest of grub;
And eminent people he'd snub.
He apparently did it for pub-
        licity.

Alexander the Great had the whim
To call; he looked over the rim
Of the tub. But the scholar was grim;
And "Kindly move out of my glim!"
Was all to be got out of him;
Which was thought at the time to be sim-
        plicity.

But what he was after, we know,
Was to get people talking, and so
To make his philosophy go,

And make the world conscious of sto-
    icity.

And what were the views of this cub?
Well, really, you know, there's the rub.
I cannot recall, like a dub.
But I know that he lived in a tub!
And there is the trouble with pub-
    licity!

MORRIS BISHOP

MONEY

Workers earn it,
Spendthrifts burn it,
Bankers lend it,
Women spend it,
Forgers fake it,
Taxes take it,
Dying leave it,
Heirs receive it,
Thrifty save it,
Misers crave it,
Robbers seize it,
Rich increase it,
Gamblers lose it . . .
I could use it.

RICHARD ARMOUR

BACK THROUGH THE LOOKING GLASS TO THIS SIDE

Yesterday, in a big market, I made seven thousand dollars
while I was flying to Dallas to speak to some lunch group
and back for a nightcap with my wife. A man from Dallas

sat by me both ways, the first from Campbell's Soup,
the other from some labeled can of his own, mostly water,
and Goldwater at that. Capt. J.J. Slaughter

of Untied Airlines kept us all in smooth air and well
and insistently informed of our progress. Miss G. Klaus
brought us bourbon on ice, and snacks. At the hotel
the lunch grouped and the group lunched. I was,
if I may say so, perceptive, eloquent, sincere.
Then back to the airport with seventeen minutes to spare.

Capt. T.V. Ringo took over with Miss P. Simbus
and that Goldwater oaf. We made it to Newark at nine
plus a few minutes lost in skirting cumulonimbus
in our descent at the Maryland-Delaware line.
"Ticker runs late," said the horoscope page. "New highs
posted on a broad front."—So the good guys

had won again! Fat, complacent, a check
for more than my father's estate in my inside pocket,
with the launched group's thanks for a good day's work,
I found my car in the lot and poked it
into the lunatic aisles of U.S.1,
a good guy coming home, the long day done.

JOHN CIARDI

BEHOLD THE DEEDS!

Being the Plaint of Adolphe Culpepper
Ferguson, Salesman of Fancy Notions,
held in durance of his Landlady for a
"failure to connect" on Saturday night)

I would that all men my hard case would know,
    How grievously I suffer for no sin:
I, Adolphe Culpepper Ferguson, for lo!
    I of my landlady am lockèd in
For being short on this sad Saturday,

Nor having shekels of silver wherewith to pay:
She turned and is departed with my key;
Wherefore, not even as other boarders free,
   I sing (as prisoners to their dungeon-stones
When for ten days they expiate a spree):
   Behold the deeds that are done of Mrs. Jones!

One night and one day have I wept my woe;
   Nor wot I, when the morrow doth begin,
If I shall have to write to Briggs & Co.,
   To pray them to advance the requisite tin
For ransom of their salesman, that he may
Go forth as other boarders go alway—
As those I hear now flocking from their tea,
Led by the daughter of my landlady
   Piano-ward. This day, for all my moans,
Dry-bread and water have been servèd me.
   Behold the deeds that are done of Mrs. Jones!

Miss Amabel Jones is musical, and so
   The heart of the young he-boarder doth win,
Playing "The Maiden's Prayer" *adagio*—
   That fetcheth him, as fetcheth the "bunko skin"
The innocent rustic. For my part, I pray
That Badarjewska maid may wait for aye
Ere sits she with a lover, as did we
Once sit together, Amabel! Can it be
   That all that arduous wooing not atones
For Saturday's shortness of trade dollars three?
   Behold the deeds that are done of Mrs. Jones!

Yea! She forgets the arm that was wont to go
   Around her waist. She wears a buckle whose pin
Galleth the crook of her young man's elbow.
   I forget not, for I that youth have been!
Smith was aforetime the Lothario gay.
Yet once, I mind me, Smith was forced to stay
Close in his room. Not calm as I was he;
But his noise brought no pleasaunce, verily.

Small ease he got of playing on the bones
Or hammering on the stope-pipe, that I see.
    Behold the deeds that are done of Mrs. Jones!

Thou, for whose fear the figurative crow
    I eat, accursed be thou and all thy kin!
Thee will I show up—yea, up I will show
    Thy too-thick buckwheats and thy tea too thin.
Aye! here I dare thee, ready for the fray:
Thou dost *not* "keep a first-class house" I say!
It does not with the advertisements agree.
Thou lodgest a Briton with a puggaree,
    And thou hast harbored Jacobses and Cohns,
Also a Mulligan. Thus denounce I thee!
    Behold the deeds that are done of Mrs. Jones!

ENVOY

Boarders! the worst I have not told to ye:
She hath stolen my trousers, that I may not flee
    Privily by the window. Hence these groans.
There is no fleeing in a *robe de nuit.*
    Behold the deeds that are done of Mrs. Jones!

H. C. Bunner

Little Lyric
(of Great Importance)

I wish the rent
Was heaven sent.

Langston Hughes

BOOM!
SEES BOOM IN RELIGION, TOO

Atlantic City, June 23, 1957 (AP)—
President Eisenhower's pastor said tonight
that Americans are living in a period of
"unprecedented religious activity" caused
partially by paid vacations, the
eight-hour day and modern conveniences.
    "These fruits of material progress,"
said the Rev. Edward L.R. Elson of the
National Presbyterian Church,
Washington, "have provided the leisure,
the energy, and the means for a level of
human and spiritual values never before
reached."

Here at the Vespasian-Carlton, it's just one
religious activity after another; the sky
is constantly being crossed by cruciform
airplanes, in which nobody disbelieves
for a second, and the tide, the tide
of spiritual progress and prosperity
miraculously keeps rising, to a level
never before attained. The churches are full,
the beaches are full, and the filling-stations
are full, God's great ocean is full
of paid vacationers praying an eight-hour day
to the human and spiritual values, the fruits,
the leisure, the energy, and the means, Lord,
the means for the level, the unprecedented level,
and the modern conveniences, which also are full.
Never before, O Lord, have the prayers and praises
from belfry and phonebooth, from ballpark and barbecue
the sacrifices, so endlessly ascended.

It was not thus when Job in Palestine
sat in the dust and cried, cried bitterly;
when Damien kissed the lepers on their wounds
it was not thus; it was not thus

when Francis worked a fourteen-hour day
strictly for the birds; when Dante took
a week's vacation without pay and it rained
part of the time, O Lord, it was not thus.

But now the gears mesh and the tires burn
and the ice chatters in the shaker and the priest
in the pulpit, and Thy Name, O Lord,
is kept before the public, while the fruits
ripen and religion booms and the level rises
and every modern convenience runneth over,
that it may never be with us as it hath been
with Athens and Karnak and Nagasaki,
nor Thy sun for one instant refrain from shining
on the rainbow Buick by the breezeway
or the Chris Craft with the uplift life raft;
that we may continue to be the just folks we are,
plain people with ordinary superliners and
disposable diaperliners, people of the stop'n'shop
'n'pray as you go, of hotel, motel, boatel,
the humble pilgrims of no deposit no return
and please adjust thy clothing, who will give to Thee,
if Thee will keep us going, our annual
Miss Universe, for Thy Name's Sake, Amen.

HOWARD NEMEROV

INTROSPECTIVE REFLECTION

I would live all my life in nonchalance and insouciance
Were it not for making a living, which is rather a nouciance.

OGDEN NASH

FATIGUE

I'm tired of Love: I'm still more tired of Rhyme.
But Money gives me pleasure all the time.

HILAIRE BELLOC

The Rich Man

The rich man has his motorcar,
    His country and his town estate.
He smokes a fifty-cent cigar
    And jeers at Fate.

He frivols through the livelong day,
    He knows not Poverty her pinch.
His lot seems light, his heart seems gay,
    He has a cinch.

Yet though my lamp burns low and dim,
    Though I must slave for livelihood—·
Think you that I would change with him?
    You bet I would!

                    Franklin P. Adams ("F.P.A.")

On Communists

What is a Communist? One who hath yearnings
For equal division of unequal earnings;
Idler or bungler, or both, he is willing
To fork out his penny and pocket your shilling.

                    Ebenezer Elliott

Art

The hen remarked to the mooley cow,
As she cackled her daily lay,
(That is, the hen cackled) "It's funny how
I'm good for an egg a day.
I'm a fool to do it, for what do I get?
My food and my lodging. My!
But the poodle gets that—he's the household pet,

And he never has laid a single egg yet—
Not even when eggs are high."

The mooley cow remarked to the hen,
As she masticated her cud,
(That is, the cow did) "Well, what then?
You quit, and your name is mud.
I'm good for eight gallons of milk each day,
And I'm given my stable and grub;
But the parrot gets that much, anyway,—
All she can gobble—and what does she pay?
Not a dribble of milk, the dub!"

But the hired man remarked to the pair,
"You get all that's coming to you.
The poodle does tricks, and the parrot can swear,
Which is better than you can do.
You're necessary, but what's the use
Of bewailing your daily part?
You're bourgeois—working's your only excuse;
You can't do nothing but just produce—
What them fellers does is ART!"

Anonymous

Spectator ab Extra

As I sat at the Café I said to myself,
They may talk as they please about what they call pelf,
They may sneer as they like about eating and drinking,
But help it I cannot, I cannot help thinking
    How pleasant it is to have money, heigh-ho!
    How pleasant it is to have money.

I sit at my table *en grand seigneur,*
And when I have done, throw a crust to the poor;
Not only the pleasure itself of good living,
But also the pleasure of now and then giving:

So pleasant it is to have money, heigh-ho!
So pleasant it is to have money.

They may talk as they please about what they call pelf,
And how one ought never to think of one's self,
How pleasures of thought surpass eating and drinking,—
My pleasure of thought is the pleasure of thinking
　　How pleasant it is to have money, heigh-ho!
　　How pleasant it is to have money.

　　　　　　　　　　　　　　ARTHUR HUGH CLOUGH

THE COMPLETE CYNIC

Diogenes, that wise old bird,
　　Walked Main Street up and down,
To lamp, as doubtless you have heard,
　　Some honest man in town.

And whether he found any
　　Has been completely hid,
But as against a penny
　　I'll bet my wad he did.

He took their names and numbers down,
　　With many secret snickers.
Diogenes sold sucker lists
　　To Hellenistic slickers.

　　　　　　　　　　　　　　KEITH PRESTON

THE ADVERTISING AGENCY SONG

When your client's hopping mad,
Put his picture in the ad.
If he still should prove refractory
Add a picture of his factory.

　　　　　　　　　　　　　　ANONYMOUS

IF I SHOULD DIE

If I should die to-night
And you should come to my cold corpse and say,
Weeping and heartsick o'er my lifeless clay—
    If I should die to-night,
And you should come in deepest grief and woe—
And say: "Here's that ten dollars that I owe,"
    I might arise in my large white cravat
    And say, "What's that?"

If I should die to-night
And you should come to my cold corpse and kneel,
Clasping my bier to show the grief you feel,
    I say, if I should die to-night
And you should come to me, and there and then
Just even hint 'bout payin' me that ten,
    I might arise the while,
    But I'd drop dead again.

BEN KING

CORRESPONDENCE BETWEEN
MR. HARRISON IN NEWCASTLE AND
MR. SHOLTO PEACH HARRISON IN HULL

Sholto Peach Harrison you are no son of mine
And do you think I bred you up to cross the River Tyne
And do you think I bred you up (and mother says the same)
And do you think I bred you up to live a life of shame
To live a life of shame my boy as you are thinking to
Down south in Kingston-upon-Hull a traveller in glue?
Come back my bonny boy nor break your father's heart
Come back and marry Lady Susan Smart
She has a mint in Anglo-Persian oil
And Sholto never more need think of toil.

You are an old and evil man my father
I tell frankly Sholto had much rather
Travel in glue unrecompensed unwed
Than go to church with oily Sue and afterwards to bed.

STEVIE SMITH

FROM A LONDON BOOKSHOP

Holy Scripture, Writ Divine,
Leather bound, at one and nine,
Satan trembles when he sees
Bibles sold as cheap as these.

ANONYMOUS

MR. BILLINGS OF LOUISVILLE

There are times in one's life which one cannot forget;
And the time I remember's the evening I met
A haughty young scion of bluegrass renown
Who made my acquaintance while painting the town:
A handshake, a cocktail, a smoker, and then
Mr. Billings of Louisville touched me for ten.

There flowed in his veins the blue blood of the South,
And a cynical smile curled his sensuous mouth;
He quoted from Lanier and Poe by the yard,
But his purse had been hit by the war, and hit hard:
I felt that he honored and flattered me when
Mr. Billings of Louisville touched me for ten.

I wonder that never again since that night
A vision of Billings has hallowed my sight;
I pine for the sound of his voice and the thrill
That comes with the touch of a ten-dollar bill:
I wonder and pine; for—I say it again—
Mr. Billings of Louisville touched me for ten.

I've heard that old Whittier sung of Miss Maud;
But all such pilosophy 's nothing but fraud;
To one who 's a bear in Chicago to-day,
With wheat going up, and the devil to pay,
These words are the saddest of tongue or of pen:
"Mr. Billings of Louisville touched me for ten."

EUGENE FIELD

LORD FINCHLEY

Lord Finchley tried to mend the Electric Light
Himself. It struck him dead: And serve him right!
It is the business of the wealthy man
To give employment to the artisan.

HILAIRE BELLOC

[DONT STEAL. THOU'LT NEVER THUS COMPETE]

Don't steal. Thou'lt never thus compete
Successfully in business. Cheat.

AMBROSE BIERCE

WHERE ARE YOU GOING,
MY PRETTY MAID

"Where are you going, my pretty maid?"
"I'm going a-milking, sir," she said.

"May I go with you, my pretty maid?"
"You're kindly welcome, sir," she said.

"What is your father, my pretty maid?"
"My father's a farmer, sir," she said.

"What is your fortune, my pretty maid?"
"My face is my fortune, sir," she said.

"Then I can't marry you, my pretty maid."
"Nobody asked you, sir," she said.

ANONYMOUS

A SUMMER MORNING

Her young employers, having got in late
From seeing friends in town
And scraped the right front fender on the gate,
Will not, the cook expects, be coming down.

She makes a quiet breakfast for herself.
The coffee-pot is bright,
The jelly where it should be on the shelf.
She breaks an egg into the morning light,

Then, with the bread-knife lifted, stands and hears
The sweet efficient sounds
Of thrush and catbird, and the snip of shears
Where, in the terraced backward of the grounds,

A gardener works before the heat of day.
He straightens for a view
Of the big house ascending stony-gray
Out of his beds moasic with the dew.

His young employers having got in late,
He and the cook alone
Receive the morning on their old estate,
Possessing what the owners can but own.

RICHARD WILBUR

from One From One Leaves Two

I pray the Lord my soul to take
If the tax collector hasn't got it before I wake.

Ogden Nash

PORTS OF CALL

~~~~~~~~~~
_____

TRIALS OF A TOURIST

It is three o'clock in the morning.
I am in a hurry.
I will have some fried fish.
It does not smell nice.
Bring some coffee now—and some wine.
Where is the toilet? There is a mistake in the bill.
You have charged me too much.
I have left my glasses, my watch and my ring, in the toilet.
Bring them.

Porter, here is my luggage.
I have only a suitcase and a bag.
I shall take this myself.
Be very careful with that.
Look out! The lock is broken.
Don't forget that.
I have lost my keys.
Help me to close this.
How much do I owe you? I did not know I had to pay.
Find me a non-smoking compartment, a corner seat, facing the
    engine.
Put the case on the rack.
Someone has taken my seat.
Can you help me to open the window.

Where is the toilet?
I have left my ticket, my gloves and my glasses in the toilet.
Can they be sent on?
Stop! I want to get off again. I have got into the wrong train.

Who is speaking?
Wrong number!
I don't understand you.
Do you speak English?
I am an Englishwoman. Does no-one here speak English?
Wait. I am looking for a phrase in my book.

My bag has been stolen.
That man is following me everywhere.
Go away. Leave me alone.
I shall call a policeman.

You are mistaken. I didn't do it.
It has nothing to do with me. I have done nothing.
Let me pass. I have paid you enough.
Where is the British Consulate?
Beware!

Bring me some cottonwool.
I think there is a mistake in your calculations.
I do not feel well.
Ring a doctor.

Can you give me something for diarrhoea?
I have a pain. Here.
I have pains all over.
I can't eat.
I do not sleep.
I think I have a temperature.
I have caught a cold.
I have been burnt by the sun.
My skin is smarting. Have you nothing to soothe it?
My nose is bleeding.
I feel giddy.

I keep vomiting.
I have been stung by sea-urchins.
I have been bitten by a dog.
I think I have food-poisoning.
You are hurting me.
I shall stay in bed.
Bring me some brandy—please.
Help!
Fire!
Thief!

ANNE TIBBLE

THE OWL AND THE PUSSY CAT

The Owl and the Pussy Cat went to sea
   In a beautiful pea-green boat.
They took some honey, and plenty of money
   Wrapped up in a five-pound note.
The Owl looked up to the stars above,
   And sang to a small guitar,
'O lovely Pussy! O Pussy, my love,
What a beautiful Pussy you are,
      You are,
      You are!
What a beautiful Pussy you are!'

Pussy said to the Owl, 'You elegant fowl!
   How charmingly sweet you sing!
O let us be married! too long we have tarried:
   But what shall we do for a ring?'
They sailed away, for a year and a day,
   To the land where the Bong-Tree grows,
And there in a wood a Piggy-wig stood,
With a ring at the end of his nose,
      His nose,
      His nose!
With a ring at the end of his nose.

'Dear Pig, are you willing to sell for one shilling
   Your ring?' Said the Piggy, 'I will.'
So they took it away, and were married next day
   By the Turkey who lives on the hill.
They dined on mince, and slices of quince,
   Which they ate with a runcible spoon;
And hand in hand, on the edge of the sand
   They danced by the light of the moon,
      The moon,
      The moon,
They danced by the light of the moon.

EDWARD LEAR

WRITTEN AFTER SWIMMING
FROM SESTOS TO ABYDOS

If, in the month of dark December,
   Leander, who was nightly wont
(What maid will not the tale remember?)
   To cross thy stream, broad Hellespont!

If, when the wint'ry tempest roar'd,
   He sped to Hero nothing loth,
And thus of old thy current pour'd,
   Fair Venus! how I pity both!

For *me*, degenerate modern wretch,
   Though in the genial month of May,
My dripping limbs I faintly stretch,
   And think I've done a feat today.

But since he crossed the rapid tide,
   According to the doubtful story,
To woo—and—Lord knows what beside,
   And swam for Love, as I for Glory;

'T were hard to say who fared the best:
   Sad mortals! thus the gods still plague you!

He lost his labor, I my jest;
   For he was drowned, and I've the ague.

GEORGE GORDON, LORD BYRON

THE LISBON PACKET

Huzza! Hodgson, we are going,
   Our embargo's off at last;
Favorable breezes blowing
   Bend the canvas o'er the mast.
From aloft the signal's streaming,
   Hark! the farewell gun is fired;
Women screeching, tars blaspheming,
   Tell us that our time's expired.
      Here's a rascal
      Come to task all,
   Prying from the custom-house;
      Trunks unpacking,
      Cases cracking,
   Not a corner for a mouse
'Scapes unsearched amid the racket,
Ere we sail on board the Packet.

Now our boatmen quit their mooring,
   And all hands must ply the oar;
Baggage from the quay is lowering,
   We're impatient—push from shore.
"Have a care! that case holds liquor—
   Stop the boat—I'm sick—O Lord!"
"Sick, ma'am, damme, you'll be sicker
   Ere you've been an hour on board."
      Thus are screaming
      Men and women,
   Gemmen, ladies, servants, Jacks;
      Here entangling,
      All are wrangling,
   Stuck together close as wax.—
Such the general noise and racket,
Ere we reach the Lisbon Packet.

Now we've reached her, lo! the captain.
    Gallant Kid, commands the crew;
Passengers their berths are clapped in,
    Some to grumble, some to spew.
"Hey day! call you that a cabin?
    Why, 'tis hardly three feet square;
Not enough to stow Queen Mab in—
    Who the deuce can harbor there?"
        "Who, sir? plenty—
        Nobles twenty
Did at once my vessel fill."—
        "Did they? Jesus,
        How you squeeze us!
Would to God they did so still:
Then I'd 'scape the heat and racket
Of the good ship Lisbon Packet."

Fletcher! Murray! Bob! where are you?
    Stretched along the decks like logs—
Bear a hand, you jolly tar, you!
    Here's a rope's end for the dogs.
Hobhouse muttering fearful curses,
    As the hatchway down he rolls,
Now his breakfast, now his verses,
    Vomits forth—and damns our souls.
        "Here's a stanza
        On Braganza—
Help!"—"A couplet?"—"No, a cup
        Of warm water—"
        "What's the matter?"
"Zounds! my liver's coming up;
I shall not survive the racket
Of this brutal Lisbon Packet."

Now at length we're off for Turkey,
    Lord knows when we shall come back!
Breezes foul and tempests murky
    May unship us in a crack.
But, since life at most a jest is,

As philosophers allow,
Still to laugh by far the best is,
Then laugh on—as I do now.
Laugh at all things,
Great and small things,
Sick or well, at sea or shore;
While we're quaffing,
Let's have laughing—
Who the devil cares for more?—
Some good wine! and who would lack it,
Even on board the Lisbon Packet?

GEORGE GORDON, LORD BYRON

PUBLIC AID FOR NIAGARA FALLS

Upon the patch of earth that clings
Near the very brink of doom,
Where the frenzied water flings
Downward to a misty gloom,

Where the earth in terror quakes
And the water leaps in foam
Plunging, frantic, from the Lakes,
Hurrying seaward, hurrying home,

Where Man's little voice is vain,
And his heart chills in his breast
At the dreadful yell of pain
Of the waters seeking rest;

There I stood, and humbly scanned
The miracle that sense appalls,
And I watched the tourist stand
Spitting in Niagara Falls.

MORRIS BISHOP

Ozymandias Revisited

I met a traveller from an antique land
Who said: Two vast and trunkless legs of stone
Stand in the desert. Near them on the sand,
Half sunk, a shatter'd visage lies, whose frown
And wrinkled lip and sneer of cold command
Tell that its sculptor well those passions read
Which yet survive, stamp'd on these lifeless things,
The hand that mock'd them and the heart that fed;
And on the pedestal these words appear:
"My name is Ozymandias, king of kings:
Look on my works, ye Mighty, and despair!"
Also the names of Emory P. Gray,
Mr. and Mrs. Dukes, and Oscar Baer
Of 17 West 4th St., Oyster Bay.

MORRIS BISHOP

Owed to New York—1906

Vulgar of manner, overfed,
Overdressed and underbred,
Heartless, Godless, hell's delight,
Rude by day and lewd by night;
Bedwarfed the man, o'ergrown the brute,
Ruled by boss and prostitute:
Purple-robed and pauper-clad,
Raving, rotting, money-mad;
A squirming herd in Mammon's mesh,
A wilderness of human flesh;
Crazed by avarice, lust and rum,
New York, thy name's "Delirium."

BYRON RUFUS NEWTON

COLOGNE

In Köln, a town of monks and bones,
And pavements fanged with murderous stones,
And rags, and hags, and hideous wenches;
I counted two-and-seventy stenches,
All well defined, and separate stinks!
Ye nymphs that reign o'er sewers and sinks,
The river Rhine, it is well known,
Doth wash your city of Cologne;
But tell me, nymphs, What power divine
Shall henceforth wash the river Rhine?

SAMUEL TAYLOR COLERIDGE

ON MY JOYFUL DEPARTURE
FROM THE SAME CITY

As I am a rhymer,
And now at least a merry one,
Mr. Mum's Rudesheimer
And the church of St. Geryon
Are the two things alone
That deserve to be known
In the body and soul-stinking town
of Cologne.

SAMUEL TAYLOR COLERIDGE

THE ALARMED SKIPPER

Many a long, long year ago,
Nantucket skippers had a plan
Of finding out, though "lying low,"
How near New York their schooners ran.

They greased the lead before it fell,
And then, by sounding through the night,
Knowing the soil that stuck, so well,
They always guessed their reckoning right.

A skipper gray, whose eyes were dim,
Could tell, by *tasting,* just the spot,
And so below he'd "dowse the glim"—
After, of course, his "something hot."

Snug in his berth, at eight o'clock,
This ancient skipper might be found;
No matter how his craft would rock,
He slept—for skippers' naps are sound!

The watch on deck would now and then
Run down and wake him, with the lead;
He'd up, and taste, and tell the men
How many miles they went ahead.

One night, 'twas Jonathan Marden's watch,
A curious wag—the peddler's son—
And so he mused (the wanton wretch),
"To-night I'll have a grain of fun.

"We're all a set of stupid fools
To think the skipper knows by *tasting*
What ground he's on—Nantucket schools
Don't teach such stuff, with all their basting!"

And so he took the well-greased lead
And rubbed it o'er a box of earth
That stood on deck—a parsnip-bed—
And then he sought the skipper's berth.

"Where are we now, sir? Please to taste."
The skipper yawned, put out his tongue,
Then ope'd his eyes in wondrous haste,
And then upon the floor he sprung!

The skipper stormed and tore his hair,
Thrust on his boots and roared to Marden,
"Nantucket's sunk; and here we are
Right over old Marm Hackett's garden!"

JAMES THOMAS FIELDS

THE DEVIL IN TEXAS

He scattered tarantulas over the roads,
Put thorns on the cactus and horns on the toads,
He sprinkled the sands with millions of ants
So the man who sits down must wear soles on his pants.
He lengthened the horns of the Texas steer,
And added an inch to the jack rabbit's ear;
He put mouths full of teeth in all of the lakes,
And under the rocks he put rattlesnakes.

He hung thorns and brambles on all of the trees,
He mixed up the dust with jiggers and fleas;
The rattlesnake bites you, the scorpion stings,
The mosquito delights you by buzzing his wings.
The heat in the summer's a hundred and ten,
Too hot for the Devil and too hot for men;
And all who remain in that climate soon bear
Cuts, bites, and stings, from their feet to their hair.

He quickened the buck of the bronco steed,
And poisoned the feet of the centipede;
The wild boar roams in the black chaparral;
It's a hell of a place that we've got for a hell.
He planted red pepper beside every brook;
The Mexicans use them in all that they cook.
Just dine with a Mexican, then you will shout,
'I've hell on the inside as well as the out!'

ANONYMOUS

Boston

I come from the city of Boston,
The home of the bean and the cod,
Where Cabots speak only to Lowells,
And Lowells speak only to God.

SAMUEL C. BUSHNELL

New Jersey Turnpike

It's been this way for some time:

   misguided through the middle
   to view the worst of it

   a dime for my waste at the
   Walt Whitman service station

   Howard Johnson's over light
     (the flavor of America)
   no truckers in sight

I paid graciously to be allowed Delaware.

RICHARD CUMBIE

The View from a Cab

An odd day. For the first time in years,
I am in New York. Riding in from
the airport on the bus, I have seen
abandoned cars spilling out their guts
onto loops of freeway cloverleaves.
The light looks dangerous. Anywhere else,
people would expect a hurricane:
the haze on the city has an edge,

like an inverted saucer. The sun
pries up one edge with a slanting ray.
I get in a cab. "This weather, huh?
I tell you what, it's them astronauts,
they're the cause of it." "How's that?" I say.
"I'm not sure," he says, "but I know this:
fuck with the moon, the sun don't like it."

HENRY TAYLOR

'¡WELLCOME, TO THE CAVES OF ARTÁ!'

'They are hollowed out in the see-coast at the municipal
terminal of Capdepera, at nine kilometers from the town
of Artá in the Island of Mallorca, with a suporizing
infinity of graceful columns of 21 meters and by down-
ward, wich prives the spectator of all animacion and
plunges in dumbness. The way going is very picturesque,
serpentine between style mountains, til the arrival at the
esplanade of the vallee called 'The Spider'. There are
good enlacements of the railroad with autobuses of ex-
cursion, many days of the week, today actually Wednes-
day and Satturday. Since many centuries renown foreing
visitors have explored them and wrote their eulogy
about, included Nort-American geoglogues.'
(From a Tourist leaflet)

Such subtile filigranity and nobless of construccion
    Here fraternise in harmony, that respiracion stops.
While all admit their impotence (though autors most formidable)
    To sing in words the excellence of Nature's underprops,
Yet stalactite and stalagmite together with dumb language
    Make hymnes to God wich celebrate the stregnth of water
        drops.

¿You, also, are you capable to make precise in idiom
    Consideracions magic of ilusions very wide?
Alraedy in the Vestibule of these Grand Caves of Artá
    The spirit of the human verb is darked and stupefyed;
So humildly you trespass trough the forest of the colums
    And listen to the grandess explicated by the guide.

From darkness into darkness, but at measure, now descending
  You remark with what esxactitude he designates each bent;
'The Saloon of Thousand Banners', or 'The Tumba of Napoleon',
  'The Grotto of the Rosary', 'The Club', 'The Camping Tent',
And at 'Cavern of the Organs' there are knocking strange
    formacions
  Wich give a nois particular pervoking wonderment.

¡Too far do not adventure, sir! For, further as you wander,
  The every of the stalactites will make you stop and say
Grand peril amenaces now, your nostrills aprehending
  An odour least delicious of lamentable decay.
Was it some poor touristers, in the depth of obscure cristal,
  Wich deceased of thier emocion on a past excursion day.

ROBERT GRAVES

ROBINSON CRUSOE'S STORY

The night was thick and hazy
  When the *Piccadilly Daisy*
Carried down the crew and captain in the sea;
  And I think the water drowned 'em
  For they never, never found 'em
And I know they didn't come ashore with me.

Oh! 'twas very sad and lonely
  When I found myself the only
Population on this cultivated shore;
  But I've made a little tavern
  In a rocky little cavern,
And I sit and watch for people at the door.

I spent no time in looking
  For a girl to do my cooking,
As I'm quite a clever hand at making stews;
  But I had that fellow Friday,

Just to keep the tavern tidy,
And to put a Sunday polish on my shoes.

I have a little garden
That I'm cultivating lard in,
As the things I eat are rather tough and dry;
For I live on toasted lizards,
Prickly pears, and parrot gizzards,
And I'm really very fond of beetle-pie.

The clothes I had were furry,
And it made me fret and worry
When I found the moths were eating off the hair;
And I had to scrape and sand 'em,
And I boiled 'em and I tanned 'em,
Till I got the fine morocco suit I wear.

I sometimes seek diversion
In a family excursion,
With the few domestic animals you see;
And we take along a carrot
As refreshment for the parrot,
And a little can of jungleberry tea.

Then we gather, as we travel,
Bits of moss and dirty gravel,
And we chip off little specimens of stone;
And we carry home as prizes
Funny bugs, of handy sizes,
Just to give the day a scientific tone.

If the roads are wet and muddy
We remain at home and study,—
For the Goat is very clever at a sum,—
And the Dog, instead of fighting,
Studies ornamental writing,
While the Cat is taking lessons on the drum.

We retire at eleven,
And we rise again at seven;
And I wish to call attention, as I close,
To the fact that all the scholars
Are correct about their collars,
And particular in turning out their toes.

CHARLES EDWARD CARRYL

A BAR ON THE PICCOLA MARINA

Verse   I'll sing you a song,
It's not very long,
Its moral may disconcert you,
Of a mother and wife
Who most of her life
Was famed for domestic virtue.
She had two strapping daughters and a rather dull son
And a much duller husband, who at sixty-one
Elected to retire
And, later on, expire.
Sing Hallelujah, Hey nonny-no, Hey nonny-no, Hey
nonny-no!

He joined the feathered choir.
Having laid him to rest
By special request
In the family mausoleum,
As his widow repaired
To the home they had shared,
Her heart sang a gay Te Deum.
And then in the middle of the funeral wake
While adding some liquor to the Tipsy Cake
She briskly cried, 'That's done.
My life's at last begun.
Sing Hallelujah, Hey nonny-no, Hey nonny-no, Hey
nonny-no!
It's time I had some fun.
Today, though hardly a jolly day,

At least has set me free,
We'll all have a lovely holiday
On the island of Capri!'

Refrain 1   In a bar on the Piccola Marina
              Life called to Mrs Wentworth-Brewster,
              Fate beckoned her and introduced her
              Into a rather queer
              Unfamiliar atmosphere.
              She'd just sit there, propping up the bar
              Beside a fisherman who sang to a guitar.
              When accused of having gone too far
              She merely cried, 'Funiculi!
              Just fancy me!
              Funicula!'
              When he bellowed 'Che Bella Signorina!'
              Sheer ecstasy at once produced a
              Wild shriek from Mrs Wentworth-Brewster,
              Changing her whole demeanour.
              When both her daughters and her son said,
              'Please come home, Mama,'
              She murmured rather bibulously, 'Who d'you think
                  you are?'
              Nobody can afford to be so lahdy-bloody-da
              In a bar on the Piccola Marina.

Interlude   Every fisherman cried.
              'Viva Viva' and 'Che Ragazza',
              When she sat in the Grand Piazza
              Everybody would rise,
              Every fisherman sighed,
              'Viva Viva che bell' Inglesi',
              Someone even said, 'Whoops-adaisy!'
              Which was quite a surprise.
              Each night she'd make some gay excuse
              And beaming with good will
              She'd just slip into something loose
              And totter down the hill.

Refrain 2   To the bar on the Piccola Marina
                   Where love came to Mrs Wentworth-Brewster,
                   Hot flushes of delight suffused her,
                   Right round the bend she went,
                   Picture her astonishment,
                   Day in, day out she would gad about
                   Because she felt she was no longer on the shelf,
                   Night out, night in, knocking back the gin
                   She'd cry, 'Hurrah!
                   Funicula
                   Funiculi
                   Funic yourself!'
                   Just for fun three young sailors from Messina
                   Bowed low to Mrs Wentworth-Brewster,
                   Said 'Scusi' and politely goosed her.
                   Then there was quite a scena.
                   Her family, in floods of tears, cried,
                   'Leave these men, Mama.'
                   She said, 'They're just high-spirited, like all Italians
                        are
                   And most of them have a great deal more to offer
                        than Papa
                   In a bar on the Piccola Marina.'

                                        NOEL COWARD

MAD DOGS AND ENGLISHMEN

In tropical climes there are certain times of day,
When all the citizens retire
To tear their clothes off and perspire.
It's one of those rules that the greatest fools obey,
Because the sun is much too sultry
And one must avoid its ultry-violet ray. . . .

The natives grieve when the white men leave their huts,
Because they're obviously definitely nuts!

Mad dogs and Englishmen
Go out in the midday sun.
The Japanese don't care to,
The Chinese wouldn't dare to,
Hindoos and Argentines sleep firmly from twelve to one,
But Englishmen detest a
Siesta.
In the Philippines there are lovely screens
To protect you from the glare.
In the Malay States there are hats like plates
Which the Britishers won't wear.
At twelve noon
The natives swoon
And no further work is done,
But mad dogs and Englishmen
Go out in the midday sun.

It's such a surprise for the Eastern eyes to see,
That though the English are effete
They're quite impervious to heat.
When the white man rides every native hides in glee,
Because the simple creatures hope he
Will impale his solar topee on a tree. . . .

It seems such a shame when the English claim the earth
That they give rise to such hilarity and mirth.

Mad dogs and Englishmen
Go out in the midday sun.
The toughest Burmese bandit
Can never understand it.
In Rangoon the heat of noon
Is just what the natives shun.
They put their Scotch or Rye down
And lie down.
In a jungle town
Where the sun beats down
To the rage of man and beast,

The English garb
Of the English sahib
Merely gets a bit more creased.
In Bangkok
At twelve o'clock
They foam at the mouth and run,
But mad dogs and Englishmen
Go out in the midday sun.

Mad dogs and Englishmen
Go out in the midday sun.
The smallest Malay rabbit
Deplores this stupid habit.
In Hongkong
They strike a gong
And fire off a noonday gun,
To reprimand each inmate
Who's in late.
In the mangrove swamps
Where the python romps
There is peace from twelve till two.
Even caribous
Lie around and snooze,
For there's nothing else to do.
In Bengal
To move at all
Is seldom, if ever done,
But mad dogs and Englishmen
Go out in the midday sun.

NOEL COWARD

BURMA-SHAVE

Every shaver
Now can snore
Six more minutes
Than before
By using
Burma-Shave

Does your husband
Misbehave
Grunt and grumble
Rant and rave
Shoot the brute
Some Burma-Shave

Are your whiskers
When you wake
Tougher than
A two-bit steak?
Try
Burma-Shave

Shaving brush
All wet
And hairy
I've passed you up
For sanitary
Burma-Shave

The answer to
A maiden's
Prayer
Is not a chin
Of stubby hair
Burma-Shave

Within this vale
Of toil
And sin
Your head grows bald
But not your chin—use
Burma-Shave

He had the ring
He had the flat
But she felt his chin
And that
Was that
Burma-Shave

Pity all
The mighty Caesars
They pulled
Each whisker out
With tweezers
Burma-Shave

Cutie invited
Varsity hop
Guy full of whiskers
Party a flop
Burma-Shave

Whiskers long
Made Samson strong
But Samson's gal
She done
Him wrong
Burma-Shave

His tenor voice
She thought divine
Till whiskers
Scratched
Sweet Adeline
Buram-Shave

The whale
Put Jonah
Down the hatch
But coughed him up
Because he scratched
Burma-Shave

If Crusoe'd
Kept his chin
More tidy
He might have found
A lady Friday
Burma-Shave

Ben
Met Anna
Made a hit
Neglected beard
Ben-Anna split
Burma-Shave

ANONYMOUS

Love

~~~~~~~

To Mistress
Margaret Hussey

Merry Margaret,
    As midsummer flower,
Gentle as falcon
Or hawk of the tower:
With solace and gladness,
Much mirth and no madness,
All good and no badness;
    So joyously,
    So maidenly,
    So womanly
    Her demeaning
    In every thing,
    Far, far passing
    That I can indite,
    Or suffice to write
Of Merry Margaret
    As midsummer flower,
Gentle as falcon
Or hawk of the tower.
    As patient and still
And as full of good will
As fair Isaphill,
Coriander,

Sweet pomander,
Good Cassander,
Steadfast of thought,
Well made, well wrought,
Far may be sought
Ere that ye can find
So courteous, so kind
As Merry Margaret,
   This midsummer flower,
Gentle as falcon
Or hawk of the tower.

JOHN SKELTON

THE PASSIONATE SHEPHERD
TO HIS LOVE

Come live with me and be my love,
And we will all the pleasures prove,
That valleys, groves, hills and fields,
And all the craggy mountains yields.

There we will sit upon the rocks,
And see the shepherds feed their flocks,
By shallow rivers to whose falls
Melodious birds sing madrigals.

And I will make thee beds of roses
With a thousand fragrant posies,
A cap of flowers, and a kirtle
Embroidered all with leaves of myrtle;

A gown made of the finest wool
Which from our pretty lambs we pull;
Fair lined slippers for the cold,
With buckles of the purest gold;

A belt of straw and ivy buds,
With coral clasps and amber studs:

And if these pleasures may thee move,
Come live with me and be my love.

The shepherds' swains shall dance and sing
For thy delight each May morning:
If these delights thy mind may move,
Then live with me and be my love.

CHRISTOPHER MARLOWE

THE NYMPH'S REPLY
TO THE SHEPHERD

If all the world and love were young,
And truth in every shepherd's tongue,
These pretty pleasures might me move,
To live with thee, and be thy love.

Time drives the flocks from field to fold,
When rivers rage, and rocks grow cold,
And Philomel becometh dumb,
The rest complains of cares to come.

The flowers do fade, and wanton fields,
To wayward winter reckoning yields,
A honey tongue, a heart of gall,
Is fancy's spring, but sorrow's fall.

Thy gowns, thy shoes, thy beds of roses,
Thy cap, thy kirtle, and thy posies,
Soon break, soon wither, soon forgotten:
In folly ripe, in reason rotten.

Thy belt of straw and ivy buds,
Thy coral clasps and amber studs,
All these in me no means can move,
To come to thee, and be thy love.

But could youth last, and love still breed,
Had joys no date, nor age no need,

Then these delights my mind might move,
To live with thee and be thy love.

Sir Walter Ralegh

When As the Rye
Reach to the Chin

When as the rye reach to the chin,
And chopcherry, chopcherry ripe within,
Strawberries swimming in the cream,
And schoolboys playing in the stream;
Then O, then O, then O my truelove said,
Till that time come again
She could not live a maid.

George Peele

A Sea Song
(*from* The Tempest)

The master, the swabber, the boatswain and I,
    The gunner and his mate,
Loved Mall, Meg, and Marian and Margery,
    But none of us cared for Kate;
    For she had a tongue with a tang,
    Would cry to a sailor, 'Go hang!'
She loved not the savour of tar nor of pitch,
Yet a tailor might scratch her where'er she did itch:
    Then to sea, boys, and let her go hang.

William Shakespeare

O Mistress Mine
(*from* twelfth night)

O mistress mine, where are you roaming?
O, stay and hear! your true love's coming,

That can sing both high and low:
Trip no further, pretty sweeting;
Journeys end in lovers meeting,
    Every wise man's son doth know.

What is love? 'tis not hereafter;
Present mirth hath present laughter;
    What's to come is still unsure:
In delay there lies no plenty;
Then come kiss me, sweet-and-twenty:
    Youth's a stuff will not endure.

WILLIAM SHAKESPEARE

WOMAN'S CONSTANCY

Now thou hast loved me one whole day,
Tomorrow when thou leav'st, what wilt thou say?
Wilt thou then Antedate some new-made vow?
    Or say that now
We are not just those persons, which we were?
Or, that oathes made in reverentiall fear
Of Love, and his wrath, any may forsweare?
Or, as true deaths, true maryages untie,
So lovers contracts, images of those,
Binde but till sleep, deaths image, them unloose?
    Or, your owne end to Justifie,
For having purpos'd change, and falsehood; you
Can have no way but falsehood to be true?
Vaine lunatique, against these scapes I could
    Dispute, and conquer, if I would,
    Which I abstaine to de,
For by to morrow, I may thinke so too.

JOHN DONNE

SONG

Goe, and catche a falling starre,
　　Get with child a mandrake roote,
Tell me, where all past yeares are,
　　Or who cleft the Divels foot,
Teach me to heare Mermaides singing,
　　Or to keep off envies stinging,
　　　　And finde
　　　　What winde
Serves to advance an honest minde.

If you beest borne to strange sights,
　　Things invisible to see,
Ride ten thousand daies and nights,
　　Till age snow white haires on thee,
Thou, when thou retorn'st, wilt tell mee
All strange wonders that befell thee,
　　　　And sweare
　　　　No where
Lives a woman true, and faire.

If thou findst one, let mee know,
　　Such a Pilgrimage were sweet;
Yet doe not, I would not goe,
　　Though at next doore wee might meet,
Though shee were true, when you met her,
And last, till you write your letter,
　　　　Yet shee
　　　　Will bee
False, ere I come, to two, or three.

　　　　　　　　　　　　　JOHN DONNE

THE APPARITION

When by thy scorne, O murdresse, I am dead,
　　And that thou thinkst thee free

From all solicitation from mee,
Then shall my ghost come to thy bed,
And thee, fain'd vestall, in worse armes shall see;
Then thy sicke taper will begin to winke,
And he, whose thou art then, being tyr'd before,
Will, if thou stirre, or pinch to wake him, thinke
    Thou call'st for more,
And in false sleepe will from thee shrinke,
And then poore Aspen wretch, neglected thou
Bath'd in cold quicksilver sweat wilt lye
    A veryer ghost than I;
What I will say, I will not tell thee now,
Lest that preserve thee; and since my love is spent,
I'had rather thou shouldst painfully repent,
Than by my threatnings rest still innocent.

JOHN DONNE

THE FLEA

Marke but this flea, and marke in this,
How little that which thou deny'st me is;
It suck'd me first, and now sucks thee,
And in this flea, our two bloods mingled bee;
Thou know'st that this cannot be said
A sinne, nor shame, nor losse of maidenhead,
    Yet this enjoyes before it wooe,
    And pamper'd swells with one blood made of two,
    And this, alas, is more than wee would doe.

Oh stay, three lives in one flea spare,
Where wee almost, yea more than maryed are.
This flea is you and I, and this
Our mariage bed, and mariage temple is;
Though parents grudge, and you, w'are met,
And cloysterd in these living walls of Jet.
    Though use make you apt to kill mee,
    Let not to that, selfe murder added bee,
    And sacrilege, three sinnes in killing three.

Cruell and sodaine, hast thou since
Purpled thy naile, in blood of innocence?
Wherein could this flea guilty bee,
Except in that drop which it suckt from thee?
Yet thou triumph'st, and saist that thou
Find'st not thy selfe, nor mee the weaker now;
   'Tis true, then learne how false, feares bee;
   Just so much honor, when you yeeld'st to mee,
   Will wast, as this flea's death tooke life from thee.

JOHN DONNE

COME, MY CELIA

Come, my Celia, let us prove,
While we can, the sports of love;
Time will not be ours forever;
He at length our good will sever.
Spend not then his gifts in vain.
Suns that set may rise again;
But if once we lose this light,
'Tis with us perpetual night.
Why should we defer our joys?
Fame and rumor are but toys.
Cannot we delude the eyes
Of a few poor household spies,
Or his easier ears beguile,
So removéd by our wile?
'Tis no sin love's fruit to steal;
But the sweet thefts to reveal,
To be taken, to be seen,
These have crimes accounted been.

BEN JONSON

Upon Julia's Clothes

Whenas in silks my Julia goes,
Then, then, methinks, how sweetly flows
The liquefaction of her clothes!

Next, when I cast mine eyes and see
That brave vibration each way free,
—O how that glittering taketh me!

Robert Herrick

To the Virgins,
To Make Much of Time

Gather ye rosebuds while ye may,
    Old Time is still a-flying:
And this same flower that smiles to-day
    To-morrow will be dying.

The glorious lamp of heaven, the sun,
    The higher he's a-getting,
The sooner will his race be run,
    And neerer he's to setting.

That age is best which is the first,
    When youth and blood are warmer;
But being spent, the worse, and worst
    Times still succeed the former.

Then be not coy, but use your time;
    And while ye may, go marry;
For having lost but once your prime,
    You may for ever tarry.

Robert Herrick

Why So Pale and Wan?

Why so pale and wan, fond lover?
    Prithee why so pale?
Will, when looking well can't move her,
    Looking ill prevail?
    Prithee why so pale?

Why so dull and mute, young sinner?
    Prithee why so mute?
Will, when speaking well can't win her,
    Saying nothing do't?
    Prithee why so mute?

Quit, quit, for shame; this will not move,
    This cannot take her;
If of herself she will not love,
    Nothing can make her:
    The devil take her!

                                    Sir John Suckling

Out Upon It! I Have Loved

Out upon it! I have loved
    Three whole days together;
And am like to love three more,
    If it prove fair weather.

Time shall moult away his wings,
    Ere he shall discover
In the whole wide world again
    Such a constant lover.

But the spite on 't is, no praise
    Is due at all to me;
Love with me had made no stays,
    Had it any been but she.

Had it any been but she,
And that very face,
There had been at least ere this
A dozen dozen in her place.

SIR JOHN SUCKLING

SONG

Love a woman? You're an ass!
'Tis a most insipid passion
To choose out for your happiness
The silliest part of God's creation.

Let the porter and the groom,
Things designed for dirty slaves,
Drudge in fair Aurelia's womb
To get supplies for age and graves.

Farewell, woman! I intend
Henceforth every night to sit
With my lewd, well-natured friend,
Drinking to engender wit.

Then give me health, wealth, mirth, and wine,
And, if busy love entrenches,
There's a sweet, soft page of mine
Does the trick worth forty wenches.

JOHN WILMOT, EARL OF ROCHESTER

UPON LEAVING HIS MISTRESS

'Tis not that I am weary grown
Of being yours, and yours alone,
But with what face can I incline
To damn you to be only mine?
You, whom some kinder power did fashion

By merit and by inclination
The joy at least of a whole nation.

Let meaner spirits of your sex
With humble aims their thoughts perplex,
And boast if by their arts they can
Contrive to make one happy man;
While moved by an impartial sense
Favours, like Nature, you dispense
With universal influence.

See the kind seed-receiving earth
To every grain affords a birth:
On her no showers unwelcome fall,
Her willing womb retains 'em all,
And shall my Caelia be confined?
No, live up to thy mighty mind,
And be the mistress of Mankind!

JOHN WILMOT, EARL OF ROCHESTER

A GENTLE ECHO ON WOMAN

(In the Doric Manner)

SHEPHERD: Echo, I ween, will in the wood reply,
And quaintly answer questions: shall I try?
              ECHO: Try.
What must we do our passion to express?
              Press.
How shall I please her, who ne'er loved before?
              Be Fore.
What most moves women when we them address?
              A dress.
Say, what can keep her chaste whom I adore?
              A door.
If music softens rocks, love tunes my lyre.
              Liar.
Then teach me, Echo, how shall I come by her?
              Buy her.

When bought, no question I shall be her dear?
Her deer.
But deers have horns: how must I keep her under?
Keep her under.
But what can glad me when she's laid on bier?
Beer.
What must I do when women will be kind?
Be kind.
What must I do when women will be cross?
Be cross.
Lord, what is she that can so turn and wind?
Wind.
If she be wind, what stills her when she blows?
Blows.
But if she bang again, still should I bang her?
Bang her.
Is there no way to moderate her anger?
Hang her.
Thanks, gentle Echo! right thy answers tell
What woman is and how to guard her well.
Guard her well.

JONATHAN SWIFT

SONG

Pious Selinda goes to prayers,
    If I but ask a favour;
And yet the tender fool's in tears,
    When she believes I'll leave her.

Would I were free from this restraint,
    Or else had hope to win her!
Would she could make of me a saint,
    Or I of her a sinner!

WILLIAM CONGREVE

I Once Was a Maid

I once was a maid, tho' I cannot tell when,
An' still my delight is in proper young men;
Some one of a troop of dragoons was my daddie,
No wonder I'm fond of a sodger laddie.

The first of my loves was a swaggering blade,
To rattle the thundering drum was his trade;
His leg was so tight, and his cheek was so ruddy,
Transported I was with my sodger laddie.

But the godly old chaplain left him in the lurch,
The sword I forsook for the sake of the church,
He ventured the soul, and I risk'd the body,
T'was then I proved false to my sodger laddie.

Full soon I grew sick of my sanctified sot.
The regiment at large for a husband I got;
From the gilded spontoon to the life I was ready,
I asked no more but a sodger laddie.

But the peace it reduced me to beg in despair,
Till I met my old boy at a Cunningham fair;
His rags regimental they fluttered so gaudy,
My heart it rejoiced at my sodger laddie.

An' now I have lived—I know not how long,
An' still I can join in a cup or a song;
But whilst with both hands I can hold the glass steady,
Here's to thee, my hero, my sodger laddie.

ROBERT BURNS

To Cloe

I could resign that eye of blue
   Howe'er its splendor used to thrill me;
And even that cheek of roseate hue—
   To lose it, Cloe, scarce would kill me.

That snowy neck I ne'er should miss,
   However much I've raved about it;
And sweetly as your lip can kiss,
   I *think* I could exist without it.

In short, so well I've learned to fast
   That, sweet my love, I know not whether
I might not bring myself at last
   To—do without you altogether.

THOMAS MOORE

translation of a poem by Martial

Jenny Kissed Me

Jenny kissed me when we met,
   Jumping from the chair she sat in;
Time, you thief, who love to get
   Sweets into your list, put that in!
Say I'm weary, say I'm sad,
   Say that health and wealth have missed me,
Say I'm growing old, but add,
   Jenny kissed me.

LEIGH HUNT

Sharing Eve's Apple

O blush not so! O blush not so!
   Or I shall think you knowing;

And if you smile the blushing while,
    Then maidenheads are going.

There's a blush for won't, and a blush for shan't,
    And a blush for having done it:
There's a blush for thought and a blush for naught,
    And a blush for just begun it.

O sigh not so! O sigh not so!
    For it sounds of Eve's sweet pippin;
By these loosened lips you have tasted the pips
    And fought in an amorous nipping.

Will you play once more at nice-cut-core,
    For it only will last our youth out,
And we have the prime of the kissing time,
    We have not one sweet tooth out.

There's a sigh for yes, and a sigh for no,
    And a sigh for I can't bear it!
O what can be done, shall we stay or run?
    O cut the sweet apple and share it!

                                        JOHN KEATS

OUR PHOTOGRAPH

She played me false, but that's not why
I haven't quite forgiven Di,
            Although I've tried:
This curl was hers, so brown, so bright,
She gave it me one blissful night,
            And—more beside!

In photo we were grouped together;
She wore the darling hat and feather
            That I adore;
In profile by her side I sat

Reading my poetry—but that
                    She'd heard before.

Why, after all, Di threw me over
I never knew, and can't discover,
                    Or even guess:
Maybe Smith's lyrics, she decided,
Were sweeter than the sweetest I did—
                    I acquiesce.

A week before their wedding-day
When Smith was called in haste away
                    To join the Staff,
Di gave to him, with tearful mien,
Our only photograph. I've seen
                    That photograph.

I've seen it in Smith's album-book!
Just think! her hat—her tender look,
                    And now that brute's!
Before she gave it, off she cut
My body, head and lyrics, but
She was obliged, the little slut,
                    To leave my boots.

FREDERICK LOCKER-LAMPSON

THE DARK-EYED GENTLEMAN

I pitched my day's leazings in Crimmercrock Lane,
To tie up my garter and jog on again,
When a dear dark-eyed gentleman passed there and said,
In a way that made all o' me color rose-red,
                    "What do I see—
                    O pretty knee!"
And he came and he tied up my garter for me.

'Twixt sunset and moonrise it was, I can mind:
Ah, 'tis easy to lose what we nevermore find!—

Of the dear stranger's home, of his name, I knew nought,
But I soon knew his nature and all that it brought.
        Then bitterly
        Sobbed I that he
Should ever have tied up my garter for me!

Yet now I've beside me a fine lissom lad,
And my slip's nigh forgot, and my days are not sad;
My own dearest joy is he, comrade, and friend,
He it is who safe-guards me, on him I depend;
        No sorrow brings he,
        And thankful I be
That his daddy once tied up my garter for me!

THOMAS HARDY

HELEN

So, how was I to know, when he invited
me to see his Trojan urns, that they
were aboard his yacht, and the crew trained to weigh
anchor at the drop of an eyelid? Admitted-
ly, if your life were fated to be blighted,
then he's the kind of blighter you might pray
heaven for. But I didn't. And anyway,
it could all have been hushed up by some half-witted
diplomat if they'd had a mind to. But no,
Troy must be taught a lesson—and beside,
there was our balance of payments problem. So
old feuds were patched, old enemies allied,
and a hundred thousand men, even though
it was a woman to blame as usual, died.

JAMES HARRISON

The Passionate Professor

But bending low, I whisper only this:
"Love, it is night."
　　　　　—Harry Thurston Peck.

Love, it is night. The orb of day
Has gone to hit the cosmic hay.
　　Nocturnal voices now we hear.
　　Come, heart's delight, the hour is near
When Passion's mandate we obey.

I would not, sweet, the fact convey
In any crude and obvious way:
　　I merely whisper in your ear—
　　　　　　　　"Love, it is night!"

Candor compels me, pet, to say
That years my fading charms betray.
　　Tho' Love be blind, I grant it's clear
　　I'm no Apollo Belvedere.
But after dark all cats are gray.
　　　　　　　　Love, it is night!

　　　　　Bert Leston Taylor ("B.L.T.")

Mia Carlotta

Giuseppe, da barber, ees greata for "mash,"
He gotta da bigga, da blacka moustache,
Good clo'es an' good styla an' playnta good cash.

W'enevra Giuseppe ees walk on da street,
Da people dey talka, "how nobby! how neat!
How softa da handa, how smalla da feet."

He leefta hees hat an' he shaka hees curls,
An' smila weeth teetha so shiny like pearls;

O, manny da heart of da seelly young girls
He gotta.
Yes, playnta he gotta
But notta
Carlotta!

Giuseppe, da barber, he maka da eye,
An' lika da steam engine puffa an' sigh,
For catcha Carlotta w'en she ees go by.

Carlotta she walka weeth nose in da air,
An' look through Giuseppe weeth far-away stare,
As eef she no see dere ees somebody dere.

Giuseppe, da barber, he gotta da cash,
He gotta da clo'es an' da bigga moustache,
He gotta da seelly young girls for da "mash,'
But notta
You bat my life, notta—
Carlotta.
I gotta!

T. A. DALY

WHEN ONE LOVES TENSELY

When one loves tensely, words are naught, my Dear!
You never felt I loved you till the day
I sighed and heaved a chunk of rock your way;
Nor I, until you clutched my father's spear
And coyly clipped the lobe from off my ear,
Guessed the sweet thought you were to shy to say—
All mute we listened to the larks of May,
Silent, we harked the laughter of the year.

Later, my Dear, I'll say you spoke enough!
Do you remember how I took you, Sweet,
And banged your head upon the frozen rill

Until I broke the ice, and by your feet
Held you submerged until your tongue was still?
When one loves tensely, one is sometimes rough.

DON MARQUIS

THE RECONCILIATION: A MODERN VERSION
ODES OF HORACE III, 9

HORACE

What time I was your one best bet
    And no one passed the wire before me,
Dear Lyddy, I cannot forget
    How you would—yes, you would—adore me.
To others you would tie the can;
    You thought of me with no aversion
In those days I was happier than
    A Persian.

LYDIA

Correct. As long as you were not
    So nuts about this Chloe person,
Your flame for me burned pretty hot—
    Mine was the door you pinned your verse on.
Your favorite name began with L,
    While I thought you surpassed by no man—
Gladder than Ilia, the well-
    Known Roman.

HORACE

On Chloe? Yes, I've got a case;
    Her voice is such a sweet soprano;
Her people come from Northern Thrace;
    You ought to hear her play piano.
If she would like my suicide—
    If she'd want me a dead and dumb thing,

Me for a glass of cyanide,
   Or something.

LYDIA

Now Calaïs, the handsome son
   Of old Ornitus, has *me* going;
He says I am his honey bun,
   He's mine, however winds are blowing;
I think that he is awful nice,
   And if the gods the signal gave him,
I'd just as lieve die once or twice
   To save him.

HORACE

Suppose I'm gone on you again,
   Suppose I've got ingrown affection
For you; I sort of wonder, then,
   If you'd have any great objection.
Suppose I pass this Chloe up
   And say: "Go roll your hoop, I'm rid o' ye!"
Would that drop sweetness in your cup?
   Eh, Lydia?

LYDIA

Why, say—though he's fair as a star,
   And you are like a cork, erratic
And light—and though I know you are
   As blustery as the Adriatic,
I think I'd rather live with you
   Or die with you, I swear to gracious.
So I will be your Mrs. Q.
   Horatius.

FRANKLIN P. ADAMS ("F.P.A.")

LIMBERICK

It's time to make love. Douse the glim.
The fireflies twinkle and dim.
   The stars lean together
   Like birds of a feather,
And the loin lies down with the limb.

CONRAD AIKEN

I LIKE THEM FLUFFY

Some like them gentle and sweet,
   Some like them haughty and proud,
Some of us like them petite,
   And some of us love the whole crowd;
Some will insist upon grace,
   And some make a point of the pelf,
But, to take a particular case,
   I do like them fluffy myself:

I like them fluffy, I freely confess,
With fluffy blue eyes and a fluffy blue dress,
   With fair fluffy hair, like Love-in-a-mist,
   And lips that declare "I want to be kissed";
      With fluffy soft cheeks, like plums on a wall,
      With a fluffy soft heart—and no brains at all.

Some like a girl that's well-read,
   Some like a shingle or crop,
But I don't care what's in her head,
   If there's plenty of hair on the top.
Give me the frivolous locks,
   Give me the Gaiety Queen,
Give me the Chocolate Box,
   And give me the Girls' Magazine!

I like them fluffy—I know it's bad taste—
With fluffy soft looks and a flower at the waist,
    With golden hair flying, like mist round the moon;
    And lips that seem sighing, "You must kiss me soon,"
        Not huffy, or stuffy, not tiny or tall,
        But fluffy, just fluffy, with no brains at all.

    Brains are all right in their place,
        But Oh, it's a shock to the heart
    If the lady postpones an embrace
        To enquire your opinions on Art!
    And to-day, as I paused on the brink,
        I own I was slightly annoyed
    When she sighed and said, "What do you think
        Of the basic assumptions of FREUD?"

"I like them fluffy," I gently replied,
"Not huffy, or stuffy, or puffy with pride,
    With downy soft eyebrows and artful blue eyes,
    The kind that the highbrows pretend to despise,
        With fluffy complexions, like plums on a wall,
        And fluffy opinions, and no brains at all."

A. P. HERBERT

from THE MIMIC MUSE

With rue my heart is laden
For many a lass I had,
For many a rouge-lipped maiden,
That's got a richer lad.

In rooms too small for leaping
Such lads as I are laid,
While richer boys are keeping
The girls that do not fade.

SAMUEL HOFFENSTEIN

from INVOCATION

Come, live with me and be my love
In statutory Christian sin,
And we shall all the pleasures prove
Of two-room flats and moral gin.

And you shall be a modern maid,
And golf upon the Attic greens,
Bisexually unafraid,
And talk about your endocrines.

And we shall to the heavens advance,
And broadcast to the quaking dawn
The age that walks in Puritan pants
With just one crucial button gone.

And we shall sing of export trade,
And celebrate the fiscal year,
And revel in the basement shade
Until the lusty riveteer,

Winds high and clear his rural horn
And the official day begins,
And we shall usher in the morn
With bowls of shredded vitamins.

And Progress shall with every flower
Of sweet expense her ardor prove,
If you will leave your dated bower,
Delightful Muse, and be my love.

SAMUEL HOFFENSTEIN

from ALWAYS TRUE TO YOU
IN MY FASHION

If a custom-tailored vet
Asks me out for something wet,
When the vet begins to pet, I cry "Hooray!"
But I'm always true to you, darlin', in my fashion,
Yes, I'm always true to you, darlin', in my way.
I enjoy a tender pass
By the boss of Boston, Mass.,
Though his pass is middle-class and notta Backa
    Bay.
But I'm always true to you, darlin', in my fashion,
Yes, I'm always true to you, darlin', in my way.
There's a madman known as Mack
Who is planning to attack,
If his mad attack means a Cadillac, okay!
But I'm always true to you, darlin', in my fashion,
Yes, I'm always true to you, darlin', in my way.

I've been asked to have a meal
By a big tycoon in steel,
If the meal includes a deal, accept I may.
But I'm always true to you, darlin', in my fashion,
Yes, I'm always true to you, darlin', in my way.
I could never curl my lip
To a dazzlin' diamond clip,
Though the clip meant "let 'er rip," I'd not say
    "Nay!'
But I'm always true to you, darlin', in my fashion,
Yes, I'm always true to you, darlin', in my way.
There's an oil man known as Tex
Who is keen to give me checks,
And his checks, I fear, mean that sex is here to stay!
But I'm always true to you, darlin', in my fashion,
Yes, I'm always true to you, darlin', in my way.

There's a wealthy Hindu priest
Who's a wolf, to say the least,
When the priest goes too far east, I also stray.
But I'm always true to you, darlin', in my fashion,
Yes, I'm always true to you, darlin', in my way.
There's a lush from Portland, Ore.,
Who is rich but sich a bore,
When the bore falls on the floor, I let him lay.
But I'm always true to you, darlin', in my fashion,
Yes, I'm always true to you, darlin', in my way.
Mister Harris, plutocrat,
Wants to give my cheek a pat,
If the Harris pat
Means a Paris hat,
Bébé, Oo-la-la!
Mais je suis toujours fidèle, darlin', in my fashion,
Oui, je suis toujours fidèle, darlin', in my way.

From Ohio Mister Thorne
Calls me up from night 'til morn,
Mister Thorne once cornered corn and that ain't hay.
But I'm always true to you, darlin', in my fashion,
Yes, I'm always true to you, darlin', in my way.
From Milwaukee, Mister Fritz
Often moves me to the Ritz,
Mister Fritz is full of Schlitz and full of play.
But I'm always true to you, darlin', in my fashion,
Yes, I'm always true to you, darlin', in my way.
Mister Gable, I mean Clark,
Wants me on his boat to park,
If the Gable boat
Means a sable coat,
Anchors aweigh!
But I'm always true to you, darlin', in my fashion,
Yes, I'm always true to you, darlin', in my way.

COLE PORTER

from YOU'RE THE TOP

You're the top!
You're the Colosseum.
You're the top!
You're the Louvre Museum.
You're a melody from a symphony by Strauss,
You're a Bendel bonnet,
A Shakespeare sonnet,
You're Mickey Mouse.
You're the Nile,
You're the Tow'r of Pisa,
You're the smile
On the Mona Lisa.
I'm a worthless check, a total wreck, a flop,
But if, Baby, I'm the bottom
You're the top!

You're the top!
You're Mahatma Gandhi.
You're the top!
You're Napoleon brandy.
You're the purple light of a summer night in
    Spain,
You're the National Gall'ry,
You're Garbo's sal'ry,
You're cellophane.
You're sublime,
You're a turkey dinner,
You're the time
Of the Derby winner.
I'm a toy balloon that is fated soon to pop,
But if, Baby, I'm the bottom
You're the top!

You're the top!
You're an Arrow collar.

You're the top!
You're a Coolidge dollar.
You're the nimble tread of the feet of Fred
   Astaire.
You're an O'Neill drama,
You're Whistler's mama,
You're Camembert.
You're a rose,
You're Inferno's Dante,
You're the nose
On the great Durante.
I'm just in the way, as the French would say
"De trop,"
But if, Baby, I'm the bottom
You're the top.

You're the top!
You're a Waldorf salad.
You're the top!
You're a Berlin ballad.
You're a baby grand of a lady and a gent,
You're an old Dutch master,
You're Mrs. Astor,
You're Pepsodent.
You're romance,
You're the steppes of Russia,
You're the pants on a Roxy usher.
I'm a lazy lout that's just about to stop,
But if, Baby, I'm the bottom
You're the top.

You're the top!
You're a dance in Bali.
You're the top!
You're a hot tamale.
You're an angel, you, simply too, too, too diveen,
You're a Botticelli,
You're Keats,
You're Shelley,

You're Ovaltine.
You're a boon,
You're the dam at Boulder,
You're the moon over Mae West's shoulder.
I'm a nominee of the G.O.P.
or GOP,
But if, Baby, I'm the bottom
You're the top.

You're the top!
You're the Tower of Babel.
You're the top!
You're the Whitney Stable.
By the River Rhine,
You're a sturdy stein of beer,
You're a dress from Saks's,
You're next year's taxes,
You're stratosphere.
You're my thoist,
You're a Drumstick Lipstick,
You're da foist
In da Irish Svipstick.
I'm a frightened frog
That can find no log
To hop,
But if, Baby, I'm the bottom
You're the top!

COLE PORTER

[MAY I FEEL SAID HE]

may i feel said he
(i'll squeal said she
just once said he)
it's fun said she

(may i touch said he
how much said she
a lot said he)
why not said she

(let's go said he
not too far said she
what's too far said he
where you are said she)

may i stay said he
(which way said she
like this said he
if you kiss said she

may i move said he
is it love said she)
if you're willing said he
(but you're killing said she

but it's life said he
but your wife said she
now said he)
ow said she

(tiptop said he
don't stop said she
oh no said he)
go slow said she

(cccome?said he
ummm said she)
you're divine!said he
(you are Mine said she)

E. E. CUMMINGS

Irish Song
(Rosie O'Grady)

When first I was courtin' sweet Rosie O'Grady,
Sweet Rosie O'Grady she whispered to me,
'Sure you shouldn't be after seducin' a lady
Before she's had time to sit down to her tea.'

With a Heigho—Top-o-the-morning—Begorrah and
    Fiddlededee.

Her cheeks were so soft and her eyes were so trustin',
She tossed her bright curls at the dusk of the day,
She said to me, 'Darlin', your breath is disgustin','
Which wasn't at all what I hoped she would say.

With a Heigho, maybe Begorrah, and possibly Fiddlededee.

Our honeymoon started so blithely and gaily
But dreams I was dreaming were suddenly wrecked
For she broke my front tooth with her father's shillelagh
Which wasn't what I had been led to expect.

With a Heigho, maybe Begorrah, and certainly Fiddlededee.

                                        Noel Coward

Major Macroo

Major Hawkaby Cole Macroo
Chose
Very wisely
A patient Griselda of a wife with a heart of gold
That never beat for a soul but him
Himself and his slightest whim.

He left her alone for months at a time
When he had to have a change
Just had to
And his pension wouldn't stretch to a fare for two
And he didn't want it to.

And if she wept she was game and nobody knew it
And she stood at the edge of the tunnel and waved as his train
   went through it.

And because it was cheaper they lived abroad
And did he care if she might be unhappy or bored?
He did not.
He'd other things to think of—a lot.

He'd fads and he fed them fat,
And she could lump it and that was that.

He'd several boy friends
And she thought it was nice for him to have them,
And she loved him and felt that he needed her and waited
And waited and never became exasperated.

Even his room
Was dusted and kept the same,
And when friends came
They went into every room in the house but that one
Which Hawkaby wouldn't have shown.

Such men as these, such selfish cruel men
Hurting what most they love and what most loves them,
Never make a mistake when it comes to choosing a woman
To cherish them and be *neglected* and not think it inhuman.

STEVIE SMITH

[He Told His Life Story to Mrs Courtly]

He told his life story to Mrs Courtly
Who was a widow. 'Let us get married shortly,'
He said. "I am no longer passionate,
But we can have some conversation before it is too late.'

Stevie Smith

Come, Live with Me
and Be My Love

Come, live with me and be my love,
And we will all the pleasures prove
Of peace and plenty, bed and board,
That chance employment may afford.

I'll handle dainties on the docks
And thou shalt read of summer frocks:
At evening by the sour canals
We'll hope to hear some madrigals.

Care on thy maiden brow shall put
A wreath of wrinkles, and thy foot
Be shod with pain: not silken dress
But toil shall tire thy loveliness.

Hunger shall make thy modest zone
And cheat fond death of all but bone—
If these delights thy mind may move,
Then live with me and be my love.

C. Day Lewis

For an Amorous Lady

"Most mammals like caresses, in the sense
in which we usually take the word,
whereas other creatures, even tame snakes,
prefer giving to receiving them."
FROM A NATURAL-HISTORY BOOK

The pensive gnu, the staid aardvark,
Accept caresses in the dark;
The bear, equipped with paw and snout;
Would rather take than dish it out.
But snakes, both poisonous and garter,
In love are never known to barter;
The worm, though dank, is sensitive:
His noble nature bids him *give*.

But you, my dearest, have a soul
Encompassing fish, flesh, and fowl.
When amorous arts we would pursue,
You can, with pleasure, bill *or* coo.
You are, in truth, one in a million,
At once mammalian and reptilian.

THEODORE ROETHKE

Pictures in the Smoke

Oh, gallant was the first love, and glittering and fine;
The second love was water, in a clear white cup;
The third love was his, and the fourth was mine;
And after that, I always get them all mixed up.

DOROTHY PARKER

One Perfect Rose

A single flow'r he sent me, since we met.
    All tenderly his messenger he chose;
Deep-hearted, pure, with scented dew still wet—
    One perfect rose.

I knew the language of the floweret;
    "My fragile leaves," it said, "his heart enclose."
Love long has taken for his amulet
    One perfect rose.

Why is it no one ever sent me yet
    One perfect limousine, do you suppose?
Ah no, it's always just my luck to get
    One perfect rose.

Dorothy Parker

Comment

Oh, life is a glorious cycle of song,
A medley of extemporanea;
And love is a thing that can never go wrong;
And I am Marie of Roumania.

Dorothy Parker

Pickin em Up
and Layin em Down

There's a long-legged girl
in San Francisco
by the Golden Gate.
She said she'd give me all I wanted
but I just couldn't wait.

I started to
Pickin em up
                    and layin em down,
Pickin em up
                    and layin em down,
Pickin em up
                    and layin em down,
gettin to the next town
Baby.

There's a pretty brown
in Birmingham
Boys, she little and cute
but when she like to tied me down
I had to grab my suit and started to
Pickin em up
                    and layin em down,
Pickin em up
                    and layin em down,
Pickin em up
                    and layin em down,
gettin to the next town
Baby.

I met that lovely Detroit lady
and thought my time had come
But just before I said "I do"
I said "I got to run" and started to
Pickin em up
                    and layin em down,
Pickin em up
                    and layin em down,
Pickin em up
                    and layin em down,
getting to the next town
Baby.

There ain't no words for what I feel
about a pretty face

But if I stay I just might miss
a prettier one some place
I start to
Pickin em up
                    and layin em down,
Pickin em up
                    and layin em down,
Pickin em up
                    and layin em down,
gettin to the next town
Baby.

                                        MAYA ANGELOU

CRABS

They are light as flakes of dandruff with scrawny legs.
Like limpets they cling to the base of each curly hair,
go lurching among the underbrush for cover.
Our passions are their weathers.
Coitus is the *Santa Maria* hitting on virgin land,
an immigrant ship coming into harbor,
free homesteads for all.
Or native crabs vs. conquistadors wrestle and nip.
Or maybe they too mingle.
As the boat glides in, there they are, the native crabs
with mandolins and bouquets of bougainvillaea
swaying on the dock singing Aloha.
For three generations we haven't seen a new face.
O the boredom, the stale genes, the incest.
Or perhaps when the two shores approach
the crabs line up to leap the gap like monkeys,
the hair always lusher on the other side.
They travel as fast as gossip.
They multiply like troubles.
They cling and persist through poison and poking and picking,
dirt and soap, torrents and drought,
like love or any other stubborn itch.

                                        MARGE PIERCY

SAMUEL SEWALL

Samuel Sewall, in a world of wigs,
Flouted opinion in his personal hair;
For foppery he gave not any figs,
But in his right and honor took the air.

Thus in his naked style, though well attired,
He went forth in the city, or paid court
To Madam Winthrop, whom he much admired,
Most godly, but yet liberal with the port.

And all the town admired for two full years
His excellent address, his gifts of fruit,
Her gracious ways and delicate white ears,
And held the course of nature absolute.

But yet she bade him suffer a peruke,
"That One be not distinguished from the All";
Delivered of herself this stern rebuke
Framed in the resonant language of St. Paul.

"Madam," he answered her, "I have a Friend
Furnishes me with hair out of His strength,
And He requires only I attend,
Unto His charity and to its length."

And all the town was witness to his trust:
On Monday he walked out with the Widow Gibbs,
A pious lady of charm and notable bust,
Whose heart beat tolerably beneath her ribs.

On Saturday he wrote proposing marriage
And closed, imploring that she be not cruel,
"Your favorable answer will oblige,
Madam, your humble servant, Samuel Sewall."

ANTHONY HECHT

PANGLOSS'S SONG:
A COMIC-OPERA LYRIC

I

Dear boy, you will not hear me speak
    With sorrow or with rancor
Of what has paled my rosy cheek
    And blasted it with canker;
'Twas Love, great Love, that did the deed
    Through Nature's gentle laws,
And how should ill effects proceed
    From so divine a cause?

Sweet honey comes from bees that sting,
    As you are well aware;
To one adept in reasoning,
Whatever pains disease may bring
Are but the tangy seasoning
    To Love's delicious fare.

II

Columbus and his men, they say,
    Conveyed the virus hither
Whereby my features rot away
    And vital powers wither;
Yet had they not traversed the seas
    And come infected back,
Why, think of all the luxuries
    That modern life would lack!

All bitter things conduce to sweet,
    As this example shows;
Without the little spirochete
We'd have no chocolate to eat,
Nor would tobacco's fragrance greet
    The European nose.

III

Each nation guards its native land
    With cannon and with sentry,
Inspectors look for contraband
    At every port of entry,
Yet nothing can prevent the spread
    Of Love's divine disease:
It round's the world from bed to bed
    As pretty as you please.

Men worship Venus everywhere,
    As plainly may be seen;
The decorations which I bear
Are nobler than the Croix de Guerre,
And gained in service of our fair
    And universal Queen.

Richard Wilbur

Ending

The love we thought would never stop
now cools like a congealing chop.
The kisses that were hot as curry
are bird-pecks taken in a hurry.
The hands that held electric charges
now lie inert as four moored barges.
The feet that ran to meet a date
are running slow and running late.
The eyes that shone and seldom shut
are victims of a power cut.
The parts that then transmitted joy
are now reserved and cold and coy.
Romance, expected once to stay,
has left a note saying GONE AWAY.

Gavin Ewart

Bacchanal

"Come live with me and be my love,"
    He said, in substance. "There's no vine
We will not pluck the clusters of,
    Or grape we will not turn to wine."

It's autumn of their second year.
    Now he, in seasonal pursuit,
With rich and modulated cheer,
    Brings home the festive purple fruit;

And she, by passion once demented
    —That woman out of Botticelli—
She brews and bottles, unfermented,
    The stupid and abiding jelly.

                            Peter De Vries

Sacred and Profane Love, Or, There's Nothing New Under the Moon Either

When bored by the drone of the wedlocked pair,
When bromides of marriage have started to wear,
Contemplate those of the crimson affair:
    "I had to see you," and "Tonight belongs to us."

Skewered on bliss of a dubious sort
Are all adventurers moved to consort
With others inspiring *this* hackneyed retort:
    "I can't fight you any longer."

Some with such wheezes have gone to the dead,
Oblivious that *Liebestod* lurked up ahead,
That pistols would perforate them as they said:
    "This thing is bigger than both of us."

Experimentation in matters of sin
Pales on the instant it's destined to win;
Paramours end as conformers begin:
   "I don't want just this—I want *you*."

Explorers are highly unlikely to hear
Novelties murmured into their ear;
Checkered with such is the checkered career:
   "It's not you I'm afraid of, it's myself."

Such liturgies standardize lovers in league
That someone will cry in the midst of intrigue,
And someone will hear in the midst of fatigue:
   "You don't want *me*—you just want sex!"

Strait is the gate and narrow the way
Closing at last on the ranging roué;
Who plucks a primrose plants a cliché:
   "We're married in the eyes of Heaven."

The dangerous life is so swiftly prosaic
You might as well marry and live in Passaic;
It ends and begins in established mosaic:
   "I'm all mixed up."

The lexicon's written for groom and for rake.
Liaisons are always a give-and-take.
Disillusionment's certain to follow a break.
   "For God's sake be careful or someone will hear you!"

PETER DE VRIES

TO HIS IMPORTUNATE MISTRESS

(Andrew Marvell Updated)

Had we but world enough, and time,
My coyness, lady, were a crime,
But at my back I always hear

Time's wingèd chariot, striking fear
The hour is nigh when creditors
Will prove to be my predators.
As wages of our picaresque,
Bag lunches bolted at my desk
Must stand as fealty to you
For each expensive rendezvous.
Obeisance at your marble feet
Deserves the best-appointed suite,
And would have, lacked I not the pelf
To pleasure also thus myself;
But aptly sumptuous amorous scenes
Rule out the rake of modest means.

Since mistress presupposes wife,
It means a doubly costly life;
For fools by second passion fired
A second income is required,
The earning which consumes the hours
They'd hoped to spend in rented bowers.
To hostelries the worst of fates
That weekly raise their daily rates!
I gather, lady, from your scoffing
A bloke more solvent in the offing.
So revels thus to rivals go
For want of monetary flow.
How vexing that inconstant cash
The constant suitor must abash,
Who with excuses vainly pled
Must rue the undishevelled bed,
And that for paltry reasons given
His conscience may remain unriven.

PETER DE VRIES

Fife Tune

(6/8) for 6 Platoon, 308th I.T.C.

One morning in Spring
We marched from Devizes
All shapes and all sizes
Like beads on a string,
But yet with a swing
We trod the bluemetal
And full to high fettle
We started to sing.

She ran down the stair
A twelve-year-old darling
And laughing and calling
She tossed her bright hair;
Then silent to stare
At the men flowing past her—
These were all she could master
Adoring her there.

It's seldom I'll see
A sweeter or prettier;
I doubt we'll forget her
In two years or three,
And lucky he'll be
She takes for a lover
While we are far over
The treacherous sea.

JOHN MANIFOLD

La, La, La!

Quickly, love, be lyrical & let
the lilting jumpy rhymes forget

Themselves to tumble giddily up
the gilded steps to the golden cup

And drink & shout & spin about
and stomp like any beerhall lout

With a hey & a haw, a haw, & a hey
There is one law we won't obey

Sweet, rest yourself upon this straw
Lie down, lie down, lie down

Thomas M. Disch

Low Church

It was after vespers one evening
When the vicar, inflamed by desire,
Beckoned a lad to the vestry,
Dismissing the rest of the choir.

He said, 'I've got something to show you,'
The boy followed hard on his heels;
Behind the locked door there was silence,
Except for some half-muffled squeals.

The vicar got two years (suspended),
The judge spoke of 'moral decay,'
The vicar is sadder and wiser,
But the choir-boy is happy and gay.

Stanley J. Sharpless

FAMILY PLEASURES

―――――――――――――――

THE JUNGLE HUSBAND

Dearest Evelyn, I often think of you
Out with the guns in the jungle stew
Yesterday I hittapotamus
I put the measurements down for you but they got lost in the
    fuss.
It's not a good thing to drink out here
You know, I've practically given it up dear.
Tomorrow I am going alone a long way
Into the jungle. It is all gray
But green on top
Only sometimes when a tree has fallen
The sun comes down plop, it is quite appalling.
You never want to go in a jungle pool
In the hot sun, it would be the act of a fool
Because it's always full of anacondas, Evelyn, not looking
    ill-fed
I'll say. So no more now, from your loving husband, Wilfred.

STEVIE SMITH

THE BREWER'S MAN

Have I a wife? Bedam I have!
But we was badly mated:

I hit her a great clout one night,
    And now we're separated.

And mornin's, going to my work,
    I meet her on the quay:
'Good mornin' to ye, ma'am,' says I;
    'To hell with ye,' says she.

                            L. A. G. STRONG

WIFE AND HOME

Who drags the fiery artist down?
What keeps the pioneer in town?
Who hates to let the seaman roam?
It is the wife, it is the home.

                            CLARENCE DAY

IN PRAISE OF COCOA,
CUPID'S NIGHTCAP

Lined written upon hearing the startling
news that cocoa is in fact a mild
aphrodisiac.

Half past nine—high time for supper
"Cocoa love?" "of course my dear."
Helen thinks it quite delicious
John prefers it now to beer.
Knocking back the sepia potion,
Hubby winks, says, "Who's for bed?"
"Shan't be long," says Hellen softly,
Cheeks a faintly flushing red.
For they've stumbled on the secret
of a love that never wanes
raft beneath the tumbled bedclothes,
cocoa coursing through their veins.

                            STANLEY J. SHARPLESS

Careless Talk

Bill
Was ill.

In his delirium
He talked about Miriam.

This was an error
As his wife was a terror

Known
As Joan.

Mark Hollis

Morning After

I was so sick last night I
Didn't hardly know my mind.
So sick last night I
Didn't know my mind.
I drunk some bad licker that
Almost made me blind.

Had a dream last night I
Thought I was in hell.
I drempt last night I
Thought I was in hell.
Woke up and looked around me—
Babe, your mouth was open like a well.

I said, Baby! Baby!
Please don't snore so loud.
Baby! Please!
Please don't snore so loud.
You jest a little bit o' woman but you
Sound like a great big crowd.

Langston Hughes

THE CUDGELED HUSBAND

As Thomas was cudgel'd one day by his wife,
He took to his heels and fled for his life:
Tom's three dearest friends came by in the squabble,
And saved him at once from the shrew and the rabble;
Then ventured to give him some sober advice—
But Tom is a person of honor so nice,
Too wise to take counsel, too proud to take warning,
That he sent to all three a challenge next morning.
Three duels he fought, thrice ventured his life;
Went home, and was cudgeled again by his wife.

JONATHAN SWIFT

CAUSE AND EFFECT

On his death-bed poor Lubin lies;
　　His spouse is in despair;
With frequent sobs and mutual cries,
　　They both express their cares.

"A different cause," says Parson Sly,
　　"The same effect may give:
Poor Lubin fears that he may die;
　　His wife, that he may live."

MATTHEW PRIOR

DUST TO DUST

After such years of dissension and strife,
Some wonder that Peter should weep for his wife;
But his tears on her grave are nothing surprising—
He's laying her dust, for fear of its rising.

THOMAS HOOD

The Saddled Ass

A certain painter, leaving in the morning,
    Was jealous of his wife . . . and being deft,
    Painted a donkey, just before he left,
Upon her navel, as a sort of warning.

A friend of his, whose honor had small heft,
At once consoled the lady thus bereft;
And leaving of the donkey not a trace
Was quick to paint another in its place.

But through a lapse of memory, alas!
He put a saddle on the patient ass.

Our friend returned, "My dear," the lady sighed,
    "Regard this proof that I've not fiddle-faddled you."
"A pox on you!" the irate husband cried,
    "And on the proof, and whosoever saddled you!"

DEEMS TAYLOR
Translation from Jean De La Fontaine

Uncle IV Surveys His Domain
from His Rocker of a Sunday Afternoon
as Aunt Dory Starts to Chop Kindling

Mister Williams
lets youn me move
tother side the house

the woman
choppin woods
mite nigh the awkerdist thing
I seen

JONATHAN WILLIAMS

A NEW WORLD SYMPHONY

What plucky sperm invented Mrs Gale?
(All starless in her first degree lay she.)

What head-of-the-river victor
plunged for her sake
down to the makings of a whale
in the amniotic sea?

Fortune the germ.
(Luck likewise it took
to get to be a sperm.)

Oh
the little bit kept its head and it flashed its tail
and there on the leaking waters—
furious, mauve, harpooned to life—
was Mrs Gale, I'm glad to say,
a beautiful daughter to Mr and Mrs Elkins,
to Mr Gale: a bouncing wife.

Time out of mind so many minds
prized out of time to consider the light of day!
Let us rejoice in the work of the sperm
and that of the fortunate egg in Mrs Elkins
(the role of its life to play)
who made Mrs Gale for our Delight
as, happily, we
freely may.

KIT WRIGHT

Reflection on Babies

A bit of talcum
Is always walcum.

Ogden Nash

MEHITABEL AND HER KITTENS

well boss
mehitabel the cat
has reappeared in her old
haunts with a
flock of kittens
three of them this time

archy she said to me
yesterday
the life of a female
artist is continually
hampered what in hell
have i done to deserve
all thes kittens

i look back on my life
and it seems to me to be
just one damned kitten
after another
i am a dancer archy
and my only prayer
is to be allowed
to give my best to my art
but just as i feel
that i am succeeding
in my life work
along comes another batch
of these damned kittens

it is not archy
that i am shy on mother love
god knows i care for
the sweet little things
curse them
but am i never to be allowed
to live my own life
i have purposely avoided
matrimony in the interests
of the higher life
but i might just
as well have been a domestic
slave for all the freedom
i have gained
i hope none of them
gets run over by
an automobile
my heart would bleed
if anything happened
to them and i found it out
but it isn t fair archy
it isn t fair
these damned tom cats have all
the fun and freedom
if i was like some of these
green eyed feline vamps i know
i would simply walk out on the
bunch of them and
let them shift for themselves
but i am not that kind
archy i am full of mother love
my kindness has always
been my curse
a tender heart is the cross i bear
self sacrifice always and forever
is my motto damn them
i will make a home
for the sweet innocent
little things

unless of course providence
in his wisdom should remove
them they are living
just now in an abandoned
garbage can just behind
a made over stable in greenwich
village and if it rained
into the can before i could
get back and rescue them
i am afraid the little
dears might drown
it makes me shudder just
to think of it
of course if i were a family cat
they would probably
be drowned anyhow
sometimes i think
the kinder thing would be
for me to carry the
sweet little things
over to the river
and drop them in myself
but a mother s love archy
is so unreasonable
something always prevents me
these terrible
conflicts are always
presenting themselves
to the artist
the eternal struggle
between art and life archy
is something fierce
yes something fierce
my what a dramatic
life i have lived
one moment up the next
moment down again
but always gay archy always gay
and always the lady too

in spite of hell
well boss it will
be interesting to note
just how mehitabel
works out her present problem
a dark mystery still broods
over the manner
in which the former
family of three kittens
disappeared
one day she was talking to me
of the kittens
and the next day when i asked
her about them
she said innocently
what kittens
interrogation point
and that was all
i could ever get out
of her on the subject
we had a heavy rain
right after she spoke to me
but probably that garbage can
leaks and so the kittens
have not yet
been drowned

DON MARQUIS

THE PERFECT CHILD

It asked for bread and butter first,
It ceased to eat before it burst.
It kept its clothing clean and neat,
It blew its nose, it wiped its feet.
Meekly repentant when it erred,
Was seldom seen and never heard.
Ordered itself with zeal intense

To those of riper years and sense.
It walked demurely through the land
With governesses hand in hand.
It fled from rowdy little boys,
It turned from vulgar books and toys,
From pantomimes and such distractions.
And gave its time to vulgar fractions.
But when it takes to married life
I shall be sorry for its wife!

ADRIAN PORTER

A SERENADE
(*from* DOMESTIC POEMS)

"Lullaby, O, lullaby!"
Thus I heard a father cry,
"Lullaby, O, lullaby!
The brat will never shut an eye;
Hither come, some power divine!
Close his lids, or open mine!"

"Lullaby, O, lullaby!
Sleep his very looks deny—
Lullaby, O lullaby!
Nature soon will stupefy—
My nerves relax—my eyes grow dim—
Who's that fallen—me or him?"

THOMAS HOOD

SALES TALK FOR ANNIE

Eat your banana, Annie dear;
    It's from a tropic tree
In lands where lurked the buccaneer
    By the Río Tilirí,

Or where the Cockscomb Mountains rise
    Above the Monkey River,
And lonely men with fevered eyes
    By turns perspire and shiver.
The parrot and the kinkajou
    And the armor-clad iguana
Have spared this golden fruit for you—
    But no, she won't even touch the lovely banana!

Eat your tapioca, please.
    In forests of Brazil
The Tupis and the Guaranis
    Have cooked it on a grill.
The poison of cassava roots
    Is thereby circumvented,
And flour and bread it constitutes.
    (It often is fermented.)
From Urubú and Urucú
    To distant Yanaoca
Indians grew this food for you,
    So for gosh sakes get going on your tapioca.

Drink your milk, my little lass.
    Oh, does it not look yummy!
A moo-cow ate the sun-lit grass
    And made it in her tummy.
The moo-cow's milk is free from faults,
    It's good for every human
(Containing sugar, fats, and salts,
    And casein and albumin.)
Here, I said to drink it, not blow in it! Listen, Annie,
    How would you like to have Father take that glass of
        milk and ram it
Down your throat? How would you like a good swift whack
        on the fanny?
    All right, go ahead and cry, damn it!

MORRIS BISHOP

INDIFFERENCE

When Grandmamma fell off the boat,
And couldn't swim (and wouldn't float),
Matilda just stood by and smiled.
I almost could have slapped the child.

HARRY GRAHAM

HENRY KING

*Who chewed bits of String, and was early
cut off in Dreadful Agonies*

The Chief Defect of Henry King
Was chewing little bits of String.
At last he swallowed some which tied
Itself in ugly Knots inside.
Physicians of the Utmost Fame
Were called at once; but when they came
They answered, as they took their Fees,
There is no Cure for this Disease.
Henry will very soon be dead.'
His Parents stood about his Bed
Lamenting his Untimely Death,
When Henry, with his Latest Breath,
Cried—'Oh, my Friends, be warned by me,
That Breakfast, Dinner, Lunch, and Tea
Are all the Human Frame requires . . .'
With that, the Wretched Child expires.

HILAIRE BELLOC

FRANKLIN HYDE
WHO CAROUSED IN THE DIRT
AND WAS CORRECTED BY HIS UNCLE

His Uncle came on Franklin Hyde
Carousing in the Dirt.
He shook him hard from Side to Side
And Hit him till it Hurt,
Exclaiming, with a Final Thud,
"Take that! Abandoned Boy!
For Playing with Disgusting Mud
As though it were a Toy!"

Moral

From Franklin Hyde's adventure, learn
To pass your Leisure Time
In Cleanly Merriment, and turn
From Mud and Ooze and Slime
And every form of Nastiness—
But, on the other Hand,
Children in ordinary Dress
May always play with Sand.

HILAIRE BELLOC

SPEAK ROUGHLY TO
YOUR LITTLE BOY

Speak roughly to your little boy,
    And beat him when he sneezes;
He only does it to annoy,
    Because he knows it teases.
        Wow! Wow! Wow!

I speak severely to my boy,
    I beat him when he sneezes;

For he can thoroughly enjoy
The pepper when he pleases!
Wow! Wow! Wow!

LEWIS CARROLL

JOHN, TOM, AND JAMES

John was a bad boy, and beat a poor cat;
Tom put a stone in a blind man's hat;
James was the boy who neglected his prayers;
They've all grown up ugly, and nobody cares.

CHARLES HENRY ROSS

MOTHER DOESN'T WANT A DOG

Mother doesn't want a dog.
Mother says they smell,
And never sit when you say sit,
Or even when you yell.
And when you come home late at night
And there is ice and snow,
You have to go back out because
The dumb dog has to go.

Mother doesn't want a dog.
Mother says they shed,
And always let the strangers in
And bark at friends instead,
And do disgraceful things on rugs,
And track mud on the floor,
And flop upon your bed at night
And snore their doggy snore.

Mother doesn't want a dog.
She's making a mistake.

Because, more than a dog, I think
She will not want this snake.

JUDITH VIORST

[As Into the Garden Elizabeth Ran]

As into the garden Elizabeth ran
Pursued by the just indignation of Ann,
She trod on an object that lay in her road,
She trod on an object that looked like a toad.

It looked like a toad, and it looked so because
A toad was the actual object it was;
And after supporting Elizabeth's tread
It looked like a toad that was visibly dead.

Elizabeth, leaving her footprint behind,
Continued her flight on the wings of the wind,
And Ann in her anger was heard to arrive
At the toad that was not any longer alive.

She was heard to arrive, for the firmament rang
With the sound of a scream and the noise of a bang,
As her breath on the breezes she broadly bestowed
And fainted away on Elizabeth's toad.

Elizabeth, saved by the sole of her boot,
Escaped her insensible sister's pursuit;
And if ever hereafter she irritates Ann,
She will tread on a toad if she possibly can.

A. E. HOUSMAN

My Papa's Waltz

The whiskey on your breath
Could make a small boy dizzy;

But I held on like death:
Such waltzing was not easy.

We romped until the pans
Slid from the kitchen shelf;
My mother's countenance
Could not unfrown itself.

The hand that held my wrist
Was battered on one knuckle;
At every step I missed
My right ear scraped a buckle.

You beat time on my head
With a palm caked hard by dirt,
Then waltzed me off to bed
Still clinging to your shirt.

THEODORE ROETHKE

from THE LITTLE ONES' A.B.C.

Refrain 1

A. Stands for Absolutely Anything,
B. Stands for Big Brass Bands,
C. Stands for Chlorophyll,
D. Stands for Dexamil,
E. Stands for Endocrine Glands,
F. and G. Don't suggest a thing to me.
Nor do H. I. J. K. L.
But after L. come M. for Mother
And Mother's going to give you Hell.

Refrain 2

A. Stands for Artichokes and Adenoids,
B. Stands for Bolts and Belts,
C. Stands for Cottage Cheese,

D. Stands for Dungarees,
E. Stands for Everything Else,
G. Of Course
Stands for Getting a Divorce
And F. Sometimes stands for Fridge,
But if I really were your mother
I'd throw myself from Brooklyn Bridge.

A. Stands for Romeo and Juliet,
B. Stands for Ku Klux Klan,
C. Stands for Bethlehem,
D. Stands for M.G.M.,
E. Stands for 'So's Your Old Man',
F. and G. Stand for Home in Tennessee
And we know H. Stands for Stoats,
But after L. come M. for Mother
And Mother'd like to slit your throats!

NOEL COWARD

TENDER-HEARTEDNESS

Billy, in one of his nice new sashes,
Fell in the fire and was burnt to ashes;
Now, although the room grows chilly,
I haven't the heart to poke poor Billy.

HARRY GRAHAM

L'ENFANT GLACÉ

When Baby's cries grew hard to bear
I popped him in the Frigidaire.
I never would have done so if
I'd known that he'd be frozen stiff.
My wife said: "George, I'm so unhappé!
Our darling's now completely *frappé!*'

HARRY GRAHAM

Ballade of Lost Objects

Where are the ribbons I tie my hair with?
    Where is my lipstick? Where are my hose—
The sheer ones hoarded these weeks to wear with
    Frocks the closets do not disclose?
Perfumes, petticoats, sports chapeaux,
    The blouse Parisian, the earring Spanish—
Everything suddenly ups and goes.
    And where in the world did the children vanish?

This is the house I used to share with
    Girls in pinafores, shier than does.
I can recall how they climbed my stair with
    Gales of giggles, on their tiptoes.
Last seen wearing both braids and bows
    (But looking rather Raggedy-Annish),
When they departed nobody knows—
    Where in the world did the children vanish?

Two tall strangers, now, I must bear with,
    Decked in my personal furbelows,
Raiding the larder, rending the air with
    Gossip and terrible radios.
Neither my friends nor quite my foes,
    Alien, beautiful, stern, and clannish,
Here they dwell, while the wonder grows:
    Where in the world did the children vanish?

Prince, I warn you, under the rose,
    Time is the thief you cannot banish.
These are my daughters, I suppose.
    But where in the world did the children vanish?

PHYLLIS McGINLEY

CHRISTMAS FAMILY REUNION

Since last the tutelary hearth
    Has seen this bursting pod of kin,
I've thought how good the family mould,
    How solid and how genuine.

Now once again the aunts are here,
    The uncles, sisters, brothers,
With candy in the children's hair,
    The grownups in each other's.

There's talk of saving room for pie;
    Grandma discusses her neuralgia.
I long for time to pass, so I
    Can think of all this with nostalgia.

PETER DE VRIES

P. G.

Good and Bad Children

Children, you are very little,
And your bones are very brittle;
If you would grow great and stately,
You must try to walk sedately.

You must still be bright and quiet,
And content with simple diet;
And remain, through all bewild'ring,
Innocent and honest children.

Happy hearts and happy faces,
Happy play in grassy places—
That was how, in ancient ages,
Children grew to kings and sages.

But the unkind and the unruly,
And the sort who eat unduly,
They must never hope for glory—
Theirs is quite a different story!

Cruel children, crying babies,
All grow up as geese and gabies,

Hated, as their age increases,
By their nephews and their nieces.

ROBERT LOUIS STEVENSON

LOOKING FORWARD

When I am grown to man's estate
I shall be very proud and great,
And tell the other girls and boys
Not to meddle with my toys.

ROBERT LOUIS STEVENSON

WHOLE DUTY OF CHILDREN

A child should always say what's true
And speak when he is spoken to,
And behave mannerly at table;
At least as far as he is able.

ROBERT LOUIS STEVENSON

SWEET LEVINSKY

Sweet Levinsky in the night
Sweet Levinsky in the light
do you giggle out of spite,
or are you laughing in delight
Sweet Levinsky, sweet Levinsky?

Sweet Levinsky, do you tremble
when the cock crows, and dissemble
as you amble to the gambol?
Why so humble when you stumble
sweet Levinsky, sweet Levinsky?

Sweet Levinsky, why so tearful,
sweet Levinsky don't be fearful,
sweet Levinsky here's your earful
of the angels chirping cheerful-
ly Levinsky, sweet Levinsky.   ·
sweet Levinsky, sweet Levinsky.

ALLEN GINSBERG

OUR BOG IS DOOD

Our Bog is dood, our Bog is dood,
They lisped in accents mild,
But when I asked them to explain
They grew a little wild.
How do you know your Bog is dood
My darling little child?

We know because we wish it so
That is enough, they cried,
And straight within each infant eye
Stood up the flame of pride,
And if you do not think it so
You shall be crucified.

Then tell me, darling little ones,
What's dood, suppose Bog is?
Just what we think, the answer came,
Just what we think it is.
They bowed their heads. Our Bog is ours
And we are wholly his.

But when they raised them up again
They had forgotten me
Each one upon each other glared
In pride and misery
For what was dood, and what their Bog
They never could agree.

Oh sweet it was to leave them then,
    And sweeter not to see,
And sweetest of all to walk alone
    Beside the encroaching sea,
The sea that soon should drown them all,
    That never yet drowned me.

STEVIE SMITH

BALLAD

The auld wife sat at her ivied door,
    (Butter and eggs and a pound of cheese)
A thing she had frequently done before;
    And her spectacles lay on her apron'd knees.

The piper he piped on the hilltop high,
    (Butter and eggs and a pound of cheese)
Till the cow said "I die," and the goose asked "Why?"
    And the dog said nothing, but search'd for fleas.

The farmer he strode through the square farmyard;
    (Butter and eggs and a pound of cheese)
His last brew of ale was a trifle hard—
    The connection of which the plot one sees.

The farmer's daughter hath frank blue eyes;
    (Butter and eggs and a pound of cheese)
She hears the rooks caw in the windy skies,
    As she sits at her lattice and shells her peas.

The farmer's daughter hath ripe red lips;
    (Butter and eggs and a pound of cheese)
If you try to approach her, away she skips
    Over tables and chairs with apparent ease.

The farmer's daughter hath soft brown hair;
    (Butter and eggs and a pound of cheese)

And I met with a ballad, I can't say where,
Which wholly consisted of lines like these.

She sat with her hands 'neath her dimpled cheeks,
   (Butter and eggs and a pound of cheese)
And spake not a word. While a lady speaks
   There is hope, but she didn't even sneeze.

She sat, with her hands 'neath her crimson cheeks;
   (Butter and eggs and a pound of cheese)
She gave up mending her father's breeks,
   And let the cat roll in her new chemise.

She sat with her hands 'neath her burning cheeks,
   (Butter and eggs and a pound of cheese)
And gazed at the piper for thirteen weeks;
   Then she follow'd him o'er the misty leas.

Her sheep follow'd her, as their tails did them,
   (Butter and eggs and a pound of cheese)
And this song is consider'd a perfect gem,
   And as to the meaning, it's what you please.

CHARLES STUART CALVERLEY

[HE THOUGHT HE SAW AN ELEPHANT]

He thought he saw an Elephant,
   That practised on a fife:
He looked again, and found it was
   A letter from his wife.
"At length I realise," he said,
   "The bitterness of Life!"

He thought he saw a Buffalo
   Upon the chimney-piece:
He looked again, and found it was
   His Sister's Husband's Niece.

"Unless you leave this house," he said,
"I'll send for the Police!"

He thought he saw a Rattlesnake
    That questioned him in Greek:
He looked again, and found it was
    The Middle of Next Week.
"The one thing I regret," he said,
    "Is that it cannot speak!"

He thought he saw a Banker's Clerk
    Descending from the bus:
He looked again, and found it was
    A Hippopotamus:
"If this should stay to dine," he said,
    "There won't be much for us!"

He thought he saw a Kangaroo
    That worked a coffee-mill:
He looked again, and found it was
    A Vegetable-Pill.
"Were I to swallow this," he said,
    "I should be very ill!"

He thought he saw a Coach-and-Four
    That stood beside his bed:
He looked again and found it was
    A Bear without a Head.
"Poor thing," he said, "Poor silly thing!
    "It's waiting to be fed!"

He thought he saw an Albatross
    That fluttered round the lamp:
He looked again, and found it was
    A Penny-Postage-Stamp.
"You'd best be getting home," he said:
    "The nights are very damp!"

He thought he saw a Garden-Door
    That opened with a key:

He looked again, and found it was
  A Double Rule of Three:
"And all its mystery," he said,
  "Is clear as day to me!"

He thought he saw an Argument
  That proved he was the Pope:
He looked again, and found it was
  A Bar of Mottled Soap.
"A fact so dread," he faintly said,
  "Extinguishes all hope!"

LEWIS CARROLL

JABBERWOCKY

'Twas brillig, and the slithy toves
  Did gyre and gimble in the wabe;
All mimsy were the borogoves,
  And the mome raths outgrabe.

'Beware the Jabberwock, my son!
  The jaws that bite, the claws that catch!
Beware the Jubjub bird, and shun
  The frumious Bandersnatch!'

He took his vorpal sword in hand:
  Long time the manxome foe he sought—
So rested he by the Tumtum tree,
  And stood awhile in thought.

And as in uffish thought he stood,
  The Jabberwock, with eyes of flame,
Came whiffling through the tulgey wood,
  And burbled as it came!

One, two! One, two! And through and through
  The vorpal blade went snicker-snack!

He left it dead, and with its head
He went galumphing back.

'And hast thou slain the Jabberwock?
    Come to my arms, my beamish boy!
O frabjous day! Callooh! Callay!'
    He chortled in his joy.

'Twas brillig, and the slithy toves
    Did gyre and gimble in the wabe;
All mimsy were the borogoves,
    And the mome raths outgrabe.

LEWIS CARROLL

THERE WAS A KING

There was a King and he had three daughters,
And they all lived in a basin of water;
        The basin bended,
        My story's ended.
If the basin had been stronger
My story would have been longer.

ANONYMOUS

SLITHERGADEE

The Slithergadee has crawled out of the sea.
He may catch all the others, but he won't catch me.
No you won't catch me, old Slithergadee,
You may catch all the others, but you wo———

SHEL SILVERSTEIN

THE SUGAR-PLUM TREE

Have you ever heard of the Sugar-Plum Tree?
    'T is a marvel of great renown!

It blooms on the shore of the Lollipop sea
    In the garden of Shut-Eye Town;
The fruit that it bears is so wondrously sweet
    (As those who have tasted it say)
That good little children have only to eat
    Of that fruit to be happy next day.

When you've got to the tree, you would have a hard time
    To capture the fruit which I sing;
The tree is so tall that no person could climb
    To the boughs where the sugar-plums swing!
But up in that tree sits a chocolate cat,
    And a gingerbread dog prowls below——
And this is the way you contrive to get at
    Those sugar-plums tempting you so:

You say but the word to that gingerbread dog
    And he barks with such terrible zest
That the chocolate cat is at once all agog,
    As her swelling proportions attest.
And the chocolate cat goes cavorting around
    From this leafy limb unto that,
And the sugar-plums tumble, of course, to the ground——
    Hurrah for that chocolate cat!

There are marshmallows, gumdrops, and peppermint canes,
    With stripings of scarlet or gold,
And you carry away of the treasure that rains
    As much as your apron can hold!
So come, little child, cuddle closer to me
    In your dainty white nightcap and gown,
And I'll rock you away to that Sugar-Plum Tree
    In the garden of Shut-Eye Town.

EUGENE FIELD

WYNKEN, BLYNKEN, AND NOD

Wynken, Blynken, and Nod one night
    Sailed off in a wooden shoe—

Sailed on a river of crystal light,
  Into a sea of dew.
"Where are you going, and what do you wish?"
  The old moon asked the three.
"We have come to fish for the herring fish
  That live in this beautiful sea;
    Nets of silver and gold have we!"
        Said Wynken,
        Blynken,
        And Nod.

The old moon laughed and sang a song,
  As they rocked in the wooden shoe,
And the wind that sped them all night long
  Ruffled the waves of dew.
The little stars were the herring fish
  That lived in that beautiful sea——
"Now cast your nets wherever you wish——
  Never afeard are we";
  So cried the stars to the fishermen three:
        Wynken,
        Blynken,
        And Nod.

All night long their nets they threw
  To the stars in the twinkling foam——
Then down from the skies came the wooden shoe,
  Bringing the fishermen home;
'T was all so pretty a sail it seemed
  As if it could not be,
And some folks thought 'twas a dream they'd dreamed
  Of sailing that beautiful sea——
  But I shall name you the fishermen three:
        Wynken,
        Blynken,
        And Nod.

Wynken and Blynken are two little eyes,
  And Nod is a little head,

And the wooden shoe that sailed the skies
   Is a wee one's trundle-bed.
So shut your eyes while your mother sings
   Of wonderful sights that be,
And you shall see the beautiful things
   As you rock in the misty sea,
   Where the old shoe rocked the fishermen three:
      Wynken,
      Blynken,
      And Nod.

Eugene Field

The Walloping Window-Blind

A capital ship for an ocean trip
   Was *The Walloping Window-blind*—
No gale that blew dismayed her crew
   Or troubled the captain's mind.
The man at the wheel was taught to feel
   Contempt for the wildest blow,
And it often appeared, when the weather had cleared,
   That he'd been in his bunk below.

The boatswain's mate was very sedate,
   Yet fond of amusement, too;
And he played hop-scotch with the starboard watch,
   While the captain tickled the crew.
And the gunner we had was apparently mad,
   For he sat on the after-rail,
And fired salutes with the captain's boots,
   In the teeth of the booming gale.

The captain sat in a commodore's hat
   And dined, in a royal way,
On toasted pigs and pickles and figs
   And gummery bread, each day.
But the cook was Dutch and behaved as such;

For the food that he gave the crew
Was a number of tons of hot-cross buns
    Chopped up with sugar and glue.

And we all felt ill as mariners will,
    On a diet that's cheap and rude;
And we shivered and shook as we dipped the cook
    In a tub of his gluesome food.
Then nautical pride we laid aside,
    And we cast the vessel ashore
On the Gulliby Isles, where the Poohpooh smiles,
    And the Anagazanders roar.

Composed of sand was that favored land,
    And trimmed with cinnamon straws;
And pink and blue was the pleasing hue
    Of the Tickletoeteaser's claws.
And we sat on the edge of a sandy ledge
    And shot at the whistling bee;
And the Binnacle-bats wore water-proof hats
    As they danced in the sounding sea.

On rubagub bark, from dawn to dark,
    We fed, till we all had grown
Uncommonly shrunk,—when a Chinese junk
    Came by from the torriby zone.
She was stubby and square, but we didn't much care,
    And we cheerily put to sea;
And we left the crew of the junk to chew
    The bark of the rubagub tree.

                          CHARLES EDWARD CARRYL

SIMON LEGREE—A NEGRO SERMON

Legree's big house was white and green,
His cotton fields were the best to be seen.
He had strong horses and opulent cattle,

And bloodhounds bold, with chains that would rattle.
His garret was full of curious things:
Books of magic, bags of gold,
And rabbits' feet on long twine strings.
But he went down to the Devil.

Legree he sported a brass-buttoned coat,
A snake-skin necktie, a blood-red shirt,
Legree he had a beard like a goat,
And a thick hairy neck, and eyes like dirt.
His puffed-out cheeks were fish-belly white,
He had great long teeth, and an appetite.
He ate raw meat, 'most every meal,
And rolled his eyes till the cat would squeal.

His fist was an enormous size
To mash poor niggers that told him lies:
He was surely a witch-man in disguise.
But he went down to the Devil.

He wore hip-boots and would wade all day,
To capture his slaves that had fled away.
But he went down to the Devil.

He beat poor Uncle Tom to death
Who prayed for Legree with his last breath.
Then Uncle Tom to Eva flew,
To the high sanctoriums bright and new;
And Simon Legree stared up beneath,
And cracked his heels, and ground his teeth:
And went down to the Devil.

He crossed the yard in the storm and gloom;
He went into his grand front room.
He said, "I killed him, and I don't care."
He kicked a hound, he gave a swear;
He tightened his belt, he took a lamp,
Went down cellar to the webs and damp.
There in the middle of the mouldy floor

He heaved up a slab; he found a door——
And went down to the Devil.

His lamp blew out, but his eyes burned bright.
Simon Legree stepped down all night——
Down, down to the Devil.
Simon Legree he reached the place,
He saw one half of the human race,
He saw the Devil on a wide green throne,
Gnawing the meat from a big ham-bone,
And he said to Mister Devil:
    "I see that you have much to eat—
    A red ham-bone is surely sweet.
    I see that you have lion's feet;
    I see your frame is fat and fine,
    I see you drink your poison wine——
    Blood and burning turpentine."

And the Devil said to Simon Legree:
    "I like your style, so wicked and free.
    Come sit and share my throne with me,
    And let us bark and revel."
And there they sit and gnash their teeth,
And each one wears a hop-vine wreath.
They are matching pennies and shooting craps,
They are playing poker and taking naps.
And old Legree is fat and fine:
He eats the fire, he drinks the wine——
Blood and burning turpentine——
    Down, down with the Devil;
        Down, down with the Devil;
            Down, down with the Devil.

VACHEL LINDSAY

MACAVITY: THE MYSTERY CAT

Macavity's a Mystery Cat: He's called the Hidden Paw—
For he's the master criminal who can defy the Law.
He's the bafflement of Scotland Yard, the Flying Squad's despair:
For when they reach the scene of crime—*Macavity's not there!*

Macavity, Macavity, there's no one like Macavity,
He's broken every human law, he breaks the law of gravity.
His powers of levitation would make a fakir stare,
And when you reach the scene of crime—*Macavity's not there!*
You may seek him in the basement, you may look up in the air—
But I tell you once and once again, *Macavity's not there!*

Macavity's a ginger cat, he's very tall and thin;
You would know him if you saw him, for his eyes are sunken in.
His brow is deeply lined with thought, his head is highly domed;
His coat is dusty from neglect, his whiskers are uncombed.
He sways his head from side to side, with movements like a snake;
And when you think he's half asleep, he's always wide awake.

Macavity, Macavity, there's no one like Macavity,
For he's a fiend in feline shape, a monster of depravity.
You may meet him in a by-street, you may see him in the square—
But when a crime's discovered, then *Macavity's not there!*

He's outwardly respectable. (They say he cheats at cards.)
And his footprints are not found in any file of Scotland Yard's.
And when the larder's looted, or the jewel-case is rifled,
Or when the milk is missing, or another Peke's been stifled,
Or the greenhouse glass is broken, and the trellis past repair—
Ay, there's the wonder of the thing! *Macavity's not there!*

And when the Foreign Office find a Treaty's gone astray,
Or when the Admiralty lose some plans and drawings by the way,
There may be a scrap of paper in the hall or on the stair—
But it's useless to investigate—*Macavity's not there!*

And when the loss has been disclosed, the Secret Service say:
"It *must* have been Macavity!"—but he's a mile away.
You'll be sure to find him resting, or a-licking of his thumbs,
Or engaged in doing complicated long division sums.

Macavity, Macavity, there's no one like Macavity,
There never was a Cat of such deceitfulness and suavity.
He always has an alibi, and one or two to spare:
At whatever time the deed took place—MACAVITY WASN'T
THERE!
And they say that all the Cats whose wicked deeds are widely
known
(I might mention Mungojerrie, I might mention Griddlebone)
Are nothing more than agents for the Cat who all the time
Just controls their operations: the Napoleon of Crime!

T. S. Eliot

The Naming of Cats

The Naming of Cats is a difficult matter,
    It isn't just one of your holiday games;
You may think at first I'm as mad as a hatter
When I tell you, a cat must have THREE DIFFERENT NAMES.
First of all, there's the name that the family use daily,
    Such as Peter, Augustus, Alonzo or James,
Such as Victor or Jonathan, George or Bill Bailey—
    All of them sensible everyday names.
There are fancier names if you think they sound sweeter,
    Some for the gentlemen, some for the dames:
Such as Plato, Admetus, Electra, Demeter—
    But all of them sensible everyday names.
But I tell you, a cat needs a name that's particular,
    A name that's peculiar, and more dignified,
Else how can he keep up his tail perpendicular,
    Or spread out his whiskers, or cherish his pride?
Of names of this kind, I can give you a quorum,
    Such as Munkstrap, Quaxo, or Coricopat,

Such as Bombalurina, or else Jellylorum—
    Names that never belong to more than one cat.
But above and beyond there's still one name left over,
    And that is the name that you never will guess;
The name that no human research can discover—
    But THE CAT HIMSELF KNOWS, and will never confess.
When you notice a cat in profound meditation,
    The reason, I tell you, is always the same:
His mind is engaged in a rapt contemplation
    Of the thought, of the thought, of the thought of his name:
      His ineffable effable
      Effanineffable
Deep and inscrutable singular Name.

T. S. ELIOT

SOLOMON GRUNDY

Solomom Grundy
Born on a Monday,
Christened on Tuesday,
Married on Wednesday,
Took ill on Thursday,
Worse on Friday,
Died on Saturday,
Buried on Sunday.
This is the end
Of Solomon Grundy.

ANONYMOUS

LITTLE ORPHANT ANNIE

Little Orphant Annie's come to our house to stay,
An' wash the cups an' saucers up, an' brush the crumbs away,
An' shoo the chickens off the porch, an' dust the hearth, an' sweep,
An' make the fire, an' bake the bread, an' earn her board-an'-keep;
An' all us other children, when the supper-things is done,

We set around the kitchen fire an' has the mostest fun
A-list'nin' to the witch-tales 'at Annie tells about,
An' the Gobble-uns 'at gits you
      Ef you
        Don't
          Watch
            Out!

Wunst they wuz a little boy wouldn't say his prayers,—
An' when he went to bed at night, away up-stairs,
His Mammy heerd him holler, an' his Daddy heerd him bawl,
An' when they turn't the kivvers down, he wuzn't there at all!
An' they seeked him in the rafter-room, an' cubby-hole, an' press,
An' seeked him up the chimbly-flue, an' ever'-wheres, I guess;
But all they ever found wuz thist his pants an' roundabout:—
An' the Gobble-uns 'll git you
      Ef you
        Don't
          Watch
            Out!

An' one time a little girl 'ud allus laugh an' grin,
An' make fun of ever' one, an' all her blood-an'-kin;
An' wunst, when they was "company," an' ole folks wuz there,
She mocked 'em an' shocked 'em, an' said she didn't care!
An' thist as she kicked her heels, an' turn't to run an' hide,
They wuz two great big Black Things a-standin' by her side,
An' they snatched her through the ceilin' 'fore she knowed what
    she's about!
An' the Gobble-uns 'll git you
      Ef you
        Don't
          Watch
            Out!

An' little Orphant Annie says, when the blaze is blue,
An' the lamp-wick sputters, an' the wind goes *woo-oo!*
An' you hear the crickets quit, an' the moon is gray,
An' the lightnin'-bugs in dew is all squenched away,—

You better mind yer parents, an' yer teachurs fond an' dear,
An' churish them 'at loves you, an' dry the orphant's tear,
An' he'p the pore an' needy ones 'at clusters all about,
Er the Gobble-uns 'll git you
        Ef you
           Don't
              Watch
                Out!

JAMES WHITCOMB RILEY

ELETELEPHONY

Once there was an elephant,
Who tried to use the telephant—
No! No! I mean an elephone
Who tried to use the telephone—
(Dear me! I am not certain quite
That even now I've got it right.)

Howe'er it was, he got his trunk
Entangled in the telephunk;
The more he tried to get it free,
The louder buzzed the telephee—
(I fear I'd better drop the song
Of elephop and telephong!)

LAURA E. RICHARDS

THE HOUSE THAT JACK BUILT

This is the knife with a handle of horn,
That killed the cock that crowed in the morn,
That wakened the priest all shaven and shorn,
That married the man all tattered and torn
Unto the maiden all forlorn,
That milked the cow with a crumpled horn
That tossed the dog over the barn,

That worried the cat
That killed the rat
That ate the malt
That lay in the house that Jack built.

ANONYMOUS

ANTIGONISH

As I was going up the stair
  I met a man who wasn't there!
He wasn't there again to-day!
  I wish, I *wish* he'd stay away!

HUGHES MEARNS

BED IN SUMMER

In winter I get up at night
And dress by yellow candle-light.
In summer, quite the other way,
I have to go to bed by day.

I have to go to bed and see
The birds still hopping on the tree,
Or hear the grown-up people's feet
Still going past me in the street.

And does it not seem hard to you,
When all the sky is clear and blue,
And I should like so much to play,
To have to go to bed by day?

ROBERT LOUIS STEVENSON

'Mips and Ma the Mooly Moo'
(*from* 'Praise To The End')

Mips and ma the mooly moo,
The likes of him is biting who,
A cow's a care and who's a coo?—
What footie does is final.

My dearest dear my fairest fair,
Your father tossed a cat in air.
Though neither you nor I was there,—
What footie does is final.

Be large as an owl, be slick as a frog,
Be good as a goose, be big as a dog.
Be sleek as a heifer, be long as a hog,—
What footie will do will be final.

Theodore Roethke

I Had But Fifty Cents

I took my girl to a fancy ball;
It was a social hop;
We waited till the folks got out,
And the music it did stop.
Then to a restaurant we went,
The best one on the street;
She said she wasn't hungry,
But this is what she eat:
A dozen raw, a plate of slaw,
A chicken and a roast,
Some applesass, and sparagrass,
And soft-shell crabs on toast.
A big box stew, and crackers too;
Her appetite was immense!
When she called for pie,

I thought I'd die,
For I had but fifty cents.

She said she wasn't hungry
And didn't care to eat,
But I've got money in my clothes
To bet she can't be beat;
She took it in so cozy,
She had an awful tank;
She said she wasn't thirsty,
But this is what she drank:
A whiskey skin, a glass of gin,
Which made me shake with fear,
A ginger pop, with rum on top,
A schooner then of beer,
A glass of ale, a gin cocktail;
She should have had more sense;
When she called for more,
I fell on the floor,
For I had but fifty cents.

Of course I wasn't hungry,
And didn't care to eat,
Expecting every moment
To be kicked into the street;
She said sh'd fetch her family round,
And some night we'd have fun;
When I gave the man the fifty cents,
This is what he done:
He tore my clothes,
He smashed my nose,
He hit me on the jaw,
He gave me a prize
Of a pair of black eyes
And with me swept the floor.
He took me where my pants hung loose,
And threw me over the fence;
Take my advice, don't try it twice
If you've got but fifty cents!

ANONYMOUS

For Those Who
Always Fear the Worst

Suppose one thing,
Suppose another,
Suppose your mother
Was a bullfrog's brother.

ANONYMOUS

Honey Moon

I need something easy,
I need something right,
I'll ask the moon
in to dinner tonight.

I'll offer him wine
and I'll offer him cheese,
I'll offer him money
to sit on my knees.

He'll shine in my windows.
He'll shine in my lap.
He'll think that I'm cute
and a little moon-trap.

KATHLEEN LELAND BAKER

[The Shades Of Night Were Falling Fast]

The shades of night were falling fast,
   And the rain was falling faster,
When through an Alpine village passed
   An Alpine village pastor:
A youth who bore mid snow and ice
   A bird that wouldn't chirrup,

And a banner with the strange device—
'Mrs. Winslow's soothing syrup'.

'Beware the pass', the old man said,
   'My bold, and desperate fellah;
Dark lowers the tempest overhead,
   And you'll want your umberella;
And the roaring torrent is deep and wide—
   You may hear how loud it washes.'
But still that clarion voice replied:
   'I've got my old goloshes.'

'Oh, stay', the maiden said, 'and rest
   (For the wind blows from the nor'ward)
Thy weary head upon my breast—
   And please don't think I'm forward.'
A tear stood in his bright blue eye,
   And he gladly would have tarried;
But still he answered with a sigh:
   'Unhappily I'm married.'

A. E. HOUSMAN

THE LAND OF COUNTERPANE

When I was sick and lay a-bed,
I had two pillows at my head,
And all my toys beside me lay
To keep me happy all the day.

And sometimes for an hour or so
I watched my leaden soldiers go,
With different uniforms and drills,
Amond the bed-clothes, through the hills;

And sometimes sent my ships in fleets
All up and down among the sheets;
Or brought my trees and houses out,
And planted cities all about.

I was the giant great and still
That sits upon the pillow-hill,
And sees before him, dale and plain,
The pleasant land of counterpane.

ROBERT LOUIS STEVENSON

FATHER WILLIAM

"You are old, Father William," the young man said,
    "And your hair has become very white;
And yet you incessantly stand on your head—
    Do you think, at your age, it is right?"

"In my youth," Father William replied to his son,
    "I feared it might injure the brain;
But, now that I'm perfectly sure I have none,
    Why, I do it again and again."

"You are old," said the youth, "as I mentioned before,
    And have grown most uncommonly fat;
Yet you turned a back-somersault in at the door—
    Pray, what is the reason of that?"

"In my youth," said the sage, as he shook his grey locks,
    "I kept all my limbs very supple
By the use of this ointment—one shilling the box—
    Allow me to sell you a couple?"

"You are old," said the youth, "and your jaws are too weak
    For anything tougher than suet;
Yet you finished the goose, with the bones and the beak—
    Pray, how did you manage to do it?"

"In my youth," said his father, "I took to the law,
    And argued each case with my wife;
And the muscular strength, which it gave to my jaw,
    Has lasted the rest of my life."

"You are old," said the youth, "one would hardly suppose
    That your eye was as steady as ever;
Yet you balanced an eel on the end of your nose—
    What made you so awfully clever?"

"I have answered three questions, and that is enough,"
    Said his father. "Don't give yourself airs!
Do you think I can listen all day to such stuff?
    Be off, or I'll kick you down stairs!"

Lewis Carroll

Nature's Blessings

The Snow Light

In the snow light,
In the swan light,
In the white-on-white light
Of a winter storm,
My delight and your delight
Keep each other warm.

The next afternoon—
And love gone so soon!—
I met myself alone
In a windless calm,
Silenced at the bone
After the white storm.

What more was to come?
Out from the cocoon,
In the silent room,
Pouring out white light,
Amaryllis bloom
Opened in the night.

The cool petals shone
Like some winter moon
Or shadow of a swan,

Echoing the light
After you were gone
Of our white-on-white.

                                          MAY SARTON

XX
(*from* TULIPS & CHIMNEYS)

spring omnipotent goddess thou dost
inveigle into crossing sidewalks the
unwary june-bug and the frivolous angleworm
thou dost persuade to serenade his
lady the musical tom-cat, thou stuffest
the parks with overgrown pimply
cavaliers and gumchewing giggly
girls and not content
Spring,with this
thou hangest canary-birds in parlor windows

spring slattern of seasons you
have dirty legs and a muddy
petticoat,drowsy is your
mouth your eyes are sticky
with dreams and you have
a sloppy body
from being brought to bed of crocuses
When you sing in your whiskey-voice
                                          the grass
rises on the head of the earth
and all the trees are put on edge

spring,
of the jostle of
thy breasts and the slobber
of your thighs
i am so very
                    glad that the soul inside me Hollers

for thou comest and your hands
are the snow
and they fingers are the rain,
and i hear
the screech of the dissonant
flowers,and most of all
i hear your stepping
                        freakish feet
                        feet incorrigible
ragging the world,

E. E. CUMMINGS

SONG

The year's at the spring,
And day's at the morn;
Morning's at seven;
The hill-side's dew-pearled;
The lark's on the wing;
The snail's on the thorn;
God's in His Heaven—
All's right with the world!

ROBERT BROWNING

FOR CITY SPRING

Now grimy April comes again,
Maketh bloom the fire-escapes,
Maketh silvers in the rain,
Maketh winter coats and capes
Suddenly all worn and shabby
Like the fur of winter bears,
Maketh kittens, maketh baby,
Maketh kissing on the stairs.
Maketh bug crawl out of crack,
Maketh ticklings down the back

As if sunlight stroked the spine
To a hurdy-gurdy's whine
And the shower ran white wine.

April, April, sing cuckoo,
April, April, maketh new
Mouse and cockroach, man and wife,
Everything with blood and life;
Bloweth, groweth, flourisheth,
Danceth in a ragged skirt
On the very stoop of Death
And will take no mortal hurt.
Maketh dogs to whine and bound,
Maketh cats to caterwaul,
Maketh lovers, all around,
Whisper in the hall.

Oh, and when the night comes down
And the shrieking of the town
Settles to the steady roar
Of a long sea-beaten shore,
April hieth, April spieth
Everywhere a lover lieth,
Bringeth sweetness, bringeth fever,
Will not stop at "I would liever,"
Will not heed, "Now God a mercy!"
Turneth Moral topsy-versy,
Bringeth he and she to bed,
Bringeth ill to maidenhead,
Bringeth joyance in its stead.
By May, by May, she lieth sped,
Yet still we praise that crocus head,
April!

STEPHEN VINCENT BENÉT

Spring
(*from* Love's Labour's Lost)

When daisies pied and violets blue
  And lady-smocks all silver-white
And cuckoo-buds of yellow hue
  Do paint the meadows with delight,
The cuckoo then, on every tree,
Mocks married men; for thus sings he,
      Cuckoo!
Cuckoo, cuckoo! O, word of fear,
Unpleasing to a married ear!

When shepherds pipe on oaten
      straws,
  And merry larks are ploughmen's
      clocks,
When turtles tread, and rooks, and daws,
  And maidens bleach their summer
      smocks,
The cuckoo then, on every tree,
Mocks married men; for thus sings he,
      Cuckoo!
Cuckoo, cuckoo! O, word of fear,
Unpleasing to a married ear!

WILLIAM SHAKESPEARE

Public Beach
(Long Island Sound)

The swart Italian with his breast of fur
Soothes bambina when her toe she stubs;
The Baltic blonde (Oh slim! my love to her!)
Adjusts the jerkin that creeps up her chubs,
But all her thought and gaze are offshore where
Two flaxhead boys swash rubber tubes adrift.

Grandpa with his babe plays Old Gray Mare:
"He learns to valk on stones. Now we make lift."

A surf of children tumbles on the sand:
Teuton, Spaniard, Negro, Chinese, Balt,
From all distemper and apartheid free.
Replete with franks and mustard, I understand:
Nakedly primed with universal salt,
Lo, a new people rises from the sea.

CHRISTOPHER MORLEY

THE PEDLAR'S SONG
(*from* THE WINTER'S TALE)

When daffodils begin to peer,
   With heigh! the doxy, over the dale,
Why, then comes in the sweet o' the year;
   For the red blood reigns in the winter's pale.

The white sheet bleaching on the hedge,
   With heigh! the sweet birds, O, how they sing!
Doth set my pugging tooth on edge;
   For a quart of ale is a dish for a king.

The lark, that tirra-lirra chants,
   With, heigh! with, heigh! the thrush and the jay,
Are summer songs for me and my aunts,
   While we lie tumbling in the hay.

WILLIAM SHAKESPEARE

ODE TO THE END OF SUMMER

Summer, adieu.
       Adieu, gregarious season.
Goodbye, 'revoir, farewell.

Now day comes late; now chillier blows the breeze on
Forsaken beach and boarded-up hotel.
Now wild geese fly together in thin lines
And Tourist Homes take down their lettered signs.

It fades—this green, this lavish interval,
This time of flowers and fruits,
Of melon ripe along the orchard wall,
Of sun and sails and wrinkled linen suits;
Time when the world seems rather plus than minus
And pollen tickles the allergic sinus.

Now fugitives to farm and shore and highland
Cancel their brief escape.
The Ferris wheel is quiet at Coney Island
And quaintness trades no longer on the Cape;
While meek-eyed parents hasten down the ramps
To greet their offspring, terrible from camps.

Turn up the steam. The year is growing older.
The maple boughs are red.
Summer, farewell. Farewell the sunburnt shoulder,
Farewell the peasant kerchief on the head.
Farewell the thunderstorm, complete with lightning,
And the white shoe that ever needeth whitening.

Farewell, vacation friendships, sweet but tenuous.
Ditto to slacks and shorts.
Farewell, O strange compulsion to be strenuous
Which sends us forth to death on tennis courts.
Farewell, Mosquito, horror of our nights;
Clambakes, iced tea, and transatlantic flights.

The zinnia withers, mortal as the tulip.
Now from the dripping glass
I'll sip no more the amateur mint julep
Nor dine al fresco on the alien grass;
Nor scale the height nor breast the truculent billow
Nor lay my head on any weekend pillow.

Unstintingly I yield myself to Autumn
And Equinoctial sloth.
I hide my swim suit in the bureau's bottom
Nor fear the fury of the after-moth.
Forswearing porch and pool and beetled garden,
My heart shall rest, my arteries shall harden.

Welcome, kind Fall, and every month with "r" in
Whereto my mind is bent.
Come, sedentary season that I star in,
O fire-lit Winter of my deep content!
Amid the snow, the sleet, the blizzard's raw gust,
I shall be cozier than I was in August.

Safe from the picnic sleeps the unlittered dell.
The last Good Humor sounds its final bell,
And all is silence.
                    Summer, farewell, farewell.

                              PHYLLIS McGINLEY

LAUGHING SONG

When the green woods laugh, with the voice of joy
And the dimpling stream runs laughing by,
When the air does laugh with our merry wit,
And the green hill laughs with the noise of it.

When the meadows laugh with lively green
And the grasshopper laughs in the merry scene,
When Mary and Susan and Emily,
With their sweet round mouths sing Ha, Ha, He.

When the painted birds laugh in the shade
Where our table with cherries and nuts is spread
Come live & be merry and join with me,
To sing the sweet chorus of Ha, Ha, He.

                              WILLIAM BLAKE

from THE TEMPEST

Where the bee sucks, there suck I,
In a cowslip's bell I lie,
There I couch when owls do cry,
On the bat's back I do fly
After summer merrily.
 Merrily, merrily, shall I live now
 Under the blossom that hangs on the bough.

        WILLIAM SHAKESPEARE

FESTE'S SONG

When that I was and a little tiny boy,
 With hey, ho, the wind and the rain;
A foolish thing was but a toy,
 For the rain it raineth every day.

But when I came to man's estate,
 With hey, ho, the wind and the rain;
'Gainst knaves and thieves men shut their gate,
 For the rain it raineth every day.

But when I came, alas! to wive,
 With hey, ho, the wind and the rain;
By swaggering could I never thrive,
 For the rain it raineth everday.

But when I came unto my beds,
 With hey, ho, the wind and the rain;
With toss-pots still had drunken heads,
 For the rain it raineth every day.

A great while ago the world begun,
 With hey, ho, the wind and the rain;

But that's all one, our play is done,
And we'll strive to please you every day.

WILLIAM SHAKESPEARE

PENNSYLVANIA DEUTSCH

The rain it raineth every day
And freezeth as it raineth:
Old Grandpapa hath hell to pay,
His motor tire he chaineth.

The power-house constraineth,
The kilowatt eke waneth,
The countryside chilblaineth,
No calory remaineth.
Lhude sing kaput! The poor old coot
Indeed he is no malamute:
Already he hath shot the chute
And his ankle spraineth.

It raineth as it freezeth,
And every roadway greaseth:
Hark how Grandpa sneezeth.
Though the drive he salteth
United Parcels halteth;
Grandpa too much malteth,
His footing double-faulteth
And on the pavement vaulteth.
Lhude sing socko,
Grandpapa is crocko.

Northeast gale appalleth
And haileth as it squalleth,
But lo, the garbage calleth.
Like the great bird on bunions free
Grandpa comes forth busily,

Where the ice him loopeth
The kitchen steps him poopeth
He trieth to grab the banister,
He falleth on his canister.

On skull and double-rumpeth
The three-point landing bumpeth.
Now noodle-strudel soupeth
And congregation groupeth:
Deep from the neck they sing, deacons caterwaul,
Grandpapa is everything, Grandpa is all.
Lhude sing skiddo:
Grandma is a widow.

CHRISTOPHER MORLEY

THE RAIN IT RAINETH

The rain it raineth on the just
    And also on the the unjust fella;
But chiefly on the just, because
    The unjust steals the just's umbrella.

LORD BOWEN

WINDOW LEDGE IN THE ATOM AGE

I have a bowl of paper whites,
    Of paper-white narcissus;
Their fragrance my whole soul delights,
    They smell delissus.
        (They grow in pebbles in the sun
        And each is like a star.)

I sit and scan the news hard by
    My paper-white narcissus;
I read how fast a plane can fly,

Against my wissus.
    (The course of speed is almost run,
    We know not where we are.)

They grow in pebbles in the sun,
    My beautiful narcissus,
Casting their subtle shade upon
    Tropical fissus.
        (No movement mars each tiny star;
        Speed has been left behind.)

I'd gladly trade the latest thing
    For paper-white narcissus;
Science, upon its airfoil wing,
    Now seems pernissus.
        (Who was it said to travel far
        Might dissipate the mind?)

I love this day, this hour, this room,
    This motionless narcissus;
I love the stillness of the home,
    I love the missus.
        (She grows pebbles in my sun
        And she is like a star.)

And though the modern world be through
    With paper-white narcissus,
I shall arise and I shall do
    The breakfast dissus.
        (The tranquil heart may yet outrun
        The rocket and the car.)

E. B. WHITE

VIRTUAL PARTICLES

Beware of thinking nothing's there
Remove all you can: despite your care

Behind remains a mindless seething
Of frenzied clones beyond conceiving.

They come in a wink, and dance about.
Whatever they meet is tracked by doubt:
What am I doing here? What should I weigh?
Such questions can lead to rapid decay.

Mourn not! The terminology's misleading:
Decay is virtual particle breeding.
And seething, though mindless, can serve noble ends:
The clone stuff, exchanged, is a bond between friends.

To be or not? The choice seems clear enough.
Hamlet vacillated—so does this stuff.

FRANK WILCZEK

TO MAKE A PRAIRIE

To make a prairie it takes a clover and one bee,—
One clover, and a bee,
And revery.
The revery alone will do
If bees are few.

EMILY DICKINSON

TWO VOICES IN A MEADOW

A MILKWEED

Anonymous as cherubs
Over the crib of God,
White seeds are floating
Out of my burst pod.
What power had I
Before I learned to yield?

Shatter me, great wind:
I shall possess the field.

A STONE

As casual as cow-dung
Under the crib of God,
I lie where chance would have me,
Up to the ears in sod.
Why should I move? To move
Befits a light desire.
The sill of Heaven would founder,
Did such as I aspire.

RICHARD WILBUR

IDEALISM

There once was a man who said, 'God
Must think it exceedingly odd
　　If he finds that this tree
　　Continues to be
When there's no one about in the Quad.'

RONALD KNOX

A REPLY

Dear Sir, Your astonishment's odd,
I am always about in the Quad;
　　And that's why this tree
　　Will continue to be,
Since observed by Yours faithfully, GOD.

ANONYMOUS

Cuckoo Song

Summer is y-comen in,
   Loudë sing, cuckoo!
Groweth seed and bloweth meed
   And spring'th the woodë now—
      Sing cuckoo!

Ewë bleateth after lamb,
   Low'th after calfë cow;
Bullock starteth, bucke farteth.
   Merry sing, cuckoo!

   Cuckoo, Cuckoo!
Well sing'st thou cuckoo:
   Ne swike thou never now!

Sing cuckoo, now! Sing cuckoo!
Sing cuckoo. Sing, cuckoo, now!

ANONYMOUS

Ancient Music

Winter is icummen in,
Lhude sing Goddamm,
Raineth drop and staineth slop,
And how the wind doth ramm!
      Sing: Goddamm.
Skiddeth bus and sloppeth us,
An ague hath my ham.
Freezeth river, turneth liver,
      Damn you, sing: Goddamm.
Goddamm, Goddamm, 'tis why I am, Goddamm.
      So 'gainst the winter's balm.
Sing goddamm, damm, sing Goddamm,
Sing goddamm, sing goddamm, DAMM.

EZRA POUND

BACCALAUREATE

Summa is i-cumen in,
    Laude sing cuccu!
Laddes rede and classe lede,
Profesor bemeth tu—
    Sing cuccu!

Scholour striveth after Aye,
    Bleteth after shepskin ewe;
Writë theseth, honoure seazeth,
    Murie sing cuccu!

Cuccu, cuccu, wel singes A. B cuccu;
    Ne flunke thu naver nu;
    Sing cuccu, nu, sing cuccu,
    Sing cuccu, Phye Betta Cappe, nu!

DAVID McCORD

BEASTLY THINGS

THE PECAN. THE TOUCAN

Very few can
Tell the Toucan
From the Pecan—
Here's a new plan:
To take the Toucan from the tree,
Requires im-mense a-gil-i-tee,
While anyone can pick with ease
The Pecans from the Pecan trees.
It's such an easy thing to do,
That even the Toucan he can too.

ROBERT WILLIAMS WOOD

THE PEN-GUIN. THE SWORD-FISH

We have for many years been bored
By that old saw about the sword
And pen, and now we all rejoice,
To see how Nature made her choice:
She made, regardless of offendin'
The Sword-fish mightier than the Penguin.

ROBERT WILLIAMS WOOD

THE ELK. THE WHELK

A roar of welcome through the welkin
Is certain proof you'll find the Elk in;
But if you listen to the shell,
In which the Whelk is said to dwell,
And hear a roar, beyond a doubt
It indicates the Whelk is out.

ROBERT WILLIAMS WOOD

ON THE ANTIQUITY OF MICROBES

Adam
Had 'em.

STRICKLAND GILLILAN

A SONNET

O lovely O most charming pug
Thy gracefull air and heavenly mug
The beauties of his mind do shine
And every bit is shaped so fine
Your very tail is most devine
Your teeth is whiter than the snow
You are a great buck and a bow
Your eyes are of so fine a shape
More like a christians than an ape
His cheeks is like the roses blume
Your hair is like the ravens plume
His noses cast is of the roman
He is a very pretty weomen
I could not get a rhyme for roman
And was oblidged to call it weoman

MARJORIE FLEMING (AGE 7)

THE EGG

Oh who that ever lived and loved
Can look upon an egg unmoved?
The egg it is the source of all.
'Tis everyone's ancestral hall.
The bravest chief that ever fought,
The lowest thief that e'er was caught,
The harlot's lip, the maiden's leg,
They each and all came from an egg.

The rocks that once by ocean's surge
Beheld the first of eggs emerge—
Obscure, defenseless, small and cold—
They little knew what eggs could hold.
The gifts the reverent Magi gave,
Pandora's box, Aladdin's cave,
Wars, loves, and kingdoms, heaven and hell
All lay within that tiny shell.

Oh, join me gentlemen, I beg,
In honoring our friend, the egg.

CLARENCE DAY

EGGOMANIA

Consider the egg. It's a miracle,
    A thing so diverse for its size
That we hardly can help growing lyrical
    When given the Pullet Surprise.

The scope of this peerless comestible
    Must drive other foods to despair
Since it's not only fully digestible
    But great for shampooing the hair.

It's boilable, poachable, fryable;
    It scrambles, it makes a sauce thicken.

It's also the only reliable
Device for producing a chicken.

FELICIA LAMPORT

[THE COMMON CORMORANT OR SHAG]

The common cormorant or shag
Lays eggs inside a paper bag
The reason you will see no doubt
Is to keep the lightning out.
But what these unobservant birds
Have never noticed is that herds
Of wandering bears may come with buns
And steal the bag to hold the crumbs.

ANONYMOUS

THE YAK

As a friend to the children commend me the Yak.
    You will find it exactly the thing:
It will carry and fetch, you can ride on its back,
    Or lead it about with a string.

The Tartar who dwells on the plains of Thibet
    (A desolate region of snow)
Has for centuries made it a nursery pet,
    And surely the Tartar should know!

Then tell your papa where the Yak can be got,
    And if he is awfully rich
He will buy you the creature—or else he will *not.*
    (I cannot be positive which.)

HILAIRE BELLOC

THE LION

The Lion, the Lion, he dwells in the waste,
He has a big head and a very small waist;
But his shoulders are stark, and his jaws they are grim,
And a good little child will not play with him.

HILAIRE BELLOC

DISASTER

'Twas ever thus from childhood's hour!
    My fondest hopes would not decay:
I never loved a tree or flower
    Which was the first to fade away!
The garden, where I used to delve
    Short-frock'd, still yields me pinks in plenty:
The peartree that I climb'd at twelve
    I see still blossoming, at twenty.

I never nursed a dear gazelle;
    But I was given a parroquet—
(How I did nurse him if unwell!)
    He's imbecile, but lingers yet.
He's green, with an enchanting tuft;
    He melts me with his small black eye:
He'd look inimitable stuff'd,
    And knows it—but he will not die!

I had a kitten—I was rich
    In pets—but all too soon my kitten
Became a full-sized cat, by which
    I've more than once been scratch'd and bitten.
And when for sleep her limbs she curl'd
    One day beside her untouch'd plateful,
And glided calmly from the world,
    I freely own that I was grateful.

And then I bought a dog—a queen!
   Ah Tiny, dear departing pug!
She lives, but she is past sixteen
   And scarce can crawl across the rug.
I loved her beautiful and kind;
   Delighted in her pert Bow-wow:
But now she snaps if you don't mind;
   'Twere lunacy to love her now.

I used to think, should e'er mishap
   Betide my crumple-visaged Ti,
In shape of prowling thief, or trap,
   Or coarse bull-terrier—I should die.
But ah! disasters have their use;
   And life might e'en be too sunshiny:
Nor would I make myself a goose,
   If some big dog should swallow Tiny.

                  CHARLES STUART CALVERLEY

THE BALLAD OF THE EMEU.

O say, have you seen at the Willows so green,—
   So charming and rurally true,—
A singular bird, with a manner absurd,
   Which they call the Australian Emeu?
             Have you
   Ever seen this Australian Emeu?

It trots all around with its head on the ground,
   Or erects it quite out of your view;
And the ladies all cry, when its figure they spy,
   O, what a sweet pretty Emeu!
             Oh! do
   Just look at that lovely Emeu!

One day to this spot, when the weather was hot,
   Came Matilda Hortense Fortescue;
And beside her there came a youth of high name,—

Augustus Florell Montague:
                    The two
Both loved that wild, foreign Emeu.

With two loaves of bread then they fed it, instead
    Of the flesh of the white cockatoo,
Which once was its food in the wild neighborhood
    Where ranges the sweet Kangaroo;
                    That too
    Is game for the famous Emeu!

Old saws and gimlets but its appetite whets
    Like the world-famous bark of Peru;
There's nothing so hard that the bird will discard,
    And nothing its taste will eschew,
                    That you
    Can give that long-legged Emeu!

The time slipped away in this innocent play,
    When up jumped the bold Montague:
"Where's that specimen pin that I gayly did win
    In raffle, and gave unto you,
                    Fortescue?"
    No word spoke the guilty Emeu!

"Quick! tell me his name whom thou gavest that same,
    Ere these hands in thy blood I imbrue!"
"Nay, dearest," she cried, as she clung to his side,
    "I'm innocent as that Emeu!"
                    "Adieu!"
    He replied, "Miss M. H. Fortescue!"

Down she dropped at his feet, all as white as a sheet,
    As wildly he fled from her view;
He thought 't was her sin,—for he knew not the pin
    Had been gobbled up by the Emeu;
                    All through
    The voracity of that Emeu!

BRET HARTE

SAGE COUNSEL

The Lion is the Beast to fight:
  He leaps along the plain,
And if you run with all your might,
  He runs with all his mane.
    I'm glad I'm not a Hottentot,
    But if I were, with outward cal-lum
    I'd either faint upon the spot
    Or hie me up a leafy pal-lum.

The Chamois is the beast to hunt:
  He's fleeter than the wind,
And when the Chamois is in front
  The hunter is behind.
    The Tyrolese make famous cheese
    And hunt the Chamois o'er the chaz-zums;
    I'd choose the former, if you please,
    For precipices give me spaz-zums.

The Polar Bear will make a rug
  Almost as white as snow:
But if he gets you in his hug,
  He rarely lets you go.
    The polar ice looks very nice
    With all the colors of a prissum:
But, if you'll follow my advice,
Stay home and learn your catechissum.

ARTHUR QUILLER-COUCH

HOW DOTH THE LITTLE CROCODILE

How doth the little crocodile
  Improve his shining tail,
And pour the waters of the Nile
  On every golden scale!

How cheerfully he seems to grin,
How neatly spreads his claws,
And welcomes little fishes in,
With gently smiling jaws!

LEWIS CARROLL

THE FAT BUDGIE

I have a little budgie
He is my very pal
I take him walks in Britain
I hope I always shall.

I call my budgie Jeffey
My grandads name's the same
I call him after grandad
Who had a feathered brain.

Some people don't like budgies
The little yellow brats
They eat them up for breakfast
Or give them to their cats.

My uncle ate a budgie
It was so fat and fair.
I cried and called him Ronnie
He didn't deem to care

Although his name was Arthur
It didn't mean a thing.
He went into a petshop
And ate up everything.

The doctors looked inside him,
To see what they could do,
But he had been too greedy
He died just like a zoo.

My Jeffrey chirps and twitters
When I walk into the room,
I make him scrambled egg on toast
And feed him with a spoon.

He sings like other budgies
But only when in trim
But most of all on Sunday
Thats when I plug him in.

He flies about the room sometimes
And sits upon my bed
And if he's really happy
He does it on my head.

He's on a diet now you know
From eating far too much
They say if he gets fatter
He'll have to wear a crutch.

It would be funny wouldn't it
A budgie on a stick
Imagine all the people
Laughing till they're sick.

So that's my budgie Jeffrey
Fat and yellow too
I love him more than daddie
And I'm only thirty two.

JOHN LENNON

IMPROMPTU

If I were a cassowary
  On the plains of Timbuctoo,
I would eat a missionary,
  Cassock, bands and hymn-book too.

SAMUEL WILBERFORCE

THE LADY AND THE BEAR

A Lady came to a Bear by a Stream
"O why are you fishing that way?
Tell me, dear Bear there by the Stream,
Why are you fishing that way?"

"I am what is known as a Biddly Bear,—
That's why I'm fishing this way.
We Biddly's are Pee-culiar Bears.
And so,—I'm fishing this way.

"And besides, it seems there's a Law:
A most, most exactious Law
Says a Bear
Doesn't dare
Doesn't dare
Doesn't DARE
Use a Hook or a Line,
Or an old piece of Twine,
Not even the end of his Claw, Claw, Claw,
Not even the end of his Claw.
Yes, a Bear has to fish with his Paw, Paw, Paw.
A Bear has to fish with his Paw."

"O it's Wonderful how with a flick of your Wrist,
You can fish out a fish, out a fish, out a fish,
If *I* were a fish I just couldn't resist
You, when you are fishing that way, that way,
When you are fishing that way."

And at that the Lady slipped from the Bank
And fell in the Stream still clutching a Plank,
But the Bear just sat there until she Sank;
As he went on fishing his way, his way,
As he went on fishing his way.

THEODORE ROETHKE

[THERE WAS A YOUNG LADY OF NIGER]

There was a young lady of Niger
Who smiled as she rode on a tiger;
    They returned from the ride
    With the lady inside,
And the smile on the face of the tiger.

COSMO MONKHOUSE

THE RED COW IS DEAD

ISLE OF WIGHT (AP)—Sir Hanson Rowbotham's favorite Red
Polled cow is dead. Grazing in the lush pastures of the
Wellow Farm, she was bitten on the udder by an adder.
    —*The Herald Tribune*

Toll the bell, fellow,
This is a sad day at Wellow:
Sir Hanson's cow is dead,
His red cow,
Bitten on the udder by an adder.

Spread the bad news! What is more sudden,
What sadder than udder stung by adder?
He's never been madder, Sir Hanson Rowbotham.

The Red Polled cow is dead.
The grass was lush at very last,
And the snake (a low sneak)
Passed, hissed,
Struck.

Now a shadow goes across the meadow,
Wellow lies fallow.
The red cow is dead, and the stories go round.
"Bit in the teat by a dog in a fit."
"A serpent took Sir Hanson's cow—
A terrible loss, a king's ransom."

A blight has hit Wight:
The lush grass, the forked lash, the quick gash
Of adder, torn bleeding udder,
The cow laid low,
The polled cow dead, the bell not yet tolled
(A sad day at Wellow),
Sir Hanson's cow,
Never again to freshen, never again
Bellow with passion—
A ruminant in death's covenant,
Smitten, bitten, gone.
Toll the bell, young fellow!

E. B. WHITE

[THE HEN IT IS A NOBLE BEAST]

The Hen it is a noble beast;
   The cow is more forlorner,
Standing in the rain
   With a leg at every corner.

WILLIAM MCGONAGALL

HOW TO TELL THE WILD ANIMALS

If ever you should go by chance
   To jungles in the East,
And if there should to you advance
   A large and tawny beast,
If he roars at you as you're dyin'
You'll know it is the Asian Lion.

Or if some time when roaming round,
   A noble wild beast greets you,
With black stripes on a yellow ground,
   Just notice if he eats you.

This simple rule may help you learn
The Bengal Tiger to discern.

If strolling forth, a beast you view,
   Whose hide with spots is peppered,
As soon as he has leapt on you,
   You'll know it is the Leopard.
'Twill do no good to roar with pain,
He'll only lep and lep again.

If when you're walking round your yard,
   You meet a creature there,
Who hugs you very, very hard,
   Be sure it is the Bear.
If you have any doubt, I guess
He'll give you just one more caress.

Though to distinguish beasts of prey
   A novice might nonplus,
The Crocodiles you always may
   Tell from Hyenas thus:
Hyenas come with merry smiles;
But if they weep, they're Crocodiles.

The true Chameleon is small,
   A lizard sort of thing;
He hasn't any ears at all,
   And not a single wing.
If there is nothing on the tree,
'Tis the Chameleon you see.

                              CAROLYN WELLS

THE FROG

What a wonderful bird the frog are—
When he stand he sit almost;
When he hop, he fly almost.

He ain't got no sense hardly;
He ain't got no tail hardly either.
When he sit, he sit on what he ain't got almost.

ANONYMOUS

APEX

The lion tamers wrestle with the lions in a cage.
With but a fragile whip they dare their charges' feral rage.
They put their heads in tigers' mouths and do not flinch a grain
But they never tried to take a cat five hundred miles to Maine.

Frank Buck he Brings 'Em Back Alive from Afric's roaring shore—
The nilghai and the elephant, the leopard and the boar.
For him to crate a rhino on a steamer is no strain
But he never drove a four-pound cat five hundred miles to Maine.

Oh, cope with the rhinoceros bare-handed and alone,
Or kick a famished grizzly if for harmless fun you hone.
Or irritate a timber wolf by feeding it cocaine,
But do NOT try to drive a cat five hundred miles to Maine.
There is no word, there is no tongue, there is no ink to tell
One-tenth of what one cat can raise of concentrated hell
When after two hours driving to mistaken qualms you yield
And take poor puss to stretch her limbs in some adjacent field.

If you have caught the antelope that leaps from crag to crag;
If you have chased a hare on foot and popped it in a bag;
If you have roped a bison or if you've outrun a moose,
You have an outside chance to catch said cat when she gets loose.

And if you've done the things set forth in stanzas two and three
You stand a chance, when Krazy from the leash has wriggled free
(Provided you are clad in steel with gloves and hat to match)
To get her back into the car without a bite or scratch.

Ye lion tamers, naturalists, and big game hunters eke,
When I'm around be chary of your tendency to speak.

To hear you boast your petty deeds gives me a shooting pain
For I have taken Krazy (phew!) five hundred miles to Maine!

NATE SALSBURY

ARCHY AT THE ZOO

the centipede adown the street
goes braggartly with scores of feet
a gaudy insect but not neat

the octopus s secret wish
is not to be a formal fish
he dreams that some time he may grow
another set of legs or so
and be a broadway music show

oh do not always take a chance
upon an open countenance
the hippopotamus s smile
conceals a nature full of guile

human wandering through the zoo
what do your cousins think of you

i worry not of what the sphinx
thinks or maybe thinks she thinks

i have observed a setting hen
arise from that same attitude
and cackle forth to chicks and men
some quite superfluous platitude

serious camel sad giraffe
are you afraid that if you laugh
those graceful necks will break in half

a lack of any mental outlet
dictates the young cetacean s spoutlet

he frequently blows like me and you
because there s nothing else to do

when one sees in the austral dawn
a wistful penguin perched upon
a bald man's bleak and desert dome
one knows tis yearning for its home

the quite irrational ichneumon
is such a fool it s almost human

despite the sleek shark s far flung grin
and his pretty dorsal fin
his heart is hard and black within
even within a dentist s chair
he still preserves a sinister air
a prudent dentist always fills
himself with gas before he drills

Don Marquis

On Buying a Horse

One white foot, try him;
Two white feet, buy him;
Three white feet, put him in the dray;
Four white feet, give him away;
Four white feet, and a white nose,
Take off his hide and feed him to the crows.

Anonymous

Riding Lesson

I learned two things
from an early riding teacher.
He held a nervous filly
in one hand and gestured
with the other, saying, "Listen.

Keep one leg on one side,
the other leg on the other side,
and your mind in the middle."

He turned and mounted.
She took two steps, then left
The ground, I thought for good.
But she came down hard, humped
her back, swallowed her neck,
and threw her rider as you'd
throw a rock. He rose, brushed
his pants and caught his breath,
and said, "See, that's the way
to do it. When you see
they're gonna throw you, get off."

HENRY TAYLOR

To a Fish

You strange, astonished-looking, angle-faced,
    Dreary-mouthed, gaping wretches of the sea,
    Gulping salt water everlastingly,
Cold-blooded, though with red your blood be graced,
And mute, though dwellers in the roaring waste;
    And you, all shapes beside, that fishy be—
    Some round, some flat, some long, all devilry,
Legless, unloving, infamously chaste:

O scaly, slippery, wet, swift, staring wights,
    What is't ye do? What life lead? eh, dull goggles?
How do ye vary your vile days and nights?
    How pass your Sundays? Are ye still but joggles
In ceaseless wash? Still nought but gapes, and bites,
    And drinks, and stares, diversified with boggles?

LEIGH HUNT

A Fish Answers

Amazing monster! that, for aught I know,
    With the first sight of thee didst make our race
    For ever stare! O flat and shocking face,
Grimly divided from the breast below!
Thou that on dry land horribly dost go
    With a split body and most ridiculous pace,
    Prong after prong, disgracer of all grace,
Long-useless-finned, haired, upright, unwet, slow!

O breather of unbreathable, sword-sharp air,
    How canst exist? How bear thyself, thou dry
And dreary sloth? What particle canst share
    Of the only blessed life, the watery?
I sometimes see of ye an actual *pair*
    Go by! linked fin by fin! most odiously.

Leigh Hunt

The Grackle

The grackle's voice is less than mellow,
His heart is black, his eye is yellow,
He bullies more attractive birds
With hoodlum deeds and vulgar words,
And should a human interfere,
Attacks that human in the rear.
I cannot help but deem the grackle
An ornithological debacle.

Ogden Nash

The Termite

Some primal termite knocked on wood
And tasted it, and found it good,

And that is why your Cousin May
Fell through the parlor floor today.

OGDEN NASH

THE COW

The cow is of the bovine ilk;
One end is moo, the other milk.

OGDEN NASH

EINE KLEINE SNAILMUSIK

The snail watchers are interested in snails from all an-
gles. . . . At the moment they are investigating the snail's
reaction to music. "We have played to them on the harp
in the garden and in the country on the pipe," said Mr.
Heaton, "and we have taken them into the house and
played to them on the piano."
The London Star

What soothes the angry snail?
What's music to his horn?
For the "Sonata Appassionata,"
He shows scorn,
And Handel
Makes the frail snail
Quail,
While Prokofieff
Gets no laugh,
And Tchaikovsky, I fear,
No tear.
Piano, pipe, and harp,
Dulcet or shrill,
Flat or sharp,
Indoors or in the garden,
Are willy-nilly
Silly

To the reserved, slow,
Sensitive
Snail,
Who prefers to live
Glissandissimo,
Pianissimo.

MAY SARTON

INHUMAN HENRY

OR

CRUELTY TO FABULOUS ANIMALS

Oh would you know why Henry sleeps,
And why his mourning Mother weeps,
And why his weeping Mother mourns?
He was unkind to unicorns.

No unicorn, with Henry's leave,
Could dance upon the lawn at eve,
Or gore the gardener's boy in spring
Or do the very slightest thing.

No unicorn could safely roar,
And dash its nose against the door,
Nor sit in peace upon the mat
To eat the dog, or drink the cat.

Henry would never in the least
Encourage the heraldic beast:
If there were unicorns about
He went and let the lion out.

The lion, leaping from its chain
And glaring through its tangled mane,
Would stand on end and bark and bound
And bite what unicorns it found.

And when the lion bit a lot
Was Henry sorry? He was not.
What did his jumps betoken? Joy.
He was a bloody-minded boy.

The unicorn is not a Goose,
And when they saw the lion loose
They grew increasingly aware
That they had better not be there.

And oh, the unicorn is fleet
And spurns the earth with all its feet.
The lion had to snap and snatch
At tips of tails it could not catch.

Returning home in temper bad,
It met the sanguinary lad,
And clasping Henry with its claws
It took his legs between its jaws.

'Down, lion, down!' said Henry, 'cease!
My legs immediately release.'
His formidable feline pet
Made no reply, but only ate.

The last words that were ever said
By Henry's disappearing head,
In accents of indignant scorn,
Were 'I am not a unicorn'.

And now you know why Henry sleeps,
And why his Mother mourns and weeps,
And why she also weeps and mourns;
So now be kind to unicorns.

A. E. HOUSMAN

BRAVE ROVER

Rover killed the goat,
He bit him through the throat,
And when it all was over
The goat's ghost haunted Rover.

And yet (the plot here thickens)
Rover killed the chickens.
They thought he was a fox—
And then he killed the cocks.

And now events moved faster:
Rover killed his master,
And then he took the life
Of his late master's wife.

And we must not forget he
Killed Rachel and killed Bettie,
Then Billie and then John.
How dogs do carry on!

To Bradford he repaired.
His great white teeth he bared
And then, with awful snarls,
Polished off Uncle Charles.

Albert in London trembled—
An aspen he resembled—
His life he held not cheap
And wept. (I heard him weep.)

Brave Rover heard him too.
He knew full well who's who,
And entered with a grin
The Fields of Lincoln's Inn.

The Elysian Fields begin
Near those of Lincoln's Inn.

'Tis there that Albert's gone.
How dogs do carry on!

MAX BEERBOHM

YE BRUTHERS DOGG

Hodain D. Dogg
& Toolie Orlen

    Ye dogg, O'Toole,
    Who hath not work
    At love nor arte
    Nor goeth schule
    Sayeth with fart
    At Gulden Rulle,
    "Be it bitch or bisquit
    Or platter stewe,
Ye palate alone shal guide yu."

    Ye dogg, Hodain,
    Forgoeth bone
    Nor doth distain
    To moanne,
    ". . . for winde & raen,
    Ye snow & fogg,
    Ye seasons, sunn,
    & world roll on,
But ye dayes a' dogg be not longe."

    Bruthers Tew,
    Ye slimm Hodain
    & fatte O'Toole,
    Beneath fense
    Diggeth hole.
    Into ye world
    Ye Bruthers danse;
    Nor wuld return
Ye fatte O'Toole & slimm Hodain.

Sune is report
Bruthers Tew
Doth run amok
I' neighborhude.
Cautions O'Toole,
"Hodain, ye may barke,
May scowle & be rude,
But do not bitte
Ye hand what giveth dogg fude."

Tho all complane
A' Bruthers Tew,
No winde nor raen
Doth drive them homme.
Then sayeth Hodain
To Bruther, "O'Toole,
Tho we hath been frende
Thru thik & thinn,
Dogg needeth sume love from Mann."

So ende ye song
A' Bruthers Tew.
Away they had flown
& back they flewe.
Reclineth i' yard
Thru seasons & sunn,
Thru winde & raen,
Ye snow, ye fogg,
O'Toole, Hodain, ye Bruthers Dogg.

JON ANDERSON

LIII
(*from* Songs About Life and Brighter Things Yet)

Of all the birds that sing and fly
Between the housetops and the sky,
The muddy sparrow, mean and small,
I like, by far, the best of all.

His lot approaches human life;
His days are full of fear and strife;
He takes the traffic as it comes,
And pounds the sullen pave for crumbs.

No bird has so unsure a span;
He fights the elements and Man;
And so harassed is all his day,
He has no time to sing or pray.

From tenement to tenement
He flees, too frail to get the rent,
And then, his checkered days to crown,
A checkered taxi runs him down.

Samuel Hoffenstein

Drive a Tractor

When it's ninety in the shade
Drive a tractor
When a seed bed must be made
Drive a tractor
For its ham strings never burst
And when dogdays are the worst
It will hardly have a thirst
Drive a tractor
When the ground is hard and dry

Drive a tractor
It will plow when horses die
Drive a tractor
Laughs at hornets, flies, and bees,
Never known to have disease
Saves you veterinary fees
Drive a tractor.

FROM *CATERPILLAR NEWS AND VIEWS*

WORDS TO LIVE BY

A GARLAND OF PRECEPTS

Though a seeker since my birth,
Here is all I've learned on earth,
This is the gist of what I know:
Give advice and buy a foe.
Random truths are all I find
Stuck like burs about my mind.
Salve a blister. Burn a letter.
Do not wash a cashmere sweater.
Tell a tale but seldom twice.
Give a stone before advice.

Pressed for rules and verities,
All I recollect are these:
Feed a cold to starve a fever.
Argue with no true believer.
Think-too-long is never-act.
Scratch a myth and find a fact.
Stitch in time saves twenty stitches.
Give the rich, to please them, riches.
Give to love your hearth and hall.
But do not give advice at all.

PHYLLIS McGINLEY

[Monday's Child Is Fair of Face]

Monday's child is fair of face,
Tuesday's child is full of grace,
Wednesday's child is full of woe,
Thursday's child has far to go,
Friday's child is loving and giving,
Saturday's child works hard for its living,
And a child that is born on the Sabbath day
Is fair and wise and good and gay.

Anonymous

[Sneeze on a Monday, You Sneeze for Danger]

Sneeze on a Monday, you sneeze for danger;
Sneeze on a Tuesday, you'll kiss a stranger;
Sneeze on a Wednesday, you sneeze for a letter;
Sneeze on a Thursday, for something better;
Sneeze on a Friday, you sneeze for sorrow;
Sneeze on a Saturday, your sweetheart to-morrow;
Sneeze on a Sunday, your safety seek,
For you will have trouble the whole of the week.

Anonymous

[They That Wash on Monday]

They that wash on Monday
    Have all the week to dry;
They that wash on Tuesday
    Are not so much awry;
They that wash on Wednesday
    Are not so much to blame;
They that wash on Thursday

Wash for shame;
They that wash on Friday
Wash for need;
And they that wash on Saturday,
Oh, slovens are indeed!

ANONYMOUS

ADVICE

Folks, I'm telling you,
birthing is hard
and dying is mean—
so get yourself
a little loving
in between.

LANGSTON HUGHES

MOTHER, MOTHER, ARE YOU ALL THERE?

The aftereffects of a mother's neglects
   May spoil her boy's orientation to sex,
But the converse is worse: if she overprotects,
   The pattern of Oedipus wrecks.

FELICIA LAMPORT

THE STAR SYSTEM

While you're a white-hot youth, emit the rays
Which, now unmarked, shall dazzle future days.
Burn for the joy of it, and waste no juice
On hopes of prompt discovery. Produce!

Then, white with years, live wisely and survive.
Thus you may be on hand when you arrive,
And, like Antares, rosily dilate,
And for a time be gaseous and great.

RICHARD WILBUR

AN ADAGE

The gardener's rule applies to youth and age:
When young 'sow wild oats', but when old, grow sage.

H. J. BYRON

THE LITTLE OLD LADY
IN LAVENDER SILK

I was seventy-seven, come August,
    I shall shortly be losing my bloom;
I've experienced zephyr and raw gust
    And (symbolical) flood and simmom.

When you come to this time of abatement,
    To this passing from Summer to Fall,
It is manners to issue a statement
    As to what you got out of it all.

So I'll say, though reflection unnerves me
    And pronouncements I dodge as I can,
That I think (if my memory serves me)
    There was nothing more fun than a man!

In my youth, when the crescent was too wan
    To embarass with beams from above,
By the aid of some local Don Juan
    I fell into the habit of love.

And I learned how to kiss and be merry—an
　　Education left better unsung.
My neglect of the waters Pierian
　　Was a scandal, when Grandma was young.

Though the shabby unbalanced the splendid,
　　And the bitter outmeasured the sweet,
I should certainly do as I then did,
　　Were I given the chance to repeat.

For contrition is hollow and wraithful,
　　And regret is no part of my plan,
And I think (if my memory's faithful)
　　There was nothing more fun than a man!

DOROTHY PARKER

GOOD AND BAD LUCK

Good luck is the gayest of all gay girls;
　　Long in one place she will not stay:
Back from your brow she strokes the curls,
　　Kisses you quick and flies away.

But Madame Bad Luck soberly comes
　　And stays—no fancy has she for flitting;
Snatches of true-love songs she hums,
　　And sits by your bed, and brings her knitting.

JOHN HAY

OF MONEY

Give money me, take friendship whoso list,
For friends are gone come once adversity.
When money yet remaineth safe in chest,
That quickly can thee bring from misery.
Fair face show friends when riches do abound;

Come time of proof, farewell, they must away.
Believe me well, they are not to be found,
If God but send thee once a lowering day.
Gold never starts aside, but in distress
Finds ways enough to ease thine heaviness.

BARNABE GOOGE

THE BENEFITS AND
ABUSE OF ALCOHOL

Three cups of wine a prudent man may take;
The first of these for constitution's sake;
The second to the girl he love the best;
The third and last to lull him to his rest,
Then home to bed! but if a fourth he pours,
That is the cup of folly, and not ours;
Loud noisy talking on the fifth attends;
The sixth breeds feuds and falling-out of friends;
Seven beget blows and faces stain'd with gore;
Eight, and the watch-patrole breaks ope the door;
Mad with the ninth, another cup goes round,
And the swill'd sot drops senseless to the ground.

RICHARD CUMBERLAND
(TRANSLATED FROM *THE DEIPNOSOPHISTS OF*
ATHENAEUS BY EUBULUS, 4TH CENT. BC)

ADVICE TO TRAVELERS

A burro once, sent by express,
His shipping ticket on his bridle,
Ate up his name and his address,
And in some warehouse, standing idle,
He waited till he like to died.
The moral hardly needs the showing:

Don't keep things locked up deep inside—
Say who you are and where you're going.

WALKER GIBSON

DIAL CALL

Deep calleth unto deep
(Said Psalm 42, vii)
But also shallow unto shallow
And gets more prompt reply.

CHRISTOPHER MORLEY

FABLE

The mountain and the
    squirrel
Had a quarrel,
And the former called the
    latter "Little Prig";
Bun replied,
'You are doubtless very big;
But all sorts of things and
    weather
Must be taken in together,
To make up a year
And a sphere

And I think it no disgrace
To occupy my place.
If I'm not so large as you,
You are not so small as I,
And not half so spry.
I'll not deny you make
A very pretty squirrel track;
Talents differ; all is well and
    wisely put;

If I cannot carry forests on
  my back,
Neither can you crack a nut."

RALPH WALDO EMERSON

THE FLY

Little Fly
Thy summer's play,
My thoughtless hand
Has brush'd away.

Am not I
A fly like thee?
Or art not thou
A man like me?

For I dance
And drink & sing:
Till some blind hand
Shall brush my wing.

If thought is life
And strength & breath:
And the want
Of thought is death;

Then am I
A happy fly,
If I live,
Or if I die.

WILLIAM BLAKE

INVENTORY

Four be the things I am wiser to know:
Idleness, sorrow, a friend, and a foe.

Four be the things I'd been better without:
Love, curiosity, freckles, and doubt.

Three be the things I shall never attain:
Envy, content, and sufficient champagne.

Three be the things I shall have till I die:
Laughter and hope and a sock in the eye.

DOROTHY PARKER

ODE ON THE DEATH OF
A FAVOURITE CAT DROWNED IN A
TUB OF GOLD FISHES

'Twas on a lofty vase's side,
Where China's gayest art had dyed
    The azure flowers, that blow;
Demurest of the tabby kind,
The pensive Selima reclined,
    Gazed on the lake below.

Her conscious tail her joy declared,
The fair round face, the snowy beard,
    The velvet of her paws,
Her coat, that with the tortoise vies,
Her ears of jet and emerald eyes,
    She saw, and purred applause.

Still had she gazed but 'midst the tide
Two angel forms were seen to glide,
    The Genii of the stream:

Their scaly armour's Tyrian hue
Through richest purple to the view
  Betrayed a golden gleam.

The hapless nymph with wonder saw:
A whisker first and then a claw,
  With many an ardent wish,
She stretched in vain to reach the prize.
What female heart can gold despise?
  What cat's averse to fish?

Presumptuous maid! with looks intent
Again she stretched, again she bent,
  Nor knew the gulf between.
(Malignant Fate sat by, and smiled)
The slippery verge her feet beguiled,
  She tumbled headlong in.

Eight times emerging from the flood
She mewed to every wat'ry god,
  Some speedy aid to send.
No dolphin came, no Nereid stirred:
Nor cruel Tom, nor Susan heard.
  A favourite has no friend!

From hence, ye beauties, undeceived,
Know, one false step is ne'er retrieved,
  And be with caution bold.
Not all that tempts your wandering eyes
And heedless hearts, is lawful prize;
  Nor all that glitters, gold.

THOMAS GRAY

MANNERS

Prig offered Pig the first chance at dessert,
So Pig reached out and speared the bigger part.

"Now that," cried Prig, "is extremely rude of you!"
Pig, with his mouth full, said, "Wha, wha' wou' 'ou do?"

"I would have taken the littler bit," said Prig.
"Stop kvetching, then it's what you've got," said Pig.

So virtue is its own reward, you see.
And that is all it's ever going to be.

HOWARD NEMEROV

PROBABLY

I am the captain of my soul;
I rule it with stern joy;
And yet I think I had more fun,
When I was cabin boy.

KEITH PRESTON

A MAXIM REVISED

Ladies, to this advice give heed—
In controlling men:
If at first you don't succeed,
Why, cry, cry, again.

ANONYMOUS

A WORD OF ENCOURAGEMENT

O what a tangled web we weave
When first we practice to deceive!
But when we've practised quite a while
How vastly we improve our style!

J. R. POPE

PLAYS

Alas, how soon the hours are over,
Counted us out to play the lover!—
And how much narrower is the stage,
Allotted us to play the sage!
But when we play the fool, how wide
The theatre expands! beside,
How long the audience sits before us!
How many prompters! what a chorus!

WALTER SAVAGE LANDOR

MIGHT AND RIGHT

Might and Right are always fighting.
In our youth it seems exciting.
Right is always nearly winning.
Might can hardly keep from grinning.

CLARENCE DAY

FATAL LOVE

Poor Hal caught his death standing under a spout,
Expecting till midnight when Nan would come out,
But fatal his patience, as cruel the dame,
And curs'd was the weather that quench'd the man's flame.

Whoe'er thou art, that read'st these moral lines,
Make love at home, and go to bed betimes.

MATTHEW PRIOR

Be Careful

I'm careful of the words I say,
To keep them soft and sweet,
I never know from day to day
Which ones I'll have to eat.

ANONYMOUS

Proverbial Advice on Marriage

Who weds a sot to get his cot,
Will lose the cot and keep the sot.

ANONYMOUS

On Tomato Ketchup

If you do not shake the bottle,
None'll come, and then a lot'll.

ANONYMOUS

Sound Advice

When in danger or in doubt,
Run in circles, scream and shout.

ANONYMOUS

Hours of Sleep

Nature requires five; custom gives seven;
Laziness takes nine, and wickedness eleven.

ANONYMOUS

Of Treason

Treason doth never prosper; what's the reason?
Why, when it prospers, none dare call it treason.

Sir John Harington

An Answer to the Parson

'Why of the sheep do you not learn peace?'
'Because I don't want you to shear my fleece.'

William Blake

Reflections on Ice-Breaking

Candy
is dandy
But liquor
is quicker.

Ogden Nash

News Item

Men seldom make passes
At girls who wear glasses.

Dorothy Parker

Twelve Articles

I
Lest it may more quarrels breed,
I will never hear you read.

II
By disputing, I will never,
To convince you once endeavor.

III
When a paradox you stick to,
I will never contradict you.

IV
When I talk and you are heedless,
I will show no anger needless.

V
When your speeches are absurd,
I will ne'er object a word.

VI
When you furious argue wrong,
I will grieve and hold my tongue.

VII
Not a jest or humorous story
Will I ever tell before ye:
To be chidden for explaining,
When you quite mistake the meaning.

VIII
Never more will I suppose,
You can taste my verse or prose.

IX
You no more at me shall fret,
While I teach and you forget.

X
You shall never hear me thunder,
When you blunder on, and blunder.

XI

Show your poverty of spirit,
And in dress place all your merit;
Give yourself ten thousand airs:
That with me shall break no squares.

XII

Never will I give advice,
Till you please to ask me thrice:
Which if you in scorn reject,
'T will be just as I expect.

Thus we both shall have our ends
And continue special friends.

JONATHAN SWIFT

BILE

IMPROMPTU ON CHARLES II

God bless our good and gracious King,
    Whose promise none relies on;
Who never said a foolish thing,
    Nor ever did a wise one.

                  JOHN WILMOT, EARL OF ROCHESTER

A SATIRICAL ELEGY ON THE
DEATH OF A LATE FAMOUS GENERAL

His Grace! impossible! what dead!
Of old age too, and in his bed!
And could that mighty warrior fall?
And so inglorious, after all!
Well, since he's gone, no matter how,
The last loud trump must wake him now:
And trust me, as the noise grows stronger,
He'd wish to sleep a little longer.
And could he be indeed so old
As by the newspapers we're told?
Threescore, I think, is pretty high;
'Twas time in conscience he should die.
This world he cumbered long enough;

He burnt his candle to the snuff;
And that's the reason, some folks think,
He left behind so great a s---k.
Behold his funeral appears,
Nor widow's sighs, nor orphan's tears,
Wont at such times each heart to pierce,
Attend the progress of his hearse.
But what of that, his friends may say.
He had those honors in his day.
True to his profit and his pride,
He made them weep before he died.
    Come hither, all ye empty things,
Ye bubbles raised by breath of kings;
Who float upon the tide of state,
Come hither, and behold your fate.
Let pride be taught by this rebuke,
How very mean a thing's a Duke;
From all his ill-got honors flung,
Turned to that dirt from whence he sprung.

JONATHAN SWIFT

EPIGRAM
ON SIR ROGER PHILLIMORE (1810–1885)
AND
HIS BROTHER, GEORGE PHILLIMORE

When Nature dreamt of making bores,
She formed a brace of Phillimores;
Sooner than make a Phillimost,
Nature herself would yield the ghost.

ANONYMOUS

To a Blockhead

You beat your pate, and fancy wit will come:
Knock as you please, there's nobody home.

Alexander Pope

On a Stone Thrown at a
Very Great Man, But Which Missed Him

Talk no more of the lucky escape of the head
    From a flint so unluckily thrown—
I think very different, with thousands indeed,
    'T was a lucky escape for the stone.

Peter Pindar (John Wolcott)

To the Sour Reader

If thou dislik'st the piece thou light'st on first,
Think that of all that I have writ the worst;
But if thou read'st my book unto the end,
And still dost this and that verse reprehend,
O perverse man! If all disgustful be,
The extreme scab take thee and thine, for me.

Robert Herrick

An Elegy on the
Death of a Mad Dog
(*from* the Vicar of Wakefield)

Good people all, of every sort,
    Give ear unto my song;
And if you find it wond'rous short,
    It cannot hold you long.

In Islington there was a man,
    Of whom the world might say,
That still a godly race he ran,
    Whene'er he went to pray.

A kind and gentle heart he had,
    To comfort friends and foes;
The naked every day he clad,
    When he put on his clothes.

And in that town a dog was found,
    As many dogs there be,
Both mongrel, puppy, whelp, and hound,
    And curs of low degree.

This dog and man at first were friends;
    But when a pique began,
The dog, to gain some private ends,
    Went mad and bit the man.

Around from all the neighbouring streets
    The wond'ring neighbours ran,
And swore the dog had lost his wits,
    To bite so good a man.

The wound it seem'd both sore and sad
    To every Christian eye;
And while they swore the dog was mad,
    They swore the man would die.

But soon a wonder came to light,
    That shew'd the rogues they lied:
The man recover'd of the bite,
    The dog it was that died.

OLIVER GOLDSMITH

ON SIR JOHN HILL, M.D., PLAYWRIGHT

For physic and farces his equal there scarce is;
His farces are physic; his physic a farce is.

DAVID GARRICK

CENSORSHIP

Damn that celibate farm, that cracker-box house
with the bed springs screaming at every stir,
even to breathe. I swear, if one of us
half turned they'd shriek, "He's getting on top of her!"

Her father, but for the marriage certificate,
would have his .30-.30 up my ass.
Her mother, certificate or not, could hate
a hole right through the wall. It was

a banshee's way to primroses that fall
of the first year in that hate-bed wired
like a burglar alarm. If I stood her against the wall,
that would quiver and creak. When we got tired

of the dog-humped floor we sneaked out for a stroll
and tumbled it out under the apple tree
just up from the spring, but the chiggers ate us whole
in that locked conspiracy of chastity

whose belts we both wore all one grated week
while virtue buzzed a blue-fly over that bitch
of a bed hair-triggered to shriek:
"They're going at it! They're doing it right now!"—which

we damned well couldn't, welted over and on
as if we were sunburned. And every night at two

her mother would get up and go to the john,
and the plumbing would howl from Hell, "We're watching
    you!"

JOHN CIARDI

INTIMATES

Don't you care for my love? she said bitterly.

I handed her the mirror, and said:
Please address these questions to the proper person!
Please make all requests to head-quarters!
In all matters of emotional importance
please approach the supreme authority direct!—
So I handed her the mirror.
And she would have broken it over my head,
but she caught sight of her own reflection
and that held her spellbound for two seconds
while I fled.

D. H. LAWRENCE

WHAT'S THAT SMELL IN THE KITCHEN?

All over America women are burning dinners.
It's lambchops in Peoria; it's haddock
in Providence; it's steak in Chicago
tofu delight in Big Sur; red
rice and beans in Dallas.
All over America women are burning
food they're supposed to bring with calico
smile on platters glittering like wax.
Anger sputters in her brainpan, confined
but spewing out missiles of hot fat.
Carbonized despair presses like a clinker
from a barbecue against the back of her eyes.
If she wants to grill anything, it's

her husband spitted over a slow fire.
If she wants to serve him anything
it's a dead rat with a bomb in its belly
ticking like the heart of an insomniac.
Her life is cooked and digested,
nothing but leftovers in Tupperware.
Look, she says, once I was roast duck
on your platter with parsley but now I am Spam.
Burning dinner is not incompetence but war.

MARGE PIERCY

DICK, A MAGGOT

As when rooting in a bin,
All powdered o'er from tail to chin,
A lively maggot sallies out,
You know him by his hazel snout:
So, when the grandson of his grandsire,
Forth issues wriggling Dick Drawcensir
With powdered rump and back and side,
You cannot blanch his tawny hide;
For 'tis beyond the pow'r of meal
The gipsy visage to conceal:
For, as he shakes his wainscot chops,
Down ev'ry mealy atom drops
And leaves the Tartar phiz, in show
Like a fresh turd just dropped on snow.

JONATHAN SWIFT

TRAVELER'S CURSE
AFTER MISDIRECTION

May they stumble, stage by stage
On an endless pilgrimage,
Dawn and dusk, mile after mile,

At each and every step, a stile;
At each and every step withal
May they catch their feet and fall;
At each and every fall they take
May a bone within them break;
And may the bone that breaks within
Not be, for variation's sake,
Now rib, now thigh, now arm, now shin,
But always, without fail, THE NECK.

ROBERT GRAVES
(translation from the Welsh)

MRS. TROLLOPE IN AMERICA

Mrs. Trollope took a doleful view
Of us, in 1832,
Whose native latitude she knew.

And every time a gentleman spit,
Not being edified a whit,
She made a plaintive note of it.

Her agitation grew so great,
At times she seemed to lie in wait
For somebody to expectorate.

But we, in 1832,
Took a broad, dispassionate view,
And spit whenever we wanted to.

HELEN BEVINGTON

THE REBEL

Oh, I'm a good old Rebel,
Now that's just what I am,
For this "fair Land of Freedom"

I don't give a damn;
I'm glad I fought agin her,
I only wish we'd won,
And I ain't axed any pardon
for anything I've done.

I fought with old Bob Lee for three years about,
Got wounded in four places and starved at Point Lookout.
I caught the rheumatism a-campin' in the snow,
An I killed a chance of Yankees and I wish I'd killed some mo'!

Three hundred thousand Yankees is dead in Southern dust,
We got three hundred thousand before they conquered us;
They died of Southern fever, of Southern steel and shot—
I wish they was three million instead of what we got.

I hate the Constitution, this great republic, too;
I hate the nasty eagle, and uniform so blue;
I hate their glorious banner, and all their flags and fuss.
Those lying, thieving Yankees, I hate 'em wuss and wuss.

I hate the Yankee nation and everything they do;
I hate the Declaration of Independence, too;
I hate the glorious Union, 'tis dripping with our blood;
I hate the striped banner, I fought it all I could.

I won't be reconstructed! I'm better now than them;
And for a carpetbagger, I don't give a damn;
So I'm off for the frontier, soon as I can go,
I'll prepare me a weapon and start for Mexico.

I can't take up my musket and fight them now no mo',
But I'm not goin' to love 'em, and that is certain sho';
And I don't want no pardon for what I was or am,
I won't be reconstructed and I don't give a damn.

INNES RANDOLPH

Speech

1

I crouch over my radio
to tune in the President,
thinking how lucky I am
not to own a television.

2

Now the rich, cultivated voice
with its cautious, measured pauses
fills my living room, fills
the wastebasket, the vase
on the mantel, the hurricane
lamps, and even fills
the antique pottery whiskey jug
beside the fireplace, nourishing
the dried flowers I have put in it.

3

"I had a responsibility,"
he says; the phrase pours
from the speaker like molasses,
flows to the rug, spreads
into a black, shining puddle,
slowly expands, covers
the rug with dark sweetness.
It begins to draw flies;
they eat all the syrup
and clamor for more.

4

I can barely hear the speech
above the buzzing of their wings.
But the Commander in Chief
has the solution: another
phrase, sweeter, thicker,

blacker, oozes out
over my living room floor:
"I have personal reasons
for wanting peace." This is more
than the flies will be able to eat;
they will stay quiet
for the rest of the speech.

5

Now, you are thinking, comes
the Good Part, the part
where the syrup proves poisonous
and kills all the flies.
My fellow Americans, that
is not at all what happened.
The flies grew fat on the phrases,
grew as large as bullfrogs.

6

They are everywhere in the house,
and the syrup continues
to feed and fatten them;
in the pottery whiskey jug,
sprouting new leaves and buds,
even the dried flowers thrive.

7

The speech
has been over for weeks now;
they go on eating,
but they stay quiet
and seem peaceful enough.
At night, sometimes,
I can hear them
making soft liquid sounds
of contentment.

HENRY TAYLOR

A DEAD STATESMAN

I could not dig: I dared not rob:
Therefore I lied to please the mob.
Now all my lies are proved untrue
And I must face the men I slew.
What tale shall serve me here among
Mine angry and defrauded young?

RUDYARD KIPLING

LORD BARRENSTOCK

Lord Barrenstock and Epicene,
What's it to me that you have been
In your pursuit of interdicted joys
Seducer of a hundred little boys?

Your sins are red about your head
And many people wish you dead.

You trod the widow in the mire
Wronged the son, deceived the sire.

You put a fence about the land
And made the people's cattle graze on sand.

Ratted from many a pool and forced amalgamation
And dealt in shares which never had a stock exchange
    quotation.

Non flocci facio, I do not care
For wrongs you made the other fellow bear:
'Tis not for these unsocial acts not these
I wet my pen. I would not have you tease,
With a repentance smug and overdue
For all the things you still desire to do,

The ears of an outraged divinity:
But oh your tie is crooked and I see
Too plain you had an éclair for your tea.

It is this nonchalance about your person—
That is the root of my profound aversion.

STEVIE SMITH

THE RATTLE BAG

As I lay, fullness of praise,
On a summer day under
Trees between field and mountain
Awaiting my soft-voiced girl,
She came, there's no denying,
Where she vowed, a very moon.
Together we sat, fine theme,
The girl and I, debating,
Trading, while I had the right,
Words with the splendid maiden.

And so we were, she was shy,
Learning to love each other,
Concealing sin, winning mead,
An hour lying together,
And then, cold comfort, it came,
A blare, a bloody nuisance,
A sack's bottom's foul seething
From an imp in shepherd's shape,
Who had, public enemy,
A harsh-horned sag-cheeked rattle.
He played, cramped yellow belly,
This bag, curse its scabby leg.
So before satisfaction
The sweet girl panicked: poor me!
When she heard, feeble-hearted,
The stones whir, she would not stay.

By Christ, no Christian country,
Cold harsh tune, has heard the like.
Noisy pouch perched on a pole,
Bell of pebbles and gravel,
Saxon rocks making music
Quaking in a bullock's skin,
Crib of three thousand beetles,
Commotion's cauldron, black bag,
Field-keeper, comrade of straw,
Black-skinned, pregnant with splinters,
Noise that's an old buck's loathing,
Devil's bell, stake in its crotch,
Scarred pebble-bearing belly,
May it be sliced into thongs.
May the churl be struck frigid,
Amen, who scared off my girl.

DAFYDD AP GWILLYM
(translated from Welsh by Joseph Clany)

A GLASS OF BEER

The lanky hank of a she in the inn over there
Nearly killed me for asking the loan of a glass of beer;
May the devil grip the whey-faced slut by the hair,
And beat bad manners out of her skin for a year.

That parboiled ape, with the toughest jaw you will see
On virtue's path, and a voice that would rasp the dead,
Came roaring and raging the minute she looked at me,
And threw me out of the house on the back of my head!

If I asked her master he'd give me a cask a day;
But she, with the beer at hand, not a gill would arrange!
May she marry a ghost and bear him a kitten, and may
The High King of Glory permit her to get the mange.

JAMES STEPHENS

I Do Not Love Thee, Doctor Fell

I do not love thee, Doctor Fell,
The reason why I cannot tell;
But this alone I know full well,
I do not love thee, Doctor Fell.

THOMAS BROWN

To R. K.

Will there never come a season
Which shall rid us from the curse
Of a prose which knows no reason
And an unmelodious verse:
When the world shall cease to wonder
At the genius of an Ass,
And a boy's eccentric blunder
Shall not bring success to pass:

When mankind shall be delivered
From the clash of magazines,
And the inkstand shall be shivered
Into countless smithereens:
When there stands a muzzled stripling
Mute, beside a muzzled bore:
When the Rudyards cease from kipling
And the Haggards ride no more?

JAMES KENNETH STEPHEN

The Candid Man

Forth went the candid man
And spoke freely to the wind—
When he looked about him he was in a far strange country.

Forth went the candid man
And spoke freely to the stars—
Yellow light tore sight from his eyes.

"My good fool," said a learned bystander,
"Your operations are mad."

"You are too candid," cried the candid man.
And when his stick left the head of the learned bystander
It was two sticks.

STEPHEN CRANE

XIII
(*from* LOVE-SONGS, AT ONCE TENDER AND INFORMATIVE)

Your little hands,
Your little feet,
Your little mouth—
Oh, God, how sweet!

Your little nose,
Your little ears,
Your eyes, that shed
Such little tears!

Your little voice,
So soft and kind;
Your little soul,
Your little mind!

SAMUEL HOFFENSTEIN

ON A PAINTED WOMAN

To youths, who hurry thus away,
How silly your desire is

At such an early hour to pay
　　Your compliments to Iris.

Stop, prithee, stop, ye hasty beaux,
　　No longer urge this race on;
Though Iris has put on her clothes,
　　She has not put her face on.

PERCY BYSSHE SHELLEY

I
(*from* SONGS ABOUT LIFE AND BRIGHTER THINGS YET)

Nothing from a straight line swerves
So sharply as a woman's curves,
And, having swerved, no might or main
Can ever put her straight again.

SAMUEL HOFFENSTEIN

TO CLOE

Cloe's the wonder of her sex,
　　'Tis well her heart is tender;
How might such killing eyes perplex,
　　With virtue to defend her!

But Nature, graciously inclined,
　　Not bent to vex but please us,
Has to her boundless beauty joined
　　A boundless will to ease us.

GEORGE GRANVILLE, LORD LANSDOWNE

WISHES OF AN ELDERLY MAN

I wish I loved the Human Race;
I wish I loved its silly face;
I wish I liked the way it walks;
I wish I liked the way it talks;
And when I'm introduced to one
I wish I thought *What Jolly Fun!*

WALTER RALEIGH

THE FOOL AND THE POET

Sir, I admit your general rule,
That every poet is a fool,
But you yourself may serve to show it,
That every fool is not a poet.

ALEXANDER POPE

Departures

The Aesthetic Point of View

As the poets have mournfully sung,
Death takes the innocent young,
  The rolling-in-money,
  The screamingly-funny,
And those who are very well hung.

W. H. Auden

Life Is Fine

I went down to the river,
I set down on the bank.
I tried to think but couldn't,
So I jumped in and sank.

I came up once and hollered!
I came up twice and cried!
If that water hadn't a-been so cold
I might've sunk and died.

But it was
Cold in that water!
It was cold!

I took the elevator
Sixteen floors above the ground.
I thought about my baby
And thought I would jump down.

I stood there and I hollered!
I stood there and I cried!
If it hadn't a-been so high
I might've jumped and died.

But it was
High up there!
It was high!

So since I'm still here livin',
I guess I will live on.
I could've died for love—
But for livin' I was born.

Though you may hear me holler,
And you may see me cry—
I'll be dogged, sweet baby,
If you gonna see me died.

Life is fine!
Fine as wine!
Life is fine!

LANGSTON HUGHES

RÉSUMÉ

Razors pain you;
Rivers are damp;
Acids stain you;
And drugs cause cramp.
Guns aren't lawful;
Nooses give;

Gas smells awful;
You might as well live.

                                        DOROTHY PARKER

A BALLADE OF SUICIDE

The gallows in my garden, people say,
Is new and neat and adequately tall.
I tie the noose on in a knowing way
As one that knots his necktie for a ball;
But just as all the neighbours—on the wall—
Are drawing a long breath to shout "Hurray!"
The strangest whim has seized me. . . . After all
I think I will not hang myself to-day.

To-morrow is the time I get my pay—
My uncle's sword is hanging in the hall—
I see a little cloud all pink and grey—
Perhaps the rector's mother will *not* call—
I fancy that I heard from Mr. Gall
That mushrooms could be cooked another way—
I never read the works of Juvenal—
I think I will not hang myself today.

The world will have another washing day;
The decadents decay; the pedants pall;
And H. G. Wells has found that children play,
And Bernard Shaw discovered that they squall;
Rationalists are growing rational—
And through thick woods one finds a stream astray,
So secret that the very sky seems small—
I think I will not hang myself today.

                    ENVOI
Prince, I can hear the trump of Germinal,
The tumbrils toiling up the terrible way;

Even to-day your royal head may fall—
I think I will not hang myself today.

G. K. Chesterson

The Despairing Lover

Distracted with care,
For Phillis the fair,
Since nothing could move her,
Poor Damon, her lover,
Resolves in despair
No longer to languish,
Nor bear so much anguish;
But, mad with his love,
To a precipice goes;
Where, a leap from above
Would soon finish his woes.

When in rage he came there,
Beholding how steep
The sides did appear,
And the bottom how deep;
His torments projecting,
And sadly reflecting
That a lover forsaken
A new love may get;
But a neck, when once broken,
Can never be set;
And, that he could die
Whenever he would;
But, that he could live
But as long as he could;
How grievous soever
This torment might grow,
He scorn'd to endeavour
To finish it so.
But bold, unconcern'd

At thoughts of the pain,
He calmly return'd
To his cottage again.

WILLIAM WALSH

A THRENODY

"The Ahkoond of Swat is dead."
                    —London Papers of Jan. 22, 1878

What, what, what,
    What's the news from Swat?
    Sad news,
    Bad news,
Comes by the cable led
Through the Indian Ocean's bed,
Through the Persian Gulf, the Red
Sea and the Med-
Iterranean—he's dead;
The Ahkoond is dead!

For the Ahkoond I mourn,
    Who wouldn't?
He strove to disregard the message stern,
    But he Ahkoodn't.
Dead, dead, dead:
    (Sorrow, Swats!)
Swats wha hae wi' Ahkoond bled,
Swats whom he hath often led
Onward to a gory bed,
Or to victory,
    As the case might be.
        Sorrow, Swats!
Tears shed,
    Shed tears like water.
Your great Ahkoond is dead!
    That Swats the matter!

Mourn, city of Swat,
Your great Ahkoond is not,
But laid 'mid worms to rot.
His mortal part alone, his soul was caught
  (Because he was a good Ahkoond)
  Up to the bosom of Mahound.
Though earthly walls his frame surround
(Forever hallowed by the ground!)

And skeptics mock the lowly mound
And say "He's now of no Ahkoond!"
  His soul is in the skies—
The azure skies that bend above his loved
  Metropolis of Swat.
  He sees with larger, other eyes,
  Athwart all earthly mysteries—
  He knows what's Swat.

Let Swat bury the great Ahkoond
  With a noise of mourning and of lamentation!
Let Swat bury the great Ahkoond
  With the noise of the mourning of the Swattish nation!'
  Fallen is at length
  Its tower of strength;
  Its sun is dimmed ere it had nooned;
    Dead lies the great Ahkoond,
  The great Ahkoond of Swat
  Is not!

GEORGE THOMAS LANIGAN

DIRCE

Stand close around, ye Stygian set,
  With Dirce in one boat conveyed!
Or Charon, seeing, may forget,
  That he is old and she a shade.

WALTER SAVAGE LANDOR

EMMELINE GRANGERFORD'S "ODE TO STEPHEN DOWLING BOTS, DEC'D"

And did young Stephen sicken,
   And did young Stephen die?
And did the sad hearts thicken,
   And did the mourners cry?

No; such was not the fate of
   Young Stephen Dowling Bots;
Though sad hearts round him thickened,
   'Twas not from sickness' shots.

No whooping-cough did rack his frame,
   Nor measles drear with spots;
Not these impaired the sacred name
   Of Stephen Dowling Bots.

Despised love struck not with woe
   That head of curly knots,
Nor stomach troubles laid him low,
   Young Stephen Dowling Bots.

O no. Then list with tearful eye,
   Whilst I his fate do tell.
His soul did from this cold world fly
   By falling down a well.

They got him out and emptied him;
   Alas it was too late;
His spirit was gone for to sport aloft
   In the realms of the good and great.

MARK TWAIN

FINNEGAN'S WAKE

Tim Finnegan lived in Walkin Street,
   A gentleman Irish mighty odd.
He had a tongue both rich and sweet,
   An' to rise in the world he carried a hod.
Now Tim had a sort of a tipplin' way,
   With the love of the liquor he was born,
An' to help him on with his work each day,
   He'd a drop of the craythur every morn.

Chorus

Whack folthe dah, dance to your partner,
   Welt the flure, yer trotters shake,
Wasn't it the truth I told you,
   Lots of fun at Finnegan's Wake.

One morning Tim was rather full,
   His head felt heavy which made him shake,
He fell from the ladder and broke his skull,
   So they carried him home his corpse to wake,
They rolled him up in a nice clean sheet,
   And laid him out upon the bed,
With a gallon of whiskey at his feet,
   And a barrel of porter at his head.

His friends assembled at the wake,
   And Mrs. Finnegan called for lunch,
First they brought in tay and cake,
   Then pipes, tobacco, and whiskey punch.
Miss Biddy O'Brien began to cry,
   'Such a neat clean corpse, did you ever see,
Arrah, Tim avourneen, why did you die?'
   'Ah, hould your gab,' said Paddy McGee.

Then Biddy O'Connor took up the job,
   'Biddy,' says she, 'you're wrong, I'm sure,'

But Biddy gave her a belt in the gob,
    And left her sprawling on the floor;
Oh, then the war did soon enrage;
    'Twas woman to woman and man to man,
Shillelagh law did all engage,
    And a row and a ruction soon began.

Then Micky Maloney raised his head,
    When a noggin of whiskey flew at him,
It missed and falling on the bed,
    The liquor scattered over Tim;
Bedad he revives, see how he rises,
    And Timothy rising from the bed,
Says, 'Whirl your liquor round like the blazes,
Thanam o'n dhoul, do ye think I'm dead?'

ANONYMOUS

IN CHRIST CHURCH, BRISTOL,
ON THOMAS TURNER, TWICE MASTER
OF THE COMPANY OF BAKERS

Like to a Baker's oven is the grave,
Wherein the bodies of the faithful have
A setting in, and where they do remain
In hopes to rise, and to be drawn again:
Blessed are they who in the Lord are dead;
Though set like dough, they shall be drawn like bread.

LORD JEFFREY

A MELANCHOLY LAY

Three Turkeys fair their last have breathed,
And now this world for ever leaved,
Their Father and their Mother too,
Will sigh and weep as well as you,

Mourning for their offspring fair,
Whom they did nurse with tender care.
Indeed the rats their bones have crunch'd,
To eternity are they launch'd;
Their graceful form and pretty eyes
Their fellow fowls did not despise,
A direful death indeed they had,
That would put any parent mad,
But she was more than usual calm
She did not give a single dam.
Here ends this melancholy lay:
Farewell poor Turkeys I must say.

MARJORIE FLEMING (AGE 8)

ON THE SETTING UP OF
MR. BUTLER'S MONUMENT
IN WESTMINSTER ABBEY

While Butler, needy wretch! was yet alive,
No generous patron would a dinner give:
See him, when starv'd to death and turn'd to dust,
Presented with a monumental bust!
The poet's fate is here in emblem shown,
He ask'd for bread, and he received a stone!

SAMUEL WESLEY, THE YOUNGER

FRAGMENT FROM
"THE MALADJUSTED: A TRAGEDY"

Upon his frustrate and unhopeful quest
    He trod the concrete road of desperation,
And in no Rest Room found he any rest
    Nor was there comfort in a Comfort Station.

He asked for beauty in a Beauty Shop
    In vain; for all their beauty was but shoddy.
So to his life he put a sudden stop.
    The Body Shop would not receive his body.

MORRIS BISHOP

OBIT ON PARNASSUS

Death before forty's no bar. Lo!
    These had accomplished their feats:
Chatterton, Burns, and Kit Marlowe,
    Byron and Shelley and Keats.

Death, the eventual censor,
    Lays for the forties, and so
Took off Jane Austen and Spenser,
    Stevenson, Hood, and poor Poe.

You'll leave a better-lined wallet
    By reaching the end of your rope
After fifty, like Shakespeare and Smollett,
    Thackeray, Dickens, and Pope.

Try for the sixties—but say, boy,
    That's when the tombstones were built on
Butler and Sheridan, the play boy,
    Arnold and Coleridge and Milton.

Three score and ten—the tides rippling
    Over the bar; slip the hawser.
Godspeed to Clemens and Kipling,
    Swinburne and Browning and Chaucer.

Some staved the debt off but paid it
    At eighty—that's after the law.
Wordsworth and Tennyson made it,
    And Meredith, Hardy, and Shaw.

But, Death, while you make up your quota,
    Please note this confession of candor—
That I wouldn't give an iota
    To linger till ninety, like Landor.

F. Scott Fitzgerald

Epitaphium Citharistriae

Stand not uttering sedately
    Trite oblivious praise above her!
Rather say you saw her lately
    Lightly kissing her last lover.

Whisper not, "There is a reason
    Why we bring her no white blossom":
Since the snowy bloom's in season
    Strow it on her sleeping bosom:

Oh, for it would be a pity
    To o'erpraise her or to flout her:
She was wild, and sweet, and witty—
    Let's not say dull things about her.

Victor Plarr

Epitaph on the Politician

Here, richly, with ridiculous display,
The Politician's corpse was laid away.
While all of his acquaintance sneered and slanged,
I wept: for I had longed to see him hanged.

Hilaire Belloc

Epitaph on a Waiter

By and by
God caught his eye.

DAVID McCORD

Epitaph–1726
On Sir John Vanbrugh,
Architect of Blenheim Palace

Under this stone, Reader, survey
Dead Sir John Vanbrugh's house of clay.
Lie heavy on him, Earth! for he
Laid many heavy loads on thee!

ABEL EVANS

On a Carrier Who
Died of Drunkenness

John Adams lies here, of the parish of Southwell,
A carrier who carried his can to mouth well;
He carried so much, and he carried so fast,
He could carry no more—so was carried at last;
For the liquor he drank, being too much for one,
He could not carry off—so he's now carrion.

GEORGE GORDON, LORD BYRON

On Peter Robinson

Here lies the preacher, judge, and poet, Peter
Who broke the laws of God, and man, and metre.

LORD JEFFREY

JOHN BUN

Here lies John Bun,
He was killed by a gun,
His name was not Bun, but Wood,
But Wood would not rhyme with gun, but Bun would.

ANONYMOUS

'HERE LIES SIR TACT'

Here lies Sir Tact, a diplomatic fellow
Whose silence was not golden, but just yellow.

TIMOTHY STEELE

AFTER GRAVE DELIBERATION . . .

When I Go
it should be by cremation,
my ashes slipped into
an 8 x 10 manila envelope
with a second (stamped and self-addressed)
inside, posted to God
in His capacity as editor
of Everything.

I stand
a better than even chance
of being returned to myself,
along with a neat note
acknowledging my insight and my craft,
regretting that I do not,
at that time, fit
His divine needs,
wishing me luck in placing myself
elsewhere.

ELIZABETH FLYNN

REQUIEM

Under the wide and starry sky
   Dig the grave and let me lie:
Glad did I live and gladly die,
   And I laid me down with a will.

This be the verse you 'grave for me:
   Here he lies where he long'd to be;
Home is the sailor, home from the sea,
   And the hunter home from the hill.

ROBERT LOUIS STEVENSON

INDEX OF TITLES AND FIRST LINES

425

INDEX OF AUTHORS